DATE DUE

DEMCO 38-296

Early American Naturalists

Early American Naturalists

EXPLORING
THE AMERICAN WEST
1804–1900

John Moring

First Cooper Square Press edition 2002

This Cooper Square Press paperback edition of *Early American Naturalists* is an original publication. It is published by arrangement with the author.

Composition and design: Barbara Werden Design

Published by Cooper Square Press
A Member of the Rowman & Littlefield Publishing Group
200 Park Avenue South, Suite 1109
New York, New York 10003-1503
www.coopersquarepress.com

Distributed by National Book Network

Library of Congress Cataloging-in-Publication Data
Moring, John, 1946–2002.
    Early American naturalists : exploring the American West, 1804–1900 / John
    Moring.—1st Cooper Square Press ed.
        p. cm.
    ISBN 0-8154-1236-3 (cloth : alk. paper)
    1. Naturalists—United States—Biography. 2. Natural history—West (U.S.)—
    History. I. Title.

QH26 .M66 2002
508.78'092'2—dc21   2002002914

♾ The paper used in this publication meets the minimum requirements of
American National Standard for Information Sciences—Permanence of
Paper for Printed Library Materials, ANSI/NISO Z39.48–1992.
Manufactured in the United States of America.

To Walter Moring,
who first showed me a track in the woods
and told me
how to tell it was made by a deer.

Contents

PART 3

THE NEW NATURALISTS

Preface

When I read David Douglas's entry in his journal for January 9, 1825, I realized how lucky I have been.

Stopping in the Galapagos Islands on his way to the Pacific coast of North America, a decade before the arrival of Charles Darwin, Douglas was amazed by the local birds. Unafraid of humans and unaccustomed to their presence, some of the small birds calmly sat on the brim of Douglas's hat. Others rested on the barrel of his shotgun. Few people back in Douglas's home in Scotland would have witnessed such an incident.

I did once. While hunting on an abandoned logging road in the woods of Maine, I stopped by a large bush that was filled with black-capped chickadees. They were singing and moving about and, suddenly, one flew over and perched on the brim of my hat. Another landed on the end of my shotgun barrel. They were unafraid and had every confidence that I posed no threat.

They were right.

I didn't dare move, hoping that the chickadees would stay where they were. Maybe others would join them.

I feel fortunate because I saw the chickadees that day. I've also been able to witness other wondrous sights of nature: flushing hundreds of quail as I walked through a wilderness meadow in northern California; staring at a pronghorn antelope as it picked its way across open plains in South Dakota; gazing at miles of colorful wildflowers that emerged from the Arizona desert following spring rains; talking to a young moose that came over to visit me along a

Maine stream; staring wide-eyed at a small, brown octopus that swam below me while scuba diving off Baja California; watching in wonder as hundreds of mule deer grazed in a mountain meadow in California; and watching an eagle soar above spawning sockeye salmon in Alaska, as white beluga whales bobbed at the surface in the distance.

But, on that day when I met the chickadees, it dawned on me that every plant, every tree, every animal that I encountered that day had been discovered long before my visit to the woods. Every species was known, every organism classified. Every biological form that I saw already could be identified by any competent naturalist. There was little new under the sun, except for the subtle nuances of chickadee behavior. Given time, there still were mysteries of science, even among the familiar species—but not the initial thrill of discovering new forms of life.

But, it wasn't always so. There were times when a naturalist could enter wild country in the West and encounter new forms of life almost everywhere. It was a feeling that most people of modern times—no matter what wonders they have witnessed—will never experience. This is an account of those naturalists who were lucky to be in the West at a time when the excitement of discovery was almost beyond our understanding today.

I want to thank my wife, Kathleen, for always making sure that I had the time to do the research, synthesize the many primary and secondary accounts, blend it together, and do the writing. Thanks also to Elizabeth Frost-Knappman, who liked this concept from the beginning and offered continual encouragement, and Bill Krohn, who has now caught the naturalist history bug, and passed on records of eastern and western naturalists. I also appreciate the assistance of staff archivists at the U.S. Military Academy, Peabody Museum at Yale University, State Historical Society of Wisconsin, Colorado Historical Society, Smith College Library, Academy of Natural Sciences of Philadelphia, the National Archives branch in College Park, Maryland, and the Harvard University Botanical Museums.

Early American Naturalists

Chapter 1

THE EARLY NATURALISTS

It was Meriwether Lewis who first coined the term *barking squirrel* to describe the black-tailed prairie dog. Lewis's friend and co-leader of the famous Corps of Discovery Expedition, William Clark, called the curious animal a "ground rat," because of its extensive burrows and tunnels. But it was one of the other members of the Lewis and Clark expedition, Sergeant John Ordway, who first used the term *prairie dog*.

In a sense, all three terms were partly accurate. This was an animal of the prairies. It lived in extensive prairie-dog "towns" constructed of elaborate burrow systems. The creature was about the size of the common gray squirrel of the East, and it barked like a dog.

But the name that eventually stuck—black-tailed prairie dog—confused scientists in the East. This small mammal was not a dog, nor a rat, nor a squirrel. It was a species new to science, and it was Lewis and Clark who first recognized the sociable, curious animals as being unique. The explorers even sent a live "barking squirrel" back to President Thomas Jefferson in the spring of 1805, and the animal (still very much alive) became the star attraction at Peale's Museum in Philadelphia.

What swayed eastern scientists concerning this animal discovery was not just a vague description of a curious animal. Rather, it was the detailed notes that Lewis and Clark kept of their encounters and their examination of the prairie dog, skins that the explorers sent back east, and the live specimen that was viewed by scientists when it was placed on display in Philadelphia.

Lewis and Clark were primarily explorers, but their place in western history as naturalists is secure. Despite the lack of formal training by either man—or any member of their party—they were able to provide meticulous notes on their collections of flora and fauna. Those who followed Lewis and Clark into the lands of the American west often did have such formal scientific training, and the American west was an Eden for naturalists. As Samuel Bowles wrote in *Our New West* in 1869, "Nature, weary of repetitions, has in the New West, created originality, freshly, uniquely, majestically." Rather than picking through familiar forms, naturalists in the west could ply their trade in virgin territory.

Scientific discovery became an important component of many of the government-sponsored exploring expeditions into the west in the last two-thirds of the nineteenth century. Naturalists often participated as important members of the exploring parties. Such scientists made important contributions in an era where Darwin's theories and the concepts of species and evolution also were evolving rapidly.

The west was a vast, beckoning ghost. In one sense, to someone crossing the Mississippi River, it felt familiar and comfortable. The land did not suddenly change when one stepped ashore on the west side of the river. But, to a trained eye, it did. Vast grasslands whistled when alerted by gentle winds and moved like any peaceful sea. The Shining Mountains, as some fur trappers called the Rocky Mountains, rose abruptly from the long, rolling plains. And great rivers swept eastward and westward, sometimes through deep canyons and, in other places, through valleys filled with rich, dark soil.

Here, the living plants and animals were often different from any seen in the east, or elsewhere in the world. There was a vast doorway that opened into this world, and it enticed dozens of brave souls who answered its siren call. As the frontier slowly moved westward, accompanied by the sounds of axes and wagon wheels, the era of new biological discoveries moved with it.

Those who traveled the uncharted lands of the west were quite varied in personality, but almost all had a passion for natural history that often had little to do with money. Some, like Thomas Nuttall and David Douglas, often wandered the country alone or attached themselves to groups of fur trappers and other armed parties who could provide some protection. It was a dangerous time, and more than a few naturalists were killed while pursuing science. Many others courted near disaster. As guides became more familiar with the new lands, European adventurers joined the pursuit of plants and, particularly, animals. Some were simply hunters who were seeking new thrills and new types of game. But others combined their collecting skills and personal finances to further scientific knowledge.

As the Civil War approached, railroad surveys and larger collecting expeditions mapped their way across the west and resulted in lengthy treatises on the region's flora and fauna. Before and after the Civil War, there were dozens of professional collectors who knew enough about natural history to seek out new forms of life and send bird skins, eggs, insects, plants, fossils, and other biological collectibles back east to government and academic notables. Spencer Baird, John Torrey, and others paid some of the collectors for their specimens. The collectors made money and the eastern scientists made their reputations. Other field collectors did it solely for science, or possibly to have some plant or animal named for them.

Late in the nineteenth century, the personal competition among several major paleontologists became legendary, each trying to beat the others to discoveries of new bones—dinosaurs and other creatures. Yet, amid this intense competition, new types of naturalists were emerging. There was a curiosity about plants and (especially) animals that would start to spread across the United States and has yet to diminish to this day. In the eighteenth and nineteenth centuries, people wanted to see animals—the more unusual, the better. Soon, it became fashionable for the professional collectors to turn their attention to the capture of animals for zoos or the hunting of specimens that could be preserved and displayed in museums of the east and Europe.

This marked a change in the role and function of the naturalists.

Whereas such men and women once focused on killing animals in order to study the creatures and their taxonomy in detail, now there were those afield who brought back live specimens, or seeds or cuttings for eastern or European zoos and botanical gardens. At the least, collections of birds and mammals were made with exhibition in mind—often the only opportunity for many people to see unusual and common plants and animals. As the nineteenth century ended, naturalists became something quite different. There were artists who depicted animals in natural settings. And, there were scientists who studied life history and behavior. These new naturalists observed the activities of animals for extended periods of time. As the century turned, quite often, new amateurs—reborn in the image of Lewis and Clark—started to make their marks on local scales. They now conducted meticulous observation and examination of plants and animals in their natural settings. Some made outstanding contributions to their fields, even though natural history was their avocation, not their vocation. Elam Bartholomew, a Kansas farmer, became an expert on plants and fungi. William Hammond was a physician whose passion was the natural history found near his army post. And Gideon Lincecum, who was a marginally trained country doctor in Texas, became noted for his biological collections and observations.

From these times emerged a new breed of naturalists. These were insightful, reflective writers, like John Muir and John Burroughs, who immersed themselves in nature and reflected on the place of humans amongst the flora and fauna and majesty of the land.

As the nineteenth century ended, the days of the early naturalists were long gone. Those observing nature had little to fear from the dangers of following game paths into roadless wilderness. Wild animals, hostile tribes, rugged terrain, and extremes of weather were no longer concerns of the new naturalists. Yet, their passion for discovery remained very much the same as it had been for Peter Custis, Thomas Nuttall, Thomas Say, Robert Kennicott, John Le Conte, and all the others who risked life and limb to discover something unique—a plant or animal that had remained hidden from the eyes of science.

Why did they do it? What leads one person to commit his or her energies to the accumulation of money through trade or business and another to spend hours exploring the woods or fields, watching a bird, examining a flowering plant, or collecting a beetle? It is a passion that sometimes defies description. Yet, Samuel Rafinesque, one of the country's most prolific describers of animals, tried to do just that:

Every step taken into the fields, groves and hills, appears to afford new enjoyments. . . . Here is an old acquaintance seen again; there a novelty or a rare plant, perhaps a new one! greets your view; you hasten to pluck it, examine it, admire and put it in your book. Then you walk on thinking what it might be, or may be made by you hereafter. You felt an exultation, you are a conqueror, you have made a conquest over Nature, you are going to add a new object, or a page to science. The peaceful conquest has cost no tears, but fills your mind with a proud sensation of not being useless on earth, of having detected another link to the creative power of God.

Part 1

TRAVELING IN THE
WILD LANDS

Chapter 2

LEWIS AND CLARK:
ENTHUSIASTIC AMATEURS

The first time that Meriwether Lewis saw a grizzly bear, he wasn't overly impressed. Bears were nothing new to him. He had encountered them in the east many times. These "white bears," as Lewis and his friend, William Clark, first called the western bear, couldn't be all that worrisome.

Even the stories that the Mandan tribe told the explorers had to be tall tales. The Mandans said their people would never attack one of these bears unless there were six, eight, or even ten warriors in the party. But Lewis assumed that these stories had to be exaggerations. After all, Lewis wrote on April 13, 1805, "The savages attack this animal with their bows and arrows and the indifferent guns with which the traders furnish them, with these they shoot with such uncertainty and at so short a distance, that they frequently miss their aim & fall a sacrefice to the bear."

Surely, trained military marksmen such as those found with the Corps of Discovery, with modern 1804 rifles, should have little trouble dispatching such animals.

"The men as well as ourselves are anxious to meet with some of these bear," Lewis wrote in his journal.

Perhaps one could read a little less confidence in Lewis's words when the party started seeing tracks of grizzlies that were apparently of "enormous size."

On April 29, two weeks after Lewis wrote those words of

confidence, he was traveling on shore with some others in the party. They spotted two bears and the men fired their rifles, wounding both animals. One bear ran off, but the other one turned and charged toward Lewis. Fortunately, the explorer was 70 to 80 yards away and he was able to reload his rifle and fire again, this time killing the bear.

Obviously, there were some tense moments, but this grizzly bear didn't seem all that ferocious. Lewis wrote in his journal, "[I]n the hands of skillful riflemen they are by no means as formidable or dangerous as they have been represented."

Lewis soon discovered that the bear—a male—was not fully grown, perhaps weighing 300 pounds. Nevertheless, the explorer spent time describing the animal in great detail in his journal.

Lewis's next encounter with a grizzly bear made him forget his earlier bravado. On May 5, William Clark and George Drewyer spotted an adult grizzly on a sandbar. It was "verry large," wrote Clark in his journal, "and a terrible looking animal, which we found very hard to kill." In fact, it took ten shots to finally dispatch the animal, five of which passed through its lungs. Even with such wounds, it was 20 minutes before the animal stopped breathing and the men could approach it.

Lewis was becoming more impressed. Hearing the shots and then the story, he examined this older brother of the grizzly bear that he had encountered a week earlier. This one weighed 500 to 600 pounds and measured 8 feet 7½ inches in length—still small compared to the largest known grizzlies.

The following week, Lewis spotted another grizzly, but "I find that the curiosity of our party is pretty well satisfied with rispect to this animal." Another incident, a week later, convinced even the most skeptical members of the exploring party that the grizzly bear was a formidable animal that was every bit as tenacious as the Mandans had claimed.

Six men of the party spotted a large grizzly and decided to go after it. Just to be safe, two of the men elected to hold their fire and stand in reserve while the others fired at the huge animal. The four men fired in unison, each ball passing through the bear at a distance of 40 yards, two of the shots through the lungs.

But it had little effect on the animal. The bear leaped up and started attacking, and the four men ran for their lives. The other two hunters fired at the approaching bear, breaking its shoulder but failing to slow its advance.

Now, all six men were running for the nearby river, empty weapons in hand. The men hid in the willows along the shore, reloaded, and fired again. But the bear was unfazed except to note the location of the panic-stricken hunters. Two of the men threw down their rifles and dove off the riverbank, landing in the water some 20 feet below. The bear leaped in after them and might have killed one of the men had another hunter not been able to shoot the grizzly through the head.

From that day on, the members of the Lewis and Clark expedition avoided attacking any grizzly bear. They had a healthy respect for the animal, *Ursus horribilis*, which was formally described by George Ord a decade later. Despite that, Meriwether Lewis had the lesson reinforced during another incident in June.

Lewis spotted a herd of buffalo that he estimated must have exceeded 1,000 in number. He killed one animal for food, but forgot to reload his rifle while he stood gazing at the huge number of animals still moving across the rolling plains. Unseen, a large grizzly bear approached to within 20 paces. Lewis calmly raised his weapon to fire when it occurred to him that it was unloaded.

The animal started approaching quickly, and there was no time to load powder and ball. The nearest tree was some 300 yards away, and the situation looked grim.

Then the bear charged at full speed, his mouth wide open.

Lewis turned and ran 80 yards to a river and jumped in. The bear, surprisingly, decided not to follow. After some growling, the animal turned and wandered off.

Lewis now had no illusions about grizzly bears, and he wrote in his journal, "I must confess that I do not like the gentleman and had reather fight two Indians than one bear."

Lewis and Clark were not the first non—Native Americans to encounter the grizzly bear. Alexander Mackenzie had described an encounter during his journey across Canada several years before, in his popular book *Voyage from Montreal.* And Bernard DeVoto, one of the more famous subsequent editors of the Lewis and Clark journals, believes that Henry Kelsey may have been the first white man to make note of the great bear in 1691. But Lewis and Clark were the first to provide a detailed description of the grizzly bear, its body proportions, its color variations, and its behavior. It is only one example of the impressive contributions that the two explorers made to natural history of the west. Lewis and Clark were not formally trained in the biological sciences, but they were enthusiastic amateurs. Their abilities to describe, collect, count, and measure plants and animals in great detail, and to compare new types of flora and fauna with existing taxonomic forms, truly made them the west's first naturalists.

The story of the Lewis and Clark expedition is a familiar one to most people. The United States acquired the Louisiana Territory—a wedge-shaped tract of land that extended from New Orleans northward across the vast Great Plains, and up the Missouri River to the Continental Divide—for $15 million, or about three cents per acre. The size of the United States doubled overnight, and the many reasons that President Thomas Jefferson had always wanted to explore this new land now became legally justified. He could send an exploring expedition into the west, even if the boundaries between Spanish lands in the south and British lands in the northwest were disputed.

Jefferson envisioned at least four initial exploring trips into these new lands, the first of which subsequently departed from St. Louis under the command of Meriwether Lewis and William Clark in May 1804.

Jefferson's instructions to the two explorers were lengthy and quite detailed. They involved exploration and mapping as primary objectives, but they also included other objectives. Jefferson specifically directed what became known as the Corps of Discovery to observe climate and geology, describe and map the fur resources, negotiate cooperative agreements with Native American tribes, describe native customs, and record and collect flora and fauna.

Specifically, Jefferson ordered the explorers to observe "the animals of the country generally, & especially those not known in the U.S. the remains and accounts of any which may [be] deemed rare or extinct."

Jefferson's motives for these natural history studies were part economic, part political, and part a reflection of his own Enlightenment curiosity. One of the economic justifications for funding the $2,500 expedition was the likely discovery of vast fur riches in the lands of the upper Missouri River. Jefferson had read Alexander Mackenzie's account of the Scottish fur trader's treks across the northern part of the continent. The president especially took notice of a statement in the epilogue of the book where Mackenzie urged the British government to "secure the trade of furs and other resources," of the western part of North America.

Jefferson took this statement quite seriously. The British were becoming firmly entrenched in the fur trade of Canada, and British ships had been exploring the Pacific coast of the continent for decades. Unchecked, Jefferson believed, British-backed fur trappers and traders would soon control the resources of the Rocky Mountains within or near the new lands of the Louisiana Purchase and have treaties and working agreements with the tribes of the region. The president showed Mackenzie's book to his secretary, Meriwether Lewis, who would eventually take a copy with him on the epic expedition of 1804–1806.

But gaining access to a valuable fur resource wasn't Jefferson's only reason for issuing orders to Lewis and Clark to study natural history. At the time, the United States was confined to the eastern portion of the continent. In 1801, two-thirds of the population of the country was living within 50 miles of the Atlantic coast. To most people, the "west" referred to places like Ohio, where the land was undeveloped and often unexploited. St. Louis seemed like a town perched at the ends of the earth. Throughout their journals, Lewis and Clark often referred to having come from "the United States," or anticipating their return to "the States."

Even though the lands of the Louisiana Purchase were now part of the United States, it meant little to Native Americans who lived there, and little to those living in the east—especially members of Congress.

The decision to purchase the Louisiana Territory may not have been constitutionally legal, and it certainly was controversial. One opponent, Senator Samuel White, warned on the floor of the Senate, "I believe it [the purchase] will be the greatest curse that could at present befall us. . . . [T]he settlement of this country will be highly injurious and dangerous to the United States." But Jefferson knew that one day the young nation would need wider boundaries, more breathing room for an expanding population that would surely come. However, at the beginning of the nineteenth century, those western lands seemed very distant and unimportant.

So, in addition to the benefits of an exploring expedition that would establish peaceful relations with Native Americans, map routes westward, and document the fur, mineral, and timber resources, Jefferson used the argument that there were abundant opportunities to expand knowledge about natural science. The scientific community of the east supported this vision, and they did have some influence with their congressional representatives.

Learning more about natural history also was a logical extension of Thomas Jefferson's personal philosophies. Perhaps no other national figure of the day personified the Enlightenment period when a curiosity about Nature was akin to becoming closer to God. To know Nature was to know God. It was through close observation of God's creations that ordinary humans could become more complete.

In many ways, Thomas Jefferson was a Renaissance man in terms of interests and abilities. But he had a special curiosity about Nature. The idea of a grand exploring expedition into uncharted lands greatly appealed to him, and it is likely that, under other circumstances, he personally would have leaped at the chance to join such an expedition. Unfortunately, he had other duties, such as running the country. But he likely saw a reflection of himself in Meriwether

Lewis. Lewis, in some ways, was an Enlightenment extension of Jefferson on this trip.

As a result of all these reasons, observation and documentation of nature always was an important component of the proposed Corps of Discovery expedition into the west. And this was to be a component of each of the early government-sponsored expeditions into the Louisiana Territory. Commanders of these expeditions of the early nineteenth century were instructed to bring back plants and animals. Yet, for decades, the biological accomplishments of most of the other expeditions ultimately would pale in comparison to those of the Lewis and Clark group, where natural history remained a priority.

Meriwether Lewis had many admirable traits that made him an ideal person to carry out Jefferson's instructions. Lewis was born near Charlottesville, Virginia, on August 18, 1774. At the time he departed up the Missouri River, he was not yet 30 years old. When he was 20, he joined the militia, then joined the regular army. In the military, he saw action against various Indian tribes while under the command of General "Mad Anthony" Wayne. It was in the army that Lewis, then an ensign, was placed under the command of Lieutenant William Clark, and the two men established a lasting friendship. Eventually, Lewis rose in rank to captain and became a regimental paymaster before being asked to serve as President Jefferson's secretary.

The Lewis family had been neighbors of Jefferson, and the president kept in touch with the young officer. Lewis always was quite comfortable in the outdoors, he was a good marksman, and he was tested in battle. Of particular interest to Jefferson, however, was that Lewis had an outdoorsman's knowledge of flora and fauna of the east but with a curiosity that bordered on the scientific. Lewis knew something about folk medicine, having learned from his mother, Lucy Meriwether Lewis, who was well known for her herb remedies in the local countryside. And Lewis was completely honest and trustworthy. Whatever Jefferson's instructions might be, Lewis did his best to follow them.

Despite Meriwether Lewis's obvious attributes, Jefferson realized that an exploring expedition such as one that he envisioned might become logistically prohibitive with only a single leader. He suggested adding a co-leader, and Lewis immediately thought of his friend and former commanding officer, William Clark.

Clark was even more at home under primitive conditions than was Lewis. Clark was born on August 1, 1770, also in Virginia, but moved with his family to Kentucky when he was 15. Four years later, he joined a group of volunteers who were fighting Indians; then he too joined the regular army and saw considerable action during the frontier Indian wars.

At the time that Clark was asked to co-lead the expedition into the Louisiana Territory, he was no longer in the army. When he received Lewis's letter, Clark knew he would accept, but he first asked the opinion of his brother, George Rogers Clark, the famous soldier. George agreed that such an expedition would be a trip of a lifetime. William took pen in hand and replied to Lewis, "This is an immense undertaking fraited with numerous difficulties, but my friend I can assure you that no man lives with whom I would prefer to undertake and share the difficulties of such a trip than yourself." William Clark was 33 years old when he left on the trip west.

The two men were quite different in several respects, but these characteristics complemented each other. Anyone reading the journals of the two men would soon distinguish their writing styles. Whereas Lewis was more flowery and verbose in his writing, Clark was more succinct and to the point. Lewis often used personal insights in his journal entries, almost as if he were writing in a private diary, while Clark used factual descriptions, almost like a ship's captain might enter into a vessel's log. The two men, however, were loyal to each other, to the men under their command, to the president, and to their mission. Lewis had an appointment as a captain, and he wanted Clark to have equal rank and authority as co-leader. Jefferson agreed. But, in an early example of bureaucratic obstruction, the War Department refused to appoint Clark to his former rank. Instead, he received a commission as a lieutenant. The military powers would not back down, even with a presidential order. However, Meriwether Lewis informed the expedition's company that both he and William Clark were captains and co-commanders and each had equal authority for the command. The matter was never questioned again.

Others in the company were selected with equal care. They had to be compatible with each other and able to work and live in stressful and even dangerous conditions for what Lewis and Clark thought might be a period of many months. Except for some discipline problems in the first few months, those personnel decisions ultimately were proven correct.

The expedition took two and a half years, close to the time period that Thomas Jefferson had predicted.

When Congress eventually approved funding for the exploring expedition, Thomas Jefferson sent Lewis to Philadelphia for training. Philadelphia was, at the time, the center of science for the country, and many of the leading figures in natural history, astronomy, and mathematics lived there. Although Lewis did not have formal training as a naturalist or medical doctor, Jefferson hoped that the leading men of science would quickly educate Lewis enough so that the scientific accomplishments of the expedition would rank in importance with the expected geographic and economic accomplishments.

Jefferson wrote letters to five leading men of science, who agreed to train Lewis in the rudiments of their fields. "It will be very useful," the president wrote to one of the scientists, "to state for him those objects on which it is most desirable he should bring in information for this purpose I ask the favor of you to prepare some notes of such particulars as may occur in his journey & which you think should draw his attention & enquiry."

Lewis arrived in Lancaster, Pennsylvania, on April 19, 1803, where he spent almost three weeks with mathematician and astronomer Andrew Ellicott, learning to accurately record positions en route. From there, he visited mathematician Robert Patterson in Philadelphia for further training with navigation instruments, including sextant, compass, and chronometer. Lewis's country folk medicine training was supplemented by more refined medical training from Dr. Benjamin Rush, perhaps the country's most respected physician. Not only did Rush advise Lewis on the contents of his medical kit, but he gave Lewis a list of medical questions to answer concerning the native tribes that might be encountered in the west. Rush also provided a supply of "Dr. Rush's pills" that Lewis would use often for ailments as diverse as constipation and diarrhea. Rush further provided a booklet of health guidelines, later popularly called "Dr. Rush's Rules of Health." Among them were:

After having had your feet chilled, it will be useful to wash them with a little spirit.

When you feel the least indisposition, do not attempt to overcome it by labor or marching. Rest in a horizontal position.

Molasses or sugar & water with a few drops of the acid of vitriol can make a pleasant & wholesome drink with your meals.

Acid of vitriol is more commonly known as sulfuric acid.

Two other scientists provided Lewis with training in natural history: Benjamin Smith Barton and Caspar Wistar. Barton was then 37 years old and the most eminent natural scientist in the country. He was a professor of botany at the College of Medicine, University of Pennsylvania, but his interests ranged into animal biology as well. He wrote the first textbook on botany published in the country, *Elements of Botany: or Outlines of the Natural History of Vegetables*, in 1803. Lewis paid $6.00 for a copy, which he later would carry on the expedition westward.

Barton and Wistar taught Lewis the rudiments of Linnaean taxonomy so that he and Clark could place specimens that they encountered en route within conventional taxonomic groupings, or at least note how unusual plants and animals differed from known species. Wistar also taught Lewis the basics of paleontology, as fossils were a particular passion for the 42-year-old scientist. In late 1803, Lewis even visited a paleontological dig site near Cincinnati that had been discovered by Dr. William Goforth. The president was thrilled when Lewis sent him several bones from the site as Jefferson, too, had a fascination with fossils and dinosaur bones.

Between Barton and Wistar, Lewis learned how to collect and preserve specimens, press samples of plants, properly skin animals, and, especially, how to observe and describe the flora and fauna. This was particularly critical, as Lewis and Clark, not being naturalists, would be turning over their samples and notes to Barton and others who would prepare formal descriptions that would be published and circulated. A pressed plant alone could not provide a true indication of coloration or height, but precise descriptions accompanying the sample would be invaluable.

For mammals and birds, proper curing of skins and notes on bones were key to later inspection by others. For fishes and other animals that could not be easily returned, meristic counts (i.e., counts of fin rays, scales along lateral lines, body proportions) would be invaluable in determining whether a particular specimen was truly unique or simply a color or form variant of a known eastern species. Accurate drawings also would prove to be invaluable, and this is where William Clark excelled. Some of his careful drawings of fishes and birds are remarkably detailed.

Lewis spent only about a month on this training, but he was able to pass much of it on to William Clark and others in the party prior to and during the initial weeks of the journey. In addition to the extensive supplies purchased for the trip, numerous reference books also were borrowed or purchased. These included Barton's textbook on botany and Mackenzie's book of his westward trip to what is now British Columbia. Other volumes known to have been transported included du Pratz's *The History of Louisiana*, which included numerous notes on natural history, a four-volume dictionary, two books on Linnaean nomenclature, Kelley's *A Practical Introduction to Spherics and Nautical Astronomy*, and two other navigation reference books.

The Lewis and Clark expedition left St. Louis on May 13, 1804. The party traveled up the Missouri River and spent the winter at Fort Mandan, their winter headquarters with the Mandan Indians, in what is today North Dakota. The men collected, observed, and described the flora and fauna as they went. It is somewhat disconcerting to the modern reader to read daily entries of animals killed by one or more members of the party. For example, on May 19, 1805, Clark reported that Lewis had killed an elk, a deer, and a beaver. At dinnertime, Clark killed three more deer and several beavers. However, the expedition, for most of its time, included from about 30 to over 50 people (the number swelled in 1804 when boat operators and other soldiers were included). Fresh meat was always in demand for such a large group. Some of that could be cured or made into jerky, but most meat taken from deer, buffalo, or elk had to be consumed quickly, so sources of fresh meat were required almost daily. However, throughout the trip, some animals were killed for a dual purpose. Not only was the meat eaten or the oil retained, but the carcasses were studied and measured for scientific records. If a specimen was unusual, the animal might be skinned and the hide retained for eastern scientists.

Prior to resuming their upriver trip in April 1805, the company spent several days packing material to be sent back to President Jefferson. On April 7, Lewis and Clark sent eight boxes and crates and a trunk back downstream to St. Louis, accompanied by six soldiers, two French hunters, and an Arikara guide.

The contents were expected to be initially examined by President Jefferson, with some of the items then transferred to scientists who could begin the task of examination, classification, and description. Among the items shipped were skeletons and hides of pronghorn antelopes and prairie dogs, horns of mule deer and bighorn sheep, and skins of hares and foxes, as well as plants, rocks, and Mandan artifacts. The latter included a bow and arrow, pots, buffalo robes, and a painted buffalo hide depicting a battle that had been fought eight years earlier between the Mandans and the Sioux and Arikara.

The shipment also included cages containing four live magpies, a sharp-tail grouse, and a black-tailed prairie dog.

All three species were first discovered by Lewis and Clark and were later described in print by other scientists. Prairie dogs particularly fascinated William Clark. On September 7, 1804, Clark and Lewis walked to a high point of ground in present-day Nebraska and encountered nearby a village of prairie dogs. Lewis would initially refer to these animals as "barking squirrels," because of the noises that they made, and Clark called them "ground rats," because of their extensive tunnel system. The men killed one animal to skin and send back east, and almost the entire company spent most of a day trying to catch a live prairie dog. They eventually resorted to pouring large quantities of water into the burrows, collected in bucketfuls from the Missouri River, to flush out an animal. The prairie-dog town covered about four acres, according to Clark, but other communities were subsequently encountered by others who estimated areas up to thousands of square miles.

Obtaining a live prairie dog in the spring was equally difficult, but the live animals sent by Lewis and Clark made their way downstream to St. Louis—a distance of some 1,000 miles—in about six weeks, arriving May 10, 1805. From there, the crates were shipped aboard a river barge to New Orleans—another 1,000 miles—where the material arrived about June 12. The prairie dog and the four magpies survived to that point. After sitting on a New Orleans dock, the crates and cages were put on a ship bound for Baltimore, then conveyed by wagon to the executive mansion where the crates were opened on August 12. A magpie and the prairie dog were still alive and healthy four months after their journey began. The president, who was at Monticello at the time, was informed of the arrival of the crates and that the animals had been placed in the president's parlor. Jefferson finally viewed the animals and the other items in October 1805, after which he sent the live animals to be displayed at Peale's Museum at Independence Hall in Philadelphia. The bird and prairie dog were still alive and being viewed by visitors until at least 1806.

In April 1805, the Lewis and Clark expedition proceeded up the Missouri River, around the Great Falls of the Missouri, in present-day Montana, across what would sometimes become known by trappers as the Great Shining Mountains (Rocky Mountains), then down the Snake and Columbia Rivers. The party reached the Pacific Ocean on November 7, 1805, near present-day Long Beach, Washington.

The company erected a small fort—Fort Clatsop—just south of the mouth of the Columbia River, where they spent the winter of 1805–1806. Compared to the bone-chilling conditions at Fort Mandan the previous winter, where frostbite was not uncommon among the men, winter on the Oregon coast was relatively mild. However, it did rain constantly, clothes were always damp and mildewed, and fleas were a constant nuisance. The temperate conditions did allow the company to collect, draw, and describe local flora and fauna and expand on their journal entries.

In the spring, the explorers returned eastward, finally reaching their first white settlement, the village of La Charette, on September 20, 1806. Soon, they were in St. Louis, and a newspaper account in the Boston *Columbia Centinel* suggested that Lewis and Clark "have kept an ample journal of their tour, which will be published and must afford much intelligence."

This brief synopsis of Lewis and Clark's historic journey does not convey the length of the endeavor (7,689 miles through unexplored terrain), the duration of the undertaking (two and a half years), or the dangers involved. Amazingly, only one man died, Sergeant Charles Floyd, of an apparent burst appendix on August 20, 1804. But every member of the party suffered injuries, illnesses, and potentially life-threatening situations. Just considering the experiences of Lewis and Clark alone, it was an eventful trip. Clark was nearly bitten by rattlesnakes on four occasions; he fell through the ice and suffered brief hypothermia, hurt his hip, endured rheumatism, "plursie," constipation, fever, and various other unspecified sicknesses, and suffered a reaction from an insect bite. Lewis was nearly bitten by a rattlesnake twice, was attacked by a grizzly bear, was swept out of a canoe by a tree limb and knocked into rapids, and fell over cliffs twice, only to cling to small bushes to avoid plunging all the way down. He was nearly poisoned when he tasted a mineral deposit and found it contained arsenic and several other toxic compounds, and suffered dysentery and an injured foot. He was nearly shot when Blackfeet tried to steal the party's weapons and two of the Indians were killed in the ensuing fight, and he *was* wounded when one of his fellow hunters mistook him for a deer, shooting the buckskin-clad Lewis through the upper thigh and buttocks.

The "journal" that soon became associated with Lewis and Clark was actually many journals. Thomas Jefferson knew that the written records of this expedition would ultimately be the most valuable accomplishment of the trip. As such, he gave Lewis and Clark specific instructions concerning the journals themselves. Jefferson wanted the explorers to make copies of their journals so that loss or damage of an individual volume would not result in the loss of important data, as would happen to journals from several other subsequent expeditions into the west, such as some of those from the Stephen Long expedition and Charles Wilkes's United States Exploring Expedition.

Several copies of these should be made at leisure times & put into the care of the most trustworthy of your attendants, to guard by multiplying them, against the accidental losses to which they will be exposed.

Jefferson further wanted one copy to be written on birch paper and, to further prevent damage to the journals, Lewis and Clark bound some in elk hide to provide a more waterproof covering.

Possibly nine individuals in the party kept journals, although not all have survived. Lewis and Clark did not specifically make duplicates of their own journals as directed, but they were instructed to make independent observations, not only of events but also of plants and animals. Jefferson, and presumably at least Lewis, knew that the most valuable information from a plant or animal encountered on the trip would be to maintain the actual specimen, pressed, skinned, or otherwise preserved, accompanied by a detailed written description. Less valuable would be such a description accompanied by drawings. Of still less value to scientists in the east would simply be a written description.

However, if two or more individuals provided their own, independent descriptions, the scientific collaboration and value would be improved. One set of observations could provide confirmation to the observations of another. It was only Meriwether Lewis's word if he described and measured an unusual frog that he might encounter. However, those data had much more validity if William Clark or another member of the party were to write down his own, independent description of the frog, and the two reports were similar. This independent collaboration was done throughout the journals, although both men did occasionally borrow each other's journal to copy entries. When this was done, however, it was generally reported in the third person, so that, from a scientific sense, the material in such instances was not confirmed through personal observation.

As a consequence of these extensive journal entries, Lewis and Clark returned home with many journals filled with meteorological observations, river height measurements, survey distances, and detailed descriptions of plants and animals. The journals that are widely known today are primarily the diary entries of daily activities. For most of the nineteenth century, the accumulated scientific data were largely unknown and unrecognized.

Part of this was due to the perception that Lewis and Clark, not being trained naturalists, could hardly have recorded much information that would advance the field of natural history. Thus, their scientific accomplishments were downplayed, filed, and essentially ignored as new, trained naturalists started to venture into the west and report their own discoveries.

Second, the unfortunate history of the publication of Lewis's and Clark's records de-emphasized the detailed observations of flora and fauna and was delayed by the unfortunate suicide of Meriwether

Lewis in 1809. Lewis was the more sensitive of the two explorers, and he was the least able to cope with the post-trip notoriety that all members of the company achieved. While Clark thrived as the new territory's principal Indian agent, with the rank of brigadier general, Lewis was ill-suited to life as governor of the Louisiana Territory.

With their new positions keeping the two men occupied, and then Lewis's death, Thomas Jefferson entrusted the publication of the journals to a Philadelphia lawyer, Nicholas Biddle. Biddle was to have been assisted by Benjamin Smith Barton in the evaluation of the scientific discoveries. But the eminent scientist was suffering from ill health and was unable to guide the non-scientist on the importance of the natural history and ethnological records. Nor was Barton all that enthusiastic about the samples and descriptions that were returned to his laboratory.

Barton was certainly prominent and knowledgeable, but this was well before Darwin's *Origin of Species* and similar controversial ideas about species and taxonomic relationships. Barton had a reputation of being somewhat over-extended, leaving many tasks unfinished. He also did not closely study many of the animal specimens that Lewis and Clark sent or brought back to the east. Part of this was due to Barton's belief—shared by many others—that most species of animals had already been discovered and described from specimens collected in the Old World. Barton and others considered that unusual examples of animals were often simply variations in color or form from those previously known animals. Few actual new species were likely to be encountered, according to this view—only forms of known animals. Even the prairie dog that was shipped to the executive mansion by Lewis and Clark in spring 1805 was examined alive by Barton, who identified the animal as *Arctomys citillus*, a rodent known from Asia. Lewis and Clark, he opined, did not discover a new species, only a range extension of a previously known species from Asia. However, close examination of the actual animal and skins sent back in 1805, and the lengthy description provided by Lewis and Clark, led George Ord to conclude that this was indeed a new species, distinct from the Asian form, and named by Ord in 1815 as *Arctomys ludoviciana*. In some instances, Barton was correct in this limited species reasoning. The magpie that survived being shipped to the east was thought by Jefferson to be different from magpies in Europe, but many today believe the western form may be, at most, only a subspecies of the common European bird.

As a result of all these factors, Nicholas Biddle was left to his own judgments as editor of Lewis's and Clark's written material. The journals that eventually were published concentrated on the daily activity narrative, with the raw data—considered of little interest to readers—largely edited out. The rather boring accounts of fin ray counts, coloration and spotting patterns, body measurements, and plant leaf branching patterns were not included. That version of the *Journals* was published in 1814 and throughout much of the remaining century, most people believed that Lewis and Clark were explorers who did not collect much in the way of important scientific data.

It was not until Elliott Coues examined the original journals and published the full material in 1893, with annotations based on decades of improved biological knowledge, that scientists and the public alike began to appreciate the natural history contributions of the two explorers. By the time that Rueben Gold Thwaites updated the full documents in 1905, the evidence was overwhelming that Lewis and Clark were responsible for significant discoveries in the field of natural history.

Two examples of such detailed records kept by the explorers are worth noting, as they are representative of the larger body of data compiled in their journals.

The bull snake, *Coluber sayi*, was first discovered by Meriwether Lewis on August 5, 1804. He took rough field notes and later entered them into legible form in his journal. He noted, "Killed a serpent on the bank of the river adjoining a large prairie," along today's South Dakota–Nebraska border. Lewis measured the snake's length and girth, and counted the number of scuta, or scale plates on the belly and on the tail. He then described in great detail the color and sounds made by the creature:

No poison teeth, therefore think him perfectly innocent; eyes, center black with a border of pale brown yellow. Color of skin on head yellow green with black specks on the extremity of the south which are pointed or triangular. Color of back, transverse stripes of black and dark brown of an inch in width. The end of the tail hard and pointed like a cock's spur. The sides are speckled with yellowish brown and black. Two rows of black spots on a light yellow ground pass throughout his whole length on the upper points of the scuta of the belly and tail one-half inch apart. This snake is vulgarly called the cow or bull snake from a bellowing noise which it is said sometimes to make resembling that animal, though as to this fact I am unable to attest it, never having heard them make that or any other noise myself.

On June 13, 1805, Private Silas Goodrich, the expedition's most accomplished angler, went fishing near the Great Falls of the Missouri where the company was temporarily delayed in their journey up the Missouri River. Goodrich caught six "very fine trout" that measured "from 16 to 23 inches in length," wrote Lewis in his journal. Lewis examined the fish closely and recorded his observations in great detail. He compared the trout to the brook trout of the east (*Salvelinus fontinalis*). "They resembled our mountain speckled trout in form and the position of their fins," he wrote. But, he continued, they differed from those eastern trout in subtle ways. Spotting patterns, he noted, "are of a deep black instead of the red or gold color of those common to the United States."

Lewis described teeth on the roof of the mouth and the tongue, the telltale slash of red at the throat, and even the color of the flesh. Anyone reading that description today would immediately recognize this as the cutthroat trout, one of the most common game fishes of the northern Rocky Mountains and Pacific Northwest. The fish was not formally described in scientific circles for another 30 years, but when Lewis's original description was compared, it was obvious that Lewis and Clark were the first to discover and describe this species. Today, we know that the cutthroat trout is found from northern California northward to Alaska, eastward to

Saskatchewan, and south to the headwaters of the Rio Grande River.

Not only did the two explorers describe this species in clear detail, but they also noted similarities as well as differences between these trout of the interior and ones found near the mouth of the Columbia River, which belong to the coastal subspecies of cutthroat trout. Today, the inland form is known as *Oncorhynchus clarki lewisi*, and the coastal form (often anadromous) is known as *Oncorhynchus clarki clarki*.

These were not the only biological discoveries credited to Lewis and Clark. In all, the two explorers are credited with discovering some 178 new species of plants, including such now familiar forms as western red cedar, Pacific yew, California rhododendron, Sitka spruce, lodgepole pine, orange honeysuckle, plains cottonwood, ponderosa pine, salmonberry, Oregon crab apple, Oregon white oak, mountain hemlock, bitterroot, and many others.

They are credited with discovering some 13 species of fishes, 50 birds, 44 mammals, and 15 reptiles, including some of the most familiar animals of the west: pocket gopher, pronghorn antelope, bighorn sheep, mule deer, mountain lion, desert cottontail, western badger, western meadowlark, black-billed magpie, western gull, Oregon jay, broad-tailed hummingbird, Pacific tree frog, western garter snake, prairie rattlesnake, blue catfish, white sturgeon, starry flounder, Montana grayling, eulachon (candlefish), and one or more subspecies of raccoon, among others. Although these species were later described by others, it is significant to note that at least two new genera, three species, two subspecies, and three common names were named after either Lewis or Clark by later scientists.

What makes the natural history contributions of Lewis and Clark even more impressive is that their meticulous descriptions and drawings of flora and fauna that could not be returned to the East are such that modern scientists can still easily identify many of the forms that were completely unknown at the time and that were first described by a pair of "enthusiastic" amateurs.

Chapter 3

PETER CUSTIS AND THE RED RIVER EXPEDITION

There was a knock at the door. Peter Custis, a doctoral student at the University of Pennsylvania, walked over, opened the door, and was handed a note by a student. Professor Benjamin Smith Barton wanted to see Peter.

It was January 1806, and as Peter slipped on his heavy coat and mittens, he wondered what his advisor wanted. It could be something bad . . . or good. Since Professor Barton had several students, he probably had some task for Peter, who was still a year away from receiving his doctorate. Whatever the reason, any student of Benjamin Barton needed to respond as soon as possible.

When he entered Barton's cramped office, the eminent botanist and naturalist explained that he had an offer for his student—a chance to go on an expedition into the unexplored lands of the new Louisiana Territory. It would be an opportunity of a lifetime, Barton explained. It was a chance to be the first trained naturalist to observe, document, and collect in the western part of the continent and to see lands never before observed by easterners.

Peter Custis didn't have to think about it long. Even though it would mean delaying the completion of his degree, he accepted immediately.

This expedition was one of four initially planned by Thomas Jefferson for the Louisiana Territory. Each was intended to explore a different part of the new lands, and the president hoped to have at least two of the groups depart in 1804. The Lewis and Clark expedition left in May of that year, but a planned expedition up the Red River (the territory's southern border with New Spain), then down the Arkansas River, kept experiencing delays. It actually would take two more years before getting under way.

Preparations for the Corps of Discovery trip were logistically complex. But the exploration of the Red River ultimately became even more difficult because one scientist after another turned down the chance to accompany the expedition.

The events surrounding all these personnel difficulties were complex and had their roots long before the acquisition of the Louisiana Territory. Thomas Jefferson wished to have at least a competent surveyor as part of the party, as well as at least one naturalist. The lack of an academically trained scientist traveling with Lewis and Clark was a nagging omission that disturbed Jefferson. He intended to remedy that criticism with his other expeditions. Jefferson had no doubts that numerous enterprising men would leap at the opportunity to explore and collect in virgin territories. Unfortunately, there seemed to be few people with the enthusiasm of a Thomas Jefferson.

Plans for a trip up the Red River, then down the Arkansas River, kept being delayed until Jefferson asked the respected mathematician and astronomer William Dunbar to lead the scientific portion of such a trip. Dunbar seemed a logical choice as a scientific leader because he had been one of the principal critics of the preparations for the Lewis and Clark expedition. Dunbar had expressed regret, in a letter to Jefferson, that the Corps of Discovery lacked "the presence of a good naturalist particularly a botanist."

But Dunbar was experiencing periodic episodes of poor health. He did agree, however, to direct the preparations for the expedition. Without Dunbar in the actual exploring party, Jefferson asked a noted druggist, chemist, and amateur geologist named George Hunter to join the party. Hunter agreed and, because he also dabbled in natural history, the president was optimistic that the Red

River trip could depart soon after Lewis and Clark headed up the Missouri River. However, Jefferson was not prepared for the difficulties that were to come in selecting a field leader to replace Dunbar—someone who was part surveyor and part scientist.

The president asked for recommendations from Andrew Ellicott, who had tutored Meriwether Lewis. Ellicott suggested two men, but neither was available. Dunbar then suggested Stephen Minor, but a formal request never came to pass. To further complicate matters, there were now concerns about a hostile band of Osages who could become a threat along the intended route of the expedition, especially along the Arkansas River. As a consequence, the plans for the trip kept being delayed and delayed.

Frustrated, Jefferson asked Dunbar and Hunter to make a brief trip up one of the Red River's lower tributaries, the Ouachita. It made sense. Hunter was prepared to go on an expedition into the new territory, and he was being paid while waiting. Dunbar's health seemed improved, and he was willing to undertake a rather short trip, if not the longer journey that was being planned. And Congress had authorized $3,000 for a Red River trip, and most of the supplies were already purchased.

So, in the fall of 1804, a few months after the departure of Lewis and Clark, William Dunbar and George Hunter accompanied a military party of 15 men up the Ouachita River. They crossed the Ouachita Mountains upriver to what is now Hot Springs, then returned. The trip took three months and was without incident, except for when one of the men accidentally wounded Hunter in an accident similar to what would befall Meriwether Lewis in 1806.

Technically, the Ouachita Expedition was the second organized exploring trip into the new western lands and the first to include scientists in the party. But neither Dunbar nor Hunter was a trained naturalist. In their notes and subsequent letters, both men regretted not having more biological training. The relatively brief Ouachita Expedition encountered wondrous plants and animals, but no member of the party felt adequate to properly describe and identify them.

When the Ouachita trip ended, Jefferson again attempted to find a scientific leader for a more extensive trip up the Red River. Dunbar agreed to continue participating in the planning of such a trip, but he was now 55 years old and the three months on the Ouachita had been too much for him to think about actually participating in anything longer. Things now seemed to start again at square one because George Hunter decided to return home. Hunter had been paid $3.00 per day for the months of waiting and planning and the trip up the Ouachita River, and although he was still interested in a longer expedition, the proposed trip now seemed to focus just on the Red River. It would no longer include the interesting Arkansas River, partly because of the continuing threat from the Osages. And even the Red River exploration seemed far in the future—at least until 1806. So Dunbar and Jefferson started to look again for a naturalist and a surveyor. But Dr. John Sibley, who was quite familiar with the lower Red River and had provided Jefferson a report of his knowledge of the river and the local tribes, also declined an offer. So, too, did surveyor Seth Pease and a Washington professor.

Dunbar was frustrated, and he wrote a letter to Jefferson wondering why "young men of talents . . . are not found in numbers," and weren't interested in going on such a great adventure. One man was interested in such a trip, a mathematician named George Davis. He even wrote to the president, asking to go. But several people who knew Davis gave him a poor recommendation because of the man's temperament, and the matter was dropped.

Eventually, Jefferson selected Thomas Freeman, a surveyor and civil engineer, to head the scientific studies. Freeman had come to the United States from Ireland in 1784, and had gained experience as a surveyor from Washington, D.C., to Florida in the 1790s. He eventually arrived in Natchez, accompanied by mathematician Andrew Ellicott, who would later become one of Meriwether Lewis's tutors. However, Ellicott and Freeman had a falling out in 1798, and they parted ways.

But Thomas Freeman made some powerful friends while in

Natchez, particularly General James Wilkinson. In 1805, Wilkinson became governor of the Louisiana Territory, and he hired Thomas Freeman to be the supervising civil engineer for a new army post. However, those Natchez friendships eventually would come back to haunt Freeman when Wilkinson and others were implicated in the Aaron Burr affair. Many individuals who worked for or took orders from Wilkinson, such as Freeman and Zebulon Pike, later would become tarred by their association with men who would become branded as traitors.

But Thomas Freeman had solid credentials, and the expedition now had a leader. The task of finding a naturalist took even longer.

With the new emphasis on just exploring the length of the Red River, a natural history survey of the Red River still remained a principal objective, and Jefferson insisted that a naturalist be found who could participate and add credibility to the scientific observations.

Jefferson was pleased to hear that Lewis and Clark had reached the Mandan villages of the Dakotas when the explorers sent men and specimens back down the Missouri River in the spring of 1805. But, as 1805 turned into 1806, and there was no further word from the Corps of Discovery, many people felt that Lewis, Clark, and the rest of the party had died somewhere in the wilderness. Further records and scientific contributions from that expedition now seemed unlikely, and the president was even more determined that the next exploring trip be one of credible scientific accomplishments.

Jefferson offered the naturalist position to Constantine Rafinesque, who was a rising star in the field of natural history, but also one of the most controversial scientists of his day. This was largely due to Rafinesque's habit of rushing into print with almost every specimen that he encountered. But Rafinesque had sailed for Europe and the offer was withdrawn. Jefferson also made an offer to naturalist William Bartram. But Bartram was then 66 years old and he, instead, recommended Alexander Wilson, a naturalist and bird expert, who seemed eager to make such a trip.

Wilson eventually would become nationally famous, but by the time Jefferson got around to responding to Bartram's suggestion, Thomas Freeman had already settled the matter. Freeman made inquiries of another surveyor, John McKee, then spent time with naturalist Benjamin Smith Barton in Philadelphia. Soon thereafter, one of Barton's doctoral students, Peter Custis, was selected as the expedition's naturalist.

Natural history as a science was undergoing great changes at the beginning of the nineteenth century, as biologists were trying to deal with the classification of plants and animals in some sort of appropriate order. What was a species? What made one animal or plant different from another? What made two forms distinctive, but related?

These were not simple questions to answer. Were two foxes different just because one had reddish-brown fur and another had gray fur? Or, were these simply two color forms of the same species, perhaps one male and one female or one from a southern climate rich in prey and the other from the north, where there might be a scarcity of food?

Most naturalists of the day used the Linnaean system of classifying plants and animals, and this continues to the present time. This taxonomic system assigns every species a Latinized name, consisting of a genus and a species. Thus, the cutthroat trout, which was discovered by Lewis and Clark in Montana, was later given a scientific name. After some changes over the years, it is now known as *Oncorhynchus clarki*. *Oncorhynchus* is the genus and *clarki* is the species. Although many plants and animals may be known by different common names around the country or the world, each plant or animal has only one, unique scientific name. Two creatures with the same genus but different species names are different, but are related, as two human brothers might be within a family.

The actual scientific name that is proposed is generally a combination of Latin terms that refer to some structure or behavior of the specimen, or it may be a Latinized form of someone's name. This could be the person who originally collected the specimen, such as in the case of Lewis's wild flax, *Linum lewisii*, which was named for

Meriwether Lewis by Frederick Pursh in 1814. Or, it could be to honor someone for their interest or involvement in science, such as when Benjamin Smith Barton named the twinleaf *Jeffersonia diphyllum*, after Thomas Jefferson, then the secretary of state. In either case, it is a high honor for someone to have a plant or animal named after them for posterity.

It also is a major achievement in the career of any naturalist to be the first to describe a new species of plant or animal. The creature that is new to science may have been collected by anyone—the actual collector is often lost to history. Rather, it is the scientist who makes careful measurements, counts of appendages or fin rays, feathers, branching patterns of plants, and other structures who receives the notoriety. Such a formal description would be published in a scientific journal or other publication that is circulated in the scientific world. With this formal description, usually accompanied by drawings (or, today, more modern illustrations), a scientist can indicate how this particular species relates to other plants or animals in the natural world and why it should be assigned a unique place in taxonomy. If it is in fact new, the initial describing scientist is allowed to propose the new scientific name.

In formal scientific circles, the name of the scientist who first described the plant or animal, along with the year, typically appear after any subsequent formal mention of the species. Thus, the botanist, entomologist, ornithologist, or zoologist who is able to publish such a description will see his or her name listed for posterity.

This is where competition can become fierce. Many eminent scientists, especially after they had made their reputations, became describers, rather than collectors as well as describers. Benjamin Barton often made arrangements with others to collect many of his specimens, especially plants. Sometimes, he paid assistants modest salaries to engage in the collecting on the condition that the specimens and notes be returned to him for formal description. It is unknown what agreement Barton had with Peter Custis, or what promises were made about any scientific credits that Custis would receive. But, on the basis of other, similar arrangements made by Barton, the botanist probably expected to receive the lion's share of formal recognition. And, of course, Peter Custis did not have much bargaining power. Barton had considerable influence over whether Peter would ever receive his doctorate.

If reputations were made by significant contributions to the scientific literature, it made sense to be able to maximize the number of new species that a taxonomist would discover or describe. But, there were two schools of thought in this evolving field of taxonomy.

During this early era of western discovery, the name of Charles Darwin was little known. Darwin's *Origin of Species* was decades in the future, and the ideas of evolving species and inherited traits were quite foreign and certainly were controversial. Benjamin Smith Barton held a more traditional view on the subject. He was of the opinion that most species of animals had already been discovered and described before the nineteenth century. As a result, any new form that was collected somewhere was likely to be just a variation of something that already was known. In this view, a bird that had the same body shape as another bird that was known from Europe was the same species, even if the North American bird had larger wings or was of a different color. For animals, especially, Barton and many other scientists believed that it was unlikely that new species would be discovered in western North America. This was the philosophy that Barton instilled in his students.

At the opposite extreme was Constantine Rafinesque, the naturalist who had been approached by Thomas Jefferson to accompany the Red River Expedition. Rafinesque was an avid collector who published hundreds of papers on mammals, fishes, birds, and other creatures, but he also was widely criticized for his insistence on classifying almost anything that he saw as being a new species. Sometimes, these descriptions were based only on a partial carcass, or a brief glimpse of a flying bird or bat, or a fish swimming through the water.

Rafinesque was 23 years old when he was approached by Jefferson, but he was already well known to most of the nation's naturalists, especially in Pennsylvania. He took a position in Sicily, stayed there for 10 years, then returned to the United States, only to be shipwrecked near his destination. He lost virtually all of his possessions, including books and manuscripts. He later resumed his exploring and collecting, but his incessant claims of new species caused many scientists to trick him into publishing accounts of bogus animals. John James Audubon once traveled with Rafinesque and painted pictures of mythical fishes that he claimed to have seen. Rafinesque promptly described these fictional creatures in scientific papers without having seen or verified Audubon's tongue-in-cheek stories. Over the years, many scientists, such as well-known botanists Asa Gray and John Torrey, tended to downplay many of Rafinesque's "discoveries," even if they turned out to be credible. The *American Journal of Science* eventually refused to consider any more of Rafinesque's submissions.

Rafinesque had an unfortunate habit of self-publishing many of his papers, writing up a new species in a short note and printing only a few copies so that he could—he hoped—receive formal credit for a discovery. Many scientists tended to disregard such publications because they circumvented the normal, but slow, peer-reviewed process.

The most noteworthy type of scientific publication (aside from book-length monographs) is the peer-reviewed scientific paper. A naturalist submits his or her manuscript to a journal or other publication which has a relatively wide distribution. The manuscript is then reviewed by two to four experts—usually anonymous—who will pass judgment on the scientific validity and significance of the paper's contents. If deemed acceptable or acceptable with revision, the paper eventually can be published. But the process can take many months, or even years, and the review process can introduce personal or professional biases in the referees' decisions. Logically, an impatient scientist, like Rafinesque, might try to avoid such a process.

But, despite the questions surrounding some of his discoveries, Rafinesque is credited with personally discovering and describing a remarkable number of new species from the eastern United States, and dozens of these have remained valid discoveries. At the time of his death, Rafinesque had published over 900 papers—an astonishing number by any scientist in any era. Rafinesque anticipated the concepts of evolving species that would become widely accepted in later years. But, at the time that Peter Custis was ready to embark on his trip up the Red River, most scientists favored the Barton (and Custis) approach to taxonomy. Eventually, almost all scientists would take a more Rafinesque approach, at least entertaining the idea that new species are still to be discovered.

It was with these two conflicting views on natural history and taxonomy that Peter Custis left by coach from Philadelphia on January 17, 1806, just three days after receiving his appointment as naturalist by Thomas Jefferson.

Although the president personally picked the military leader of the expedition, Captain Richard Sparks, Thomas Freeman was the scientific leader. Both Freeman and Custis kept journals of the trip and both men jointly collected the scientific data, whether it was biological in nature—Custis's specialty—or meteorological or geographical—Freeman's expertise. Like Lewis and Clark, Peter Custis took several reference books with him on the trip. These included two volumes of Linnaean taxonomy, du Pratz's *History of Louisiana*, three books on botany, several recent issues of popular scientific journals, Thomas Jefferson's notes on the *State of Virginia*, and Sibley's report to the president on Sibley's knowledge of the lower Red River.

The Red River expedition departed Fort Adams, 60 miles downstream from Natchez, on April 19, 1806, with the objective now of exploring the Red River to its source, while mapping and collecting plants and animals along its length. Because of more last-minute delays, the trip stopped and the actual redeparture was further postponed until a week later. On April 26, the party finally sailed downstream with Freeman, Custis, and Sparks, Lieutenant Humphreys, two noncommissioned officers, 17 soldiers recruited from the army garrisons at Fort Adams and New Orleans, and an African-

American servant. The party moved downstream, then into the Red River using two specially built, flat-bottomed boats that were designed by Dunbar, and a pirogue—a boat fashioned from canoes connected by wooden planks.

The expedition was delayed when it encountered low water levels at times but, even so, the river was a half mile wide and 84 feet deep at its mouth. The water was a reddish-brown color due to the high sediment content eroded from the surrounding banks. By May 3, the expedition reached the mouth of the Black River, about 26 miles upstream, where the river width was now reduced to a quarter mile and the depth was now 42 feet. The red-colored river banks on each side rose to 14 feet above the water and then kept increasing in height to as much as 25 feet.

On May 19, the party reached Natchitoches, having passed by the Red River Rapids, an old Franciscan mission that had been first constructed in 1690, and scattered settlements. Essentially, Natchitoches was the last outpost of western expansion along the Red River although, unlike what Lewis and Clark were encountering along the upper Missouri River, Freeman and Custis kept seeing scattered dwellings and tribal villages. Native Americans had been living along the river for centuries, moving camps to follow the migrations of animals. The tribes were now being joined by settlers of French, Spanish, and African descent in scattered houses and shacks. Relatively speaking, communications were more advanced along the Red River than anywhere that Lewis and Clark would encounter. But upstream from Natchitoches, the river would become wild and relatively unexplored. To prepare for the difficulties that might await them, the expedition rested and re-outfitted with the assistance of Dr. John Sibley. It was there that Freeman, Sparks, and Custis learned that Spanish troops had been alerted to their presence.

Reports came from residents as well as travelers between Natchitoches and the Mississippi River that a detachment of Spanish soldiers was moving toward the Red River.

From the initial days of planning an expedition up the Red River, Thomas Jefferson had worried about a confrontation with the

Spaniards. The upper reaches of the river originated in a murky area of land claims between the two nations. The Spanish had a network of spies and paid informers throughout the lower Mississippi drainage including, it would turn out, General James Wilkinson. Any time that traders attempted to establish an overland trade route to Santa Fe, the Spaniards moved quickly to stop them. The minute that the Red River Expedition departed from Fort Adams, Spanish officials were alerted. And, when the party of armed men started up the Red River, messages were sent by informants and Spanish troops were alerted at Bayou Pierre.

Jefferson had tried to avoid such a situation. His original plan was to have the expedition depart in 1804, and he requested an exploring passport from the Spaniards. He stressed the scientific mission of the trip and even offered to include Spaniards in the party to demonstrate its peaceful intentions. But the request was denied. A year later, William Claiborne, the Orleans territorial governor, again requested such a passport. This time it was approved by the local official, but he was overruled by higher-ranking Spanish authorities. The Spaniards were adamant in their claims to the upper Red River, based on the explorations of de Soto and La Salle, who first visited the region hundreds of years earlier.

Apparently, Jefferson and Dunbar continued to worry because, while the Red River party rested at Natchitoches from May 19 to June 2, they were joined by another group of 20 soldiers sent from Fort Claiborne and led by Lieutenant John DuForest.

When this larger party of over 40 armed men left Natchitoches in seven boats, everyone had concerns. Some reports placed the Spanish troops only 150 miles away. Peter Custis wrote in his journal, "It is expected that the Spaniards will endeavor to stop us."

Despite the ever-present worries about a possible armed confrontation upriver, Freeman and Custis continued to survey the river and collect plants and animals. Peter Custis's particular interest was botany. Although he noted the presence of various animals along the Red River, most of his biological observations were focused on trees and shrubs.

This was logical, because botany was a particular objective recommended by William Dunbar and Benjamin Smith Barton. The former supervised Peter Custis's preparations for the trip, and the latter man was Custis's mentor. As a consequence, it was quite reasonable that young Peter Custis would concentrate on the botanical features of the region. Custis identified cottonwood, pecan, cypress, mulberry, red cedar, hickory, ash, oak, and other familiar eastern trees along the Red River.

Above Natchitoches, the river narrowed to only 70 yards in width and the banks were thickly vegetated. "The trees are so covered with vines and creeping plants, as to present an impermeable mass of vegetation, while the low banks of the river are edged with willows," wrote Freeman.

Soon after passing through this stretch, the party encountered two beautiful lakes, but then a series of swampy bayous and large "rafts" that were composed of downed logs, tree stumps, and sandbars that made upstream passage extremely difficult. It took 14 days to pass through this stretch that the men called "The Great Swamp."

Eventually, the river became clear and the explorers reached the Coushatta village on June 26. The tribal members were peaceful and helpful, but also reported that Spanish troops were now only 25 miles away, traveling overland to reach the Red River.

Despite the danger from the Spaniards, the exploring party decided to rest for two weeks with the Coushatta Creek tribe and resupply food stocks. After the difficult days in the swamp, the men were exhausted. And, the stopover gave Peter Custis more time to do collecting. Fishing in the river one day, he encountered several large catfish "of from 15 to 70 pounds weight, equal in taste and flavor to any caught within the U. States."

On July 25, the party entered a village of the Caddo tribe, upstream from the mouth of the Little River. There they learned that Spanish troops had recently entered the village and had cut down a flagpole from which was flying an American flag. The banner had been given to a chief as a present during the man's earlier trip downriver. The Caddos estimated there had been 1,000 soldiers and they were seeking a party of Americans on the river. According to the Caddos, the soldiers threatened to kill or imprison the Americans if they resisted.

The Spanish troops were less than three days away.

On July 28, the expedition members heard gunshots upriver. The next day, the explorers encountered advanced segments of the main body. The Americans took cover in a stand of cottonwoods, with firearms cocked. The exploring party of 40 men found themselves facing a force of at least 300 Spaniards at a location that is today known as Spanish Bluff.

Sparks, Freeman, Custis, and others met with Spanish officers for an extended period of negotiation while the others crouched in readiness. It must have been an eventful time for 25-year-old graduate student Peter Custis, who had thought he would be spending his time collecting plants and animals while on a simple river excursion.

The Spaniards wanted the explorers to turn around, and when Thomas Freeman asked for their reasoning in writing, the officers refused. With overwhelming odds against them, the Red River Exploring Party left Spanish Bluff the following day, July 30, 1806, pointing their boats downstream. By August 23, they were again in Natchitoches. Soon thereafter, they reached the Mississippi River.

The modified objective of the expedition, to explore the Red River to its source, was far from accomplished. Ultimately, only half of the length of the river (615 miles) was explored.

When members of the party returned to civilization, several events combined to work against them. Messengers sent downriver quickly spread the word about the incident at Spanish Bluff. William Claiborne, the territorial governor, even rode a horse to Natchitoches to hear the news firsthand from Sparks and Freeman. This led to face-to-face negotiations with Spanish commanders and months of threats and counterthreats, most of it directed at the disputed border between the two countries and the treatment of the exploring party. This, in turn, would simmer into revelations about the Aaron Burr–James Wilkinson scandal as all their secret plans for the southwest became known.

As the conspiracy net was cast around Wilkinson, it fell around almost anyone who had been a friend or associate of the general, or anyone who had been involved with the Spaniards.

One of these men was Zebulon Pike, who had been sent into the western lands on July 15, 1806, on direct orders from Wilkinson. Pike's route took him along the Osage River, across the Great Plains, along the Arkansas River, into present-day Colorado, then south to the headwaters of the Rio Grande.

Pike, like Freeman and Custis, was supposed to have returned via the Red River. Instead, he was captured and imprisoned by the Spanish. Whether he intentionally ventured well into New Spain or traveled there accidentally is a matter of dispute. But, the fact that he traveled under orders from Wilkinson placed Pike under suspicion. Zebulon Pike was subsequently court-martialed—and ultimately exonerated—but he was tarnished in the public eye because of his association with the general.

Another person so tarnished was Thomas Freeman. His previous friendship with the general, coupled with the embarrassing confrontation with Spanish troops on the Red River, cast a cloud over what success the expedition did have in its four-month trip.

Added to this was poor timing. In the midst of the tensions between the United States and Spain, Lewis and Clark and the other members of their party returned to a hero's welcome in St. Louis in September 1806. Most people had assumed the men had died long before. But now, here came the explorers, back from an adventure that had taken them almost 7,700 miles, to the other side of the continent. They had encountered dozens of native tribes and had established peaceful relations with most of them. They returned home with specimens of new and unusual plants and animals, Native American artifacts, and notebooks filled with exciting accounts of adventures. They found rich beaver grounds and brought back notes on geology, meteorology, botany, zoology, and ethnology.

As explorers, Lewis and Clark became national heroes. Many years later, their accomplishments as naturalists would become equally noteworthy.

Compared to Lewis and Clark, the accomplishments of the Red

River expedition seemed rather sparse. The party never reached the headwaters of the Red River, but only mapped a portion of the river. The records of natural history, as seen by Custis, seemed to reflect plants and animals that were largely already known in the east, and it appeared to many that the party had turned tail and run after being confronted by Spanish troops in land that most people believed belonged to the United States. And, finally, one of the leaders was associated with a traitor.

Rather than returning to an appreciative reception by the public, the names of Peter Custis and Thomas Freeman were delegated to the footnotes of American history. The resultant report of the expedition, which was edited by Nicholas King in 1807 and based on Custis's four reports and Freeman's surveys, tended to be under-supported by President Jefferson, and it eventually settled into obscurity in archives.

Thomas Freeman, despite the difficulties surrounding General Wilkinson, remained a personal favorite of Thomas Jefferson. He was a competent mapmaker and scientific leader. As a result, the president appointed Freeman to lead a new expedition up the Arkansas River, and Freeman again worked with William Dunbar to plan the trip. It was scheduled to depart in 1807, but Congress withheld funding and plans were again canceled. Instead, Thomas Freeman was appointed to a series of surveying jobs with the federal government in the early nineteenth century.

Peter Custis completed his government report-writing obligations by October 1806 and returned to the University of Pennsylvania to complete his degree. He received his M.D. in May 1807, writing his thesis on "bilious fever." His career as a naturalist, however, started to fade away. In 1807, Custis worked on some plants stored in Benjamin Barton's herbarium, especially a collection from Virginia. But specimens collected along the Red River were largely ignored. Custis would only have one scientific paper published, and that was more of a general description of the lower Red River in the *Philadelphia Medical and Physical Journal.*

As a loyal student, Peter Custis dutifully turned over his notes and specimens to his advisor, Barton. Unfortunately, because of health problems and other reasons, Barton did little with the plant specimens. Many of the samples literally decayed and rotted away. The remaining plants were later described by others, including Constantine Rafinesque, Alexander Wilson, and Frederick Pursh. Those natural history luminaries were given access to the samples and received the lasting credit.

Even Peter Custis's major discovery, the three-toed amphiuma, which was later determined to be in an entirely new family, was formally described in a scientific paper by Benjamin Barton. Custis's mentor received the professional notoriety, and he even changed the proposed scientific name that had been suggested by Custis.

This intense competition and infighting between naturalists probably led to Peter Custis moving to North Carolina and devoting his time exclusively to medicine. Soon, he no longer had contact with his former professor. Benjamin Smith Barton's name has remained a familiar one throughout history, but the name of Peter Custis is largely forgotten.

It was unfortunate as well as fortunate that the natural history records of the Red River expedition were not widely circulated. It was unfortunate because, among the botanical and zoological records were dozens of new species—particularly plants, but also some animals, such as the Mississippi kite. The accounts of the expedition also provide the earliest scientific picture of a land inhabited by such diverse biota as buffalo, bald cypress, and the western Carolina parakeet—the latter now extinct.

It is difficult to provide an exact listing of species collected by Peter Custis, but he recorded the names of some 56 trees and 120 species of plants. He made 18 detailed descriptions of plants that Custis believed were new to science—despite Barton's misgivings about encountering new forms of life. Custis made the first botanical collections in and above the Great Swamp. And, he identified almost two dozen types of mammals and three dozen forms of birds. Many of his identifications were incorrect, but sufficient plant material was collected to earn him admiration from later naturalists.

But, by the same token, it was fortunate that many of Custis's identifications were not widely circulated because of those many inaccuracies. Custis often used names to identify a specimen, but these names—especially of animals—were typically just that: a name, sometimes scientific, sometimes common, and sometimes entirely vague. Whereas Lewis and Clark were less familiar with the members of the botanical and zoological world, they thoroughly described new biota in their notes. Peter Custis, however, recommended by Professor Barton as a naturalist, attempted to identify everything in terms of a known species or form of plant or animal.

The result is that Custis probably was the first to encounter new species. But, in many cases, we may never know which animals he observed. Whereas Lewis and Clark provided extensive notes, descriptions, and even drawings of many of the animals that they encountered, Peter Custis often just recorded a name. As an example, he noted that he collected "catfish *(Silurus catus)* very abundant and of a very large size." Sometimes, he mentioned a length, such as a $3^1/_2$-foot specimen taken in the Red River at Natchitoches that was "seven inches between the eyes."

Today, we know that several species of the catfish family were native to the Red River and some of them reach large sizes, such as the blue catfish, channel catfish, and flathead catfish. Lewis and Clark first reported large catfish that likely were channel and blue catfish two years earlier along the Missouri River, even though the two fish species were not formally described by taxonomists until 1818 and 1840, respectfully. Did Peter Custis also encounter one or all of those large catfish along the Red River? It seems likely, but he only mentioned an old name for European catfish and he provided no distinguishing characteristics for his catfish.

Part of the difficulty, too, was Barton's belief that, essentially, a catfish was a catfish. Since the name *Silurus catus* was a long-established name for a catfish, anything that resembled a catfish in form also had to be *Silurus catus*, even if the new specimen was smaller or larger in size, or of a different color. Thus, to Barton's student, anything that resembled a catfish was simply identified by the same name. Small catfish were dismissed as being young specimens.

Large catfish were considered the same species, only larger in size because of abundant food supplies. Scientific names have changed over the years, but *Silurus catus* was never found in the Red River and modern scientists are left to wonder what new species Peter Custis might have encountered, yet failed to recognize as unique. In a similar manner, Custis identified a brightly colored snake as *Columber rhomboideus*, referring to the common king snake of the east. We know today that this could not have been true, but the serpent was undoubtedly a new find, the milk snake. Peter Custis might have been credited with making a new discovery, but he assumed that a snake with bands of red, yellow, white, and black had to be the familiar king snake. Instead, the lasting notoriety went to someone else who took the time to carefully note how the two snakes differed in appearance. In all fairness to Peter Custis, however, most experienced naturalists of the day likely would have made the same misidentifications, especially given the state of knowledge of the time.

Peter Custis's obvious talents were with plants, trees, and shrubs, even though he had the opportunity to make a name for himself as a zoologist as well. So, although the presence of a trained naturalist with the Red River expedition stifled criticism of Lewis and Clark's scientific discoveries, to modern scientists it is the detailed notes of Lewis and Clark that are today more valuable, rather than the simple names applied by a pre-Darwinian scientist.

For the field of natural history to proceed in the west, it would take naturalists with a new approach—individuals who would entertain the possibility that plants and animals in unexplored lands were not always familiar forms. These living things could easily be something new to science. One of these new naturalists was already en route from England, bound for Philadelphia. When he arrived there in 1808, Thomas Nuttall was hired by Benjamin Smith Barton to work on plants in Barton's herbarium and to engage in field collecting. But, unlike all other protégés of the eminent professor, Thomas Nuttall would eventually use a new approach to natural science, especially in the west.

Chapter 4

THOMAS NUTTALL AND THE
WILDERNESS COLLECTORS

Richard Henry Dana, who would later write the classic *Two Years before the Mast*, was standing on a beach near San Diego in 1836 when he saw a man walking toward him.

The man was middle-aged and was "wearing a sailor's pea-jacket, with a wide straw hat, and barefooted, with his trousers rolled up to his knees," Dana later wrote in his journal. The man seemed oblivious to Dana and his shipmates along the long, sandy strand. Instead, the barefooted beachcomber was intently searching the shore and trapped pools. Occasionally, he would stop, bend over, and pick up a shell or a stone. Head bowed, the man would carefully inspect the object for a minute or two, then either discard it or put it in a pocket of his pea jacket.

The solitary figure on the beach was in his own world, unaware that others were watching him with curiosity. But Dana noted something distinct about the man's walk and, as the beachcomber approached, Dana recognized him. It was Thomas Nuttall, formerly the renowned instructor of natural history at Harvard.

Dana had been a student of Nuttall's at Harvard, but he was amazed to see his old professor on the other side of the continent, far from the academic confines of Cambridge, Massachusetts. Dana wrote that his former teacher was "the last person I should have expected to have seen on the coast of California. . . . I had left him quietly seated in the chair of Botany and Ornithology in Harvard University, and the next I saw of him, he was strolling about San Diego beach."

By sheer coincidence, Nuttall had hitched a ride from Monterey on the *Pilgrim*, the same ship that had carried Richard Henry Dana to California. Dana was now working aboard the *Alert*, a larger vessel that was soon to sail for the East Coast, and Nuttall had booked passage. The second mate aboard the *Pilgrim* told Dana that they had "an old gentleman on board" who knew Dana back in his college days. But, try as he might, Dana could not think who that passenger might be. The mate couldn't remember the man's name, but he was "sort of an oldish man, with white hair, and spent all of his time in the bush, and along the beach, picking up flowers and shells and such truck, and had a dozen boxes and barrels full of them."

When Dana recognized the distinct walk of Thomas Nuttall on the beach, the sailor/writer mentally kicked himself, as the unnamed beachcomber could only have been one man—one of the greatest field naturalists ever to travel across the American west.

Nuttall had been spending his time in San Diego, waiting for the *Alert* to deport, doing what he normally did with his time, examining and discovering new forms of nature. Collecting specimens on the beach was exactly what he had been doing for most of his 27 years in North America, and he was happiest when he was walking lands never examined by naturalists, seeing living plants and animals that, perhaps, had never been viewed by humans.

Nuttall was a printer by trade, a product of his family's printing business, and he was expected to pursue the trade back in his native England. But, like many people who were fascinated by natural history, Nuttall's mind tended to drift toward scientific questions, even when he was working with printing presses. He was fascinated by the living things that he saw around his Yorkshire home.

In his free time, Thomas wandered the fields and marshes, and he became particularly adept at identifying flowers. Perhaps because printers must develop an eye for detail to be successful in their trade, Nuttall—although an amateur—became quite knowledgeable about the local flora and fauna.

The English, particularly, always have been interested in hobbies and outside pursuits that might be quite removed from one's workday vocation. Thus, to his family, Nuttall's preoccupation with natural history seemed harmless enough. But, when 21-year-old Thomas announced that he was going to North America to discover new plants, his family was shocked.

Nuttall arrived in Philadelphia in 1808—just two years after the return of Lewis and Clark from their trip across the continent, and the return of Peter Custis from the Red River expedition. Philadelphia was not only a cultural center of the United States, it was its center for science as well. Yet, despite these modern attributes, Pennsylvania was still a relatively unexplored territory—especially for naturalists. Woods were largely uncut, and natural systems were still often just that.

To support himself, Nuttall secured work as a printer. But, on Sundays, he often would be found in the fields and woods near Philadelphia, collecting plants, many of which were new to him. One day, Nuttall collected what he thought was a passionflower. But, unable to confirm its identification, an acquaintance suggested that the budding botanist purchase a copy of Benjamin Smith Barton's *Elements of Botany*—the standard reference at the time.

Unable to find a copy, Nuttall went right to the source—Barton—in his office at the University of Pennsylvania. Barton was a professor at the medical school and a renowned lecturer in botany. He was president of the Linnaean Society and vice president of the American Philosophical Society. Although the Englishman was young and academically untrained, Barton readily recognized that Nuttall was quite intelligent and his self-taught knowledge of botany was impressive. Barton took on the young printer as a student.

With Peter Custis and subsequent assistants now gone, Barton was in need of help. Most of Lewis and Clark's botanical specimens remained unexamined, as were many of Custis's Red River collections. And, Benjamin Smith Barton was primarily a describer rather than a collector (and a procrastinating describer at that). His continued reputation depended on having a consistent supply of specimens collected by enthusiastic assistants, especially new varieties of plant life taken from virgin lands. As was the case with Peter Custis, many of those field collectors placed themselves in harm's way to obtain those specimens, yet it was Barton who received the lion's share of the fame.

To Barton, Thomas Nuttall was obviously highly intelligent and motivated. He knew enough to recognize new forms of plant life, as well as closely related variations. Yet, as Barton once remarked to an acquaintance, Nuttall was "a young man distinguished by innocence of character." In essence, Nuttall was a pure naturalist, innocent in the ways of scientific infighting.

Given an opportunity to pursue his passion for natural history, Nuttall had little knowledge or interest in who would get credit for discoveries and whose reputation might be enhanced. Barton suggested that Nuttall explore the coast of Delaware to enhance Barton's herbarium collection. Thomas readily obliged, even though he was bitten so badly by mosquitoes that people avoided the Englishman because he appeared to have contracted smallpox. Because Nuttall was such a meticulous observer of nature, he was able to discover several new or rare plants in Delaware, even though the area had been visited by eastern botanists in the past.

Thomas Nuttall would have liked nothing better than to spend his days wandering through wild places. So, when Barton made Nuttall an offer to undertake a massive, two-year trip into largely uncollected lands, Nuttall jumped at the chance.

Barton had the young botanist sign a formal contract that was very one-sided. Nuttall agreed to undertake a journey of several thousand miles, much of it on foot, that would consume his efforts for about two years. This collecting trip would take Nuttall through the northern Appalachian Mountains to the Great Lakes, then to Lake Winnipeg in Manitoba, up the Saskatchewan River, down the

Missouri River, and through Illinois, Indiana, Kentucky, and Virginia before returning to Philadelphia. West of Pittsburgh, there were few roads, especially in the uncollected lands west of the Mississippi River. A man traveling alone was at the mercy of the elements, terrain, wild animals, hostile tribes, and dangerous outcasts of society who were now moving into the fringes of the American west.

Nuttall readily agreed.

While en route, the young naturalist was to carry paper and plant presses for preserving flora and alcohol for preserving fauna. He was to collect "plants, animals, vegetables, minerals, Indian curiosities, etc." and ship them back to Barton in Philadelphia. Exactly how Nuttall was expected to do this from unexplored and uncivilized lands was not spelled out.

Nuttall agreed.

Furthermore, Nuttall was not to discuss his collections or any aspects of science with others unless given express permission by Barton, and Barton would keep all journals and notes of Thomas's travels.

Nuttall agreed, and for his efforts, he was outfitted with supplies and paid $8.00 per month.

Barton was quite pleased to have another competent assistant in the field collecting for him. Nuttall signed a work-for-hire contract, and he would receive little or no recognition for his collections. Barton (whose health was not sufficient to do such collecting anymore) retained the specimens and notes and would receive the glory of describing and naming a plethora of new species from areas never explored by scientists.

"I have no doubt," Barton wrote of Nuttall, "should his life be spared, that he will add much to our knowledge of geography [and] the natural history . . . of all countries through which he is directed to pass."

Outfitted and primed for an adventure of a lifetime, Nuttall left Philadelphia on April 12, 1810. He was 24 years old and a neophyte at living in remote areas. He left with a rifle and a trunk full of clothes and collecting supplies: a plant press and paper, thermometer, steel pen, weighing scales, five blank notebooks, and a German botany book. On that first day, he wrote in his journal, "Winter reluctantly yields to the smiling aspect of spring."

From Philadelphia, he traveled west to Pittsburgh, then collected along Lakes Erie and Huron, finally crossing Lake Michigan by boat before traveling largely on foot through Wisconsin and the upper Mississippi drainage.

Along the way, he contracted a fever that would plague him for much of his journey; it quite possibly could have been malaria. Between overnight stays with hospitable settlers, he would arrange to have his trunk shipped on ahead while he collected on foot. Sometimes the trunk awaited him at the next stage station or farm. Sometimes it was missing and Nuttall would have to backtrack to find it. But, whether traveling new ground or retracing his own footsteps, Thomas Nuttall kept his eyes to the ground, always in search of curiosities—both animal and plant.

After hitching a ride in a canoe, Nuttall arrived at Mackinac Island (Michilimackinac), where he made an fortunate acquaintance. The Mackinac Trading Post was as wild and woolly a place as anywhere in North America. Yet, Nuttall continued to collect plants, including salmonberry. There, among the trappers, traders, and dregs of society, Nuttall made friends with Wilson Price Hunt, who was organizing a group of trappers and traders to travel up the Missouri River. Hunt convinced Nuttall that Benjamin Barton's optimistic route, traced on a rough map spread out on a table at the University of Pennsylvania, was quite impractical. Instead, Hunt offered Nuttall a ride. More important, the botanist would be afforded much more protection while traveling with a large group of armed men.

It was September 1810 by the time Thomas reached St. Louis. There, he awaited the arrival of Hunt and his party. Nuttall arrived almost in the footsteps of Lewis and Clark. It only had been four years since the two explorers and amateur naturalists had returned down the Missouri River with a collection of plants and animals.

But Lewis and Clark had been faced with numerous tasks—not just scientific collecting. Nuttall would have the time and opportunity to concentrate on just the natural history pursuits.

Hunt's group was working for John Jacob Astor, who was intent on carving out the lion's share of the fur trade in the upper Missouri River, as well as the Rocky Mountains and greater Pacific Northwest. But, Astor had considerable competition. Fur trappers typically led a solitary existence, working for themselves or for emerging, larger operations. The British, particularly the Hudson Bay Company, had long established a presence in the Northwest. Now, entrepreneurs, such as Astor and Manuel Lisa, were trying to do the same in the relatively new lands of the Louisiana Purchase.

Hunt was the field captain of what Astor hoped would be a permanent series of trading forts up the Missouri River—a merging of independent and contract trappers and buyers, and a delivery system downriver to St. Louis. But, it was now well into fall, and Hunt's group would not head upriver until spring. So Thomas Nuttall spent the winter months collecting flora and fauna in the area near St. Louis. It was a productive time, despite the long historical presence of humans along the Mississippi River. The lands were still ripe for natural history discoveries. Nuttall found various types of peas, poppies, a false indigo plant, and the western mugwort. Each was carefully described, pressed, and shipped to Barton in Philadelphia. While traveling in the area, he also met briefly with two other legends of western explorations: 77-year-old Daniel Boone, who was returning from a beaver trapping trip, and John Colter, former member of Lewis and Clark's Corps of Discovery and a fur-trapping explorer who had worked for Manuel Lisa.

Hunt's party left St. Louis in March 1811, accompanied by Nuttall and another botanist, John Bradbury. It was a fortunate association for Nuttall because Bradbury, a competent field scientist, had been sent by the Liverpool Botanical Society to the Western Hemisphere to collect new species of cotton and other plants. The two shared the field collecting and their mutual enthusiasm for collecting in virgin territories. Bradbury would later write of his adventures in his book,

Travels in the Interior of America in the Years 1809, 1810, and 1811.

The lands of the Louisiana Purchase were rugged and the traveling was difficult. But Nuttall was oblivious to it all. He collected white evening primrose, ragwort, various milkweeds, saltbush, and dozens of other new or unusual species. For much of the trip upriver, Nuttall and Bradbury were the first trained naturalists to appear on the scene and, except for some species of plants and animals encountered by Lewis and Clark, they were the first naturalists to collect specimens in any sort of concerted manner. They definitely were the first to appreciate the undescribed biodiversity and complexity of the western lands.

En route to the Mandan villages, where Lewis and Clark had spent the winter of 1804–1805, Nuttall's behavior continued to amuse the rugged frontier trappers who were focused on furs and hides. They called the botanist "*le fou.*" Nuttall often wandered off and became lost because he was so preoccupied with his collecting. Once, when the Hunt party had a brief confrontation with a band of Sioux, the trappers double-checked their rifles and powder.

Nuttall's rifle, which he had carried with him all the way from Philadelphia, was found to be completely plugged with mud. It turned out that Nuttall often had used the weapon as a spade or shovel for digging up plants. He did occasionally notice the dried mud in the barrel, but thought little of it. To him, the mud was a handy place for storing seeds that he collected. The weapon, in his mind, was more useful as a botanical tool. Besides, he had little need to fire it.

Fortunately, the fur trappers made their point quite vocally—if Nuttall actually had tried to fire the weapon, the barrel likely would have exploded and Nuttall's legacy would have ended as one who had collected several dozen species of plants for someone else, and had died as a historical footnote.

At the Arikara Village, Hunt and the two naturalists parted ways. The Astor Party of fur trappers was heading overland. But fortune and friendship again smiled on Thomas Nuttall. Heading farther upstream was entrepreneur Manuel Lisa, who had become friends with Nuttall while the two had been stage passengers one and a half years before.

Lisa had established a trading fort farther up the Missouri, near the Bighorn River. He invited his friend to accompany Lisa's own party of fur trappers, who also were joined for a time by Toussaint Charbonneau, his wife Sacajawea, and their son—all three veterans of the Lewis and Clark expedition. Also accompanying Lisa's men was Henry Marie Breckinridge, an eastern lawyer who would later write of his adventures in his *Journal of a Voyage up the River Missouri, Performed in Eighteen Hundred and Eleven.*

Breckinridge was like most people who encountered Nuttall in the field. He was amazed by the Englishman's complete preoccupation with science:

> *He appears singularly devoted and which seems to engross every thought to the total disregard of his own personal safety and sometimes to the inconvenience of the party he accompanies. When the boat touches shore, he leaps out and no sooner is his attention arrested by a plant or flower than everything else is forgotten.*

Even John Bradbury, although almost as passionate in his botanical collecting, was taken back by Nuttall's zeal. Bradbury also wrote of his adventures in his own book, and the section on his Missouri River travels was filled with examples of Nuttall becoming lost or narrowly avoiding disaster.

Preoccupied with searching the prairies and woods, Nuttall once found himself separated from the rest of the party, but he was led back to safety when the other men burned a dead tree to provide a signal fire. Numerous times, the trappers had to delay their departure from shore when Nuttall wandered off and failed to return. Another time, he was apparently so preoccupied to notice lightning flashes all around him, including one strike that landed near his feet.

Even more revealing was Nuttall's disappearance once the party reached Manuel Lisa's fort, which was being operated at the time by Meriwether Lewis's brother, Reuben. Eager to venture into an unexplored Eden, Nuttall wandered from plant to shrub, tree to meadow, his eyes downward, observing nature. Eventually, he had traveled about 100 miles from his companions. His food and other supplies were gone, and he finally collapsed from exhaustion. Fortunately, luck again intervened and a passing Mandan found him, placed him in a canoe, and returned him to Lisa's fort.

White travelers to the Rocky Mountains found Nuttall's exploits amusing, but sometimes irritating. The naturalist was a friend of Hunt and Lisa—therefore, the others were expected to watch over him. The Native American tribes, however, were simply bewildered.

Native Americans routinely collected plants that had some edible or medicinal value. But they were confused by someone who spent hours in the fields and obviously delighted in bringing back seemingly useless plants. Even when tribes were otherwise hostile, they believed that Nuttall (as well as Bradbury) had some very strong medicine, and either was very brilliant, or was touched in the head. Perhaps it was a combination of all three.

In any event, the tribes all knew about the naturalist. They watched him wander the countryside and they dared not approach too closely. Except for isolated incidents where individuals broke into Nuttall's containers that held specimens and drank the preserving alcohol, all the tribes left him alone.

John Bradbury did not have as complete a disregard for his own safety and comfort as did Nuttall, and he left the Mandan villages (in modern-day North Dakota) in the spring, bothered by the incessant swarms of mosquitoes and the desire to return to England. Bradbury returned to St. Louis on one of Lisa's keelboats, and, after the War of 1812 ended, he returned to England where his published journal became quite popular. Eventually, he returned to St. Louis, where he made a new home.

Nuttall was not so inclined to leave. To him, the prairie was a "magnificent garden." He stayed on collecting until the end of summer 1811, discovering a new species of bat and other small animals, as well as numerous new plants and beetles. He even compiled a small collection of rocks from the upper Missouri River.

In the fall, Nuttall hitched a ride downstream to St. Louis, then continued on to New Orleans. There, he dutifully fulfilled the terms of his contract with Benjamin Barton. Although Barton fully expected his field assistant to return to Philadelphia with his specimens, then remain and describe the collection to be published under Barton's name, Nuttall did not return.

Thomas had long since realized that Barton had taken advantage of the younger man's desire to collect flora and fauna and to explore the natural history of uncharted lands of the west. Yet, except for slight alterations in Barton's overly ambitious itinerary, Nuttall kept his part of the contract. He shipped a treasure trove of material back to Barton, along with his journal notes—enough samples to keep any scientist busy for years.

Nuttall probably would never have received much credit for his endeavors if he had waited for Barton's acknowledgments in scientific publications. Peter Custis and many others had learned that lesson the hard way. Also, Barton tended to promise more than he could deliver. At the time of Nuttall's arrival in New Orleans, Barton still had considerable material unprocessed and undescribed from the Lewis and Clark expedition that had returned five years before. When Barton died in 1815, much of the Corps of Discovery material was still stored away, undescribed. Many of the specimens were forgotten until they were rediscovered in 1896. Now, Thomas Nuttall had provided Barton with even more specimens—easily years, if not decades, of steady work for Barton or his assistants.

But Nuttall didn't plan to wait for Barton to formally describe these latest specimens, with only the possibility of passing on recognition to the collector. Instead, Thomas Nuttall collected duplicate specimens, seeds, and even living plants for many of the plants that he shipped to Barton. These he either sold to earn money for his two years of effort, or he retained to include in his own scientific publications.

Benjamin Smith Barton was not happy, and he repeatedly told others that Nuttall had cheated the distinguished professor. Nuttall felt otherwise, and for the remainder of his life, he refused to mention his mentor's name.

Whatever the legalities or ethics of either man's actions, the discoveries of new flora in western North America came into print earlier than they would have if left solely to Barton. But Nuttall still failed to receive his full measure of credit because of more scientific politics. When he arrived in New Orleans, rumors of war were rampant. With the center of science in the United States now an inhospitable location for him, Nuttall booked passage back to England where he remained for three years.

During his absence, another botanist who worked for Barton, Frederick Pursh, was given access to the Nuttall specimens, along with others collected by Lewis and Clark, John Clayton, Peter Custis, Benjamin Barton, and many others—most held in Barton's herbarium collection at the University of Pennsylvania. Pursh largely ignored matters of attribution to collectors because—after all—the specimens belonged to Benjamin Barton, and the professor was reluctant to provide additional credit to those who he felt had abandoned him, such as Custis and Nuttall. Pursh had established a solid reputation prior to moving to New York in 1807. And, because Pursh's resultant work, *Flora Americae Septentrionalis,* essentially doubled the previously known numbers of species from North America, it became an extremely useful reference. It was Pursh who became famous—not those who did much of the collecting. As a result, when Thomas Nuttall published, in London, his *Catalogue of New and Interesting Plants Collected in Upper Louisiana and Principally of the River Missouri, North America,* Pursh was already associated with the formal descriptions. His was the name listed with many of the scientific names and, by implication, their discovery. Nuttall largely was ignored in the eyes of natural historians.

Nonetheless, Thomas Nuttall had become noticed because of his field collections and his knowledge of North American flora. His *Catalogue* steadily became a standard reference to flora of the American west, and he was elected a member of the Linnaean Society of London.

When he returned to Philadelphia in 1815, Nuttall had solid credentials as an authority on botany. He was no longer just an enthusiastic amateur. He made ends meet by becoming a commercial collector—selling specimens and seeds to botanical gardens, private collectors, and botanists in the United States, as well as at least one wealthy client in London.

As always, Nuttall sought out the new and the unusual. He collected in areas of the South, as well as Pennsylvania, Ohio, and Kentucky—even though those regions had been searched by others for years—finding a new type of needle grass, a gerardia, an ironweed, a blue-eyed Mary, a variety of mint, and many others. Eventually, Nuttall returned to Philadelphia and became friends with Thomas Say, another passionate naturalist who would make his own important mark in the natural history of the west.

Say and Nuttall collected together, and the two spent long hours at Peale's Museum in Philadelphia—unquestionably the leading exhibitor and collection of flora and fauna. Peale's had been where many of Lewis and Clark's animal curiosities were stored and displayed, and it was where the live barking squirrel—the black-tailed prairie dog—was seen by thousands after it was shipped back east in the spring of 1805.

Peale's collections of specimens, hides, skins, eggs, plants, and other biota fascinated Say and Nuttall. Their enthusiasm for natural history was contagious. The two even slept in the museum on occasion, and they edited and printed the Academy of Natural Sciences of Philadelphia's *Journal.*

In 1818, Nuttall reinforced his own reputation by publishing *Genera of North American Plants and a Catalogue of the Species through 1817,* which improved on Frederick Pursh's work from 1814. But, unlike Pursh and Barton and some others who had evolved into describers rather than field collectors *and* describers, Thomas Nuttall never lost his burning curiosity that could only be quenched by plunging into the field. He was the first field botanist to actually collect and describe his own specimens from the west, and he was innovative in another way as well. His *Genera of North American Plants* was published in English, rather than the traditional scholarly Latin. Thus, his works became useful guides for amateur collectors as well as academics.

This was not an easy task. Publication of such a volume was not readily encouraged, and Nuttall had to finance the printing with his own funds. He even turned to his former profession as a printer and actually did some of the printing of the book. The result was a volume that was cordially received in North America, but enthusiastically embraced by Europeans. Eventually, it was that notoriety that would indirectly enhance Nuttall's American reputation as well.

Field collecting was never far from Thomas's mind. And, when Thomas Say and Nuttall worked together in Philadelphia, they hoped also to collect together with a new, government-sponsored expedition that was being planned for the west in 1819 and 1820. Ultimately, Nuttall was disappointed because Say was chosen to accompany Major Stephen Long's trip to the Great Plains and the Rocky Mountains—and Nuttall was not.

The rationale was that Dr. William Baldwin, a medical doctor and competent botanist, could perform dual roles on the trip: physician and scientist. Ultimately, the Long expedition was delayed, and Dr. Baldwin died before the trip could resume. He was replaced by another physician/scientist, Edwin James, who would prove to be invaluable, not only in his dual roles, but also as a geologist as well as compiler of the expedition's records.

Disappointed at not being able to travel to what would ultimately become a trip along the Platte River and beyond, Nuttall decided to finance his own expedition, although a decidedly less ambitious one. He solicited $50 each from a number of friends and, armed with this small nest egg, he spent the next 18 months collecting in what was then considered the largely unexplored southwest—what is today Arkansas and Oklahoma.

Nuttall left Philadelphia on October 2, 1818, traveled by boat down the Ohio River, and later teamed up with another amateur botanist, Dr. Daniel Drake, who would later hire a young painter named John James Audubon. After entering the Mississippi River, accompanied by a man and his son, their flatboat ran aground on a river sandbar. Over the next several weeks, Nuttall experienced enough adventures to fill several books: encounters with river

pirates, bouts with fever, disorientation in canebrakes and bram-
bles—but always collecting and observing.

At Fort Smith, Arkansas, Nuttall teamed up with army physician
Dr. Thomas Russell, another amateur botanist. Together, Nuttall
and Russell discovered several new plants, including a poppy, a
violet variation of the blue-eyed Mary, and the prairie iris (celestial
lily). Taking advantage of every opportunity, Nuttall joined a detail
of soldiers on May 16 that was heading up the Red River to disperse
some squatters who were occupying Osage treaty lands. Thomas was
now retracing some of the territory covered by Peter Custis and the
Red River expedition some 13 years earlier. Unfortunately, Nuttall
became infatuated with the beauty of the open plains, which he
called "delightful prairies." Wandering about, he again became disoriented and, finally, completely lost. By the time he returned to
where the soldiers had been, they were gone.

Undaunted, Nuttall walked for miles, eventually staying with a
settler until he could join a party of travelers that was returning to
Fort Smith. Unfortunately, the return trip also was delayed when all
the travelers became lost for a time.

In addition to his extensive notes on natural history subjects,
Nuttall recorded numerous observations on his encounters with
Osage Indians. But not all of the interactions were positive. One
Osage stole the botanist's pen knife, and he blamed other Osages
when his supplies started to disappear.

Nuttall next joined a trapper named Lee who was traveling to the
headwaters of the Canadian River. But the trip seemed more like a
string of misadventures. Once, about to bathe in a small creek, Nuttall almost sat on a poisonous snake. Then, the two men drank some
bad water and neither one could sit astride a horse. And, when Nuttall contracted a fever that left him further incapacitated, it was Lee
who actually did some of the collecting. Some passing Osages fed
the two men, but then promptly stole some of the travelers' belong-
ings. After that, dealing with inclement weather and encounters
with quicksand seemed to be quite routine.

But, despite the difficulties, the natural history contributions of the trip were substantial, even though the region had been covered by several naturalists in the previous decades. Nuttall retained his botanical samples, gave the fossils to Thomas Say and the fishes to Charles Lesueur, one of the country's leading ichthyologists.

When his friend, Thomas Say, returned from the arduous Long expedition, Nuttall could share equally colorful stories about collecting in wild lands. While Say was busy helping Edwin James and Stephen Long prepare a report of their trip through the Great Plains, Nuttall published the diary of his own trip, *A Journal of Travels into the Arkansas Territory during the Year 1919*, one of his few personal journals that remain in existence. And, when Say left to accompany Long on a second expedition, Thomas Nuttall accepted a position that would be the envy of any naturalist—a post at Harvard University.

In 1822, he was appointed the curator of the Harvard Botanical Garden and an instructor of botany and natural history. Although Nuttall would receive increases in pay during his years at Harvard, he never was appointed a professor. One reason was that when the former curator, William Dandridge Peck, died, Harvard did not have sufficient funds to pay his replacement a professor's salary. Instead, Nuttall began at a salary of $500 per year, plus course fees paid by students who enrolled in his classes.

Perhaps more important, despite Nuttall's solid credentials as a botanist and scientist, he lacked formal academic training and degrees. From Harvard's standpoint, Thomas Nuttall may have been a genius, but he was only a self-trained genius.

During Nuttall's decade at Harvard, he was considered a good teacher, obviously inspired, and apparently inspiring to students. Forty students enrolled in his first class, and class sizes slowly increased. Many young minds pointed to Nuttall as their inspiration for escaping the confines of Cambridge, Massachusetts, and leaping into fieldwork. Their teacher lectured at Yale and at Philadelphia's Academy of Natural Sciences and published on a variety of topics. Harvard was appreciative; Nuttall's salary eventually doubled, and he was awarded an honorary master of arts degree.

Yet, it was an unsettled time in his life. He longed to return to the west and to pursue field collecting. Harvard tried to accommodate him by giving the naturalist several leaves of absence. He used those sabbaticals to collect in North Carolina, Florida, and Alabama. On one such trip, he returned to Pennsylvania. Among other specimens, he collected and gave a rare white butterfly to his friend Thomas Say, who had become, arguably, the nation's leading authority on insects. But, when Say left for an extended residence at New Harmony, a utopian community in Indiana, Nuttall returned to Harvard and resumed teaching.

Philadelphia always had been the center of science and discovery, but the departure of Say and Nuttall, among others, signaled a change in the focus of natural history in North America. Now, more and more talented professionals were working in Boston, New York, Indiana, Kentucky, Tennessee, and elsewhere.

Despite Nuttall's preoccupation with biological subjects, his social life became quite different for a man who never had many concerns for personal comfort. While traveling, he generally relied on the hospitality of others to board him. While living in Philadelphia, he once lived in the basement of a house. Now, at Harvard, he lived in a university-owned boarding house and was considered an eligible bachelor.

Nuttall was not an unattractive man, but he was relatively short, with a receding hairline and round, prominent chin. His hair was typically unkempt and he walked with a slight stoop, from years of peering downward at plants. Yet, he was a professional man and, obviously, a scientist of great intellect. Although he was pleasant enough in a social scene, he seldom carried on long conversations with anyone who was not passionate about natural science.

He did, however, gain a reputation as an eccentric.

His room was only accessible by means of a rope ladder, which he pulled up to keep others out. He had a trap door in the closet ceiling by which he could leave his room unnoticed. And, he took his meals through a hole in the kitchen wall.

Yet, despite these eccentricities, he continued to build his scientific reputation. He wrote a textbook, *Introduction to Systematic and*

Physiological Botany, and was elected president of the Boston Society of Natural Sciences—an honor that he declined. He also became an expert in a new field—ornithology.

A friend, James Brown—who founded the Boston publishing company, Little, Brown—suggested that Nuttall publish a field guide to birds. This he did in 1832: *Manual of Ornithology of the United States and Canada.* It became the most popular birder's guide in the United States and was repeatedly reissued until the twentieth century. The book even was noticed abroad. When John James Audubon returned from England in 1832, he went to Thomas Nuttall for suggestions on birding locations and to borrow some of Nuttall's bird skins. Audubon even carried a copy of Nuttall's guide book during his North American travels, calling it "a gem."

Despite these distractions, Nuttall became restless. He wanted to return to the American west and collect in areas of the country that he believed were rapidly being settled by humans.

The chance came in 1832 when entrepreneur Nathaniel Jarvis Wyeth led an unsuccessful expedition up the Missouri River. After Wyeth returned, he started making preparations for another expedition to the west. When Wyeth presented several specimens of plants that he had collected to his friend Thomas Nuttall, he asked the naturalist to go along on the future trip.

Nuttall immediately agreed, and resigned his position at Harvard.

When the plans for the trip finally materialized, another naturalist also agreed to go up the Missouri: 24-year-old John Townsend, a physician, pharmacist, and amateur botanist from Philadelphia who would later recount his adventures in a book, *Narrative of a Journey across the Rocky Mountains.* The American Philosophical Society and other organizations helped purchase supplies for Nuttall and Townsend in return for bird specimens for their collections, and Townsend and Nuttall happily collected their way across the Great Plains, sometimes by boat and often on foot. They were joined for a while by Captain William Drummond Stewart, a British veteran of the Battle of Waterloo, who later would make his own mark in the field of natural history. Also joining the Wyeth group was fur trader Milton Sublette and several missionaries, including Marcus Whitman, who were heading for the Pacific Northwest.

The Wyeth expedition traveled up the Missouri, then across the Rocky Mountains in a route that took them near what would later become the Oregon Trail. Wyeth's group eventually established the trading post of Fort Hall. They endured difficult traveling across lava beds near the Snake River, then paddled down the Columbia River in canoes—just as Lewis and Clark had done almost three decades before—to the fur trading post at Fort Vancouver. Along the way, Townsend and Nuttall were able to collect specimens from many new, unspoiled regions. The two naturalists discovered new species and rediscovered others that only had been seen by Lewis and Clark.

True to form, Nuttall became lost on several occasions. But, even when he was completely disoriented, he turned his gaze downward and continued to collect plants and animals until rescuers found him. Descending the Columbia River, a storm struck and most of the plant specimens and drying papers became soaked. It took the men hours to spread out and dry all the material.

No one would ever accuse John Townsend of lacking enthusiasm for collecting in the wilds. But he paled in comparison to Nuttall's single-purpose determination. As Townsend wrote of his companion, "Throughout the whole of our long journey, I have had constantly to admire the ardor and perfect indefatigability with which he has devoted himself to the grand object of his tour. No difficulty, no danger, no fatigue has ever daunted him."

Even by the evening campfire, while others slept, talked, or played the fiddle, Nuttall was working on his specimens, organizing them in probable taxonomic groups, adding to his notes, and thinking about plants that he had seen that day.

From Fort Vancouver, Townsend and Nuttall journeyed up the Willamette Valley where Nuttall met several members of John Jacob Astor's fur trading party who had accompanied Thomas up the Missouri River in 1811. The trappers were settled into the less strenuous life in the mild Oregon climate. From Oregon, quite impulsively, but following a lifelong dream, Nuttall left the others and made two trips to Hawaii, each time returning to California. Townsend remained behind, arranging to ship their specimens back to Philadelphia. Whether it was a rain forest in Hawaii, a hillside in the Willamette Valley, or a beach at Monterey, Nuttall always had his eyes cast downward, discovering new plants, birds, and shells that others had never seen or, at least, had never noticed.

He was still collecting when he met his former student, Richard Henry Dana, on the beach at San Diego.

Whether he knew it at the time or not, this would be Nuttall's last trip to the west. He stooped to collect shellfish and other creatures literally to the moment that he stepped aboard the small launch that took him out to the *Alert*, then back to New York in September 1836. Among trunks full of other specimens, Nuttall carried 21 new types of shells and 15 new crustaceans with him—all collected in San Diego while he waited for the *Alert* to depart. When he tried to pay for his fare, the *Alert's* Boston owners rejected his money, waiving the charge in the name of the advancement of science.

For a few years after his return to the east, Nuttall worked on describing the specimens from his most recent collections. Sometimes, he did this where many of the specimens were held—in Philadelphia. Other times, he worked at the Harvard campus. He traveled widely in the South and completed work on several important natural history accounts, including *North American Sylva*. Finally, in 1842, Thomas Nuttall returned to England.

Except for a final trip to Boston and Philadelphia during 1847–1848, he would remain in England for the rest of his life, having inherited an estate passed down from his uncle. The terms of the will required that Nuttall remain in England permanently. With the acceptance of the inheritance, Nuttall's days of wilderness collecting largely ended. He died on September 10, 1859, at the age of 72.

Crew members aboard the *Alert* were not permitted to intermingle with the passengers on the homeward voyage from California to the East Coast. But, sometimes at night, when Richard Henry Dana was on watch, his old professor would come up on deck to talk.

Back at Harvard, Nuttall had little time for anyone who wasn't serious about natural history. And he had little regard for people whom he called "closet naturalists." These were people who seldom collected or observed nature in the field. Instead, closet naturalists made their reputations by publishing from the fruits of others' efforts. Thomas Nuttall would never be called a closet naturalist. He was the exact opposite. Washington Irving, in his classic work, *Astoria*, described Nuttall's behavior in the field: "All his enthusiasm was awakened at beholding a new world, opening upon him in the boundless prairies, clad in the variegated ruse of unknown flowers."

Crew members aboard the *Alert* called the naturalist "Old Curiosity," and, on the homeward voyage, Nuttall asked to spend time on unexplored Staten Island, near the tip of Cape Horn, so he could collect again in untouched lands. Nuttall was "hopping around, bright as a bird," wrote Dana. "[A] more desolate looking spot I never wish to set eyes upon, bare, broken and girt with rocks and ice. Mr. N. said he should like to go ashore upon the island and examine a spot probably no human being had ever set foot upon."

The captain of the *Alert* was less enthusiastic than was "Old Curiosity," especially with foul weather approaching, but he did allow a brief stopover in the name of science.

The written legacy of Thomas Nuttall is astounding. Despite the lack of acknowledgment from Barton and Pursh, Nuttall made his own mark and others responded by naming numerous new species after the wilderness collector: Nuttall's cockle, Nuttall's poor-will, the olive-sided flycatcher (*Nuttallornis borealis*), Nuttall's dogwood, and Nuttall's woodpecker are just a few of the plants and animals that still carry his name.

But Nuttall, Say, and others were indicative of a new breed of naturalists who were then actively following in the footsteps of Lewis and Clark, but with a particular eye toward plants and animals. Soon, associates of Nuttall, such as John Townsend and William Gambel, and former students at Harvard, were carving their own niches in western natural history.

Chapter 5

THOMAS SAY AND EDWIN JAMES:
THE LONG EXPEDITION

Goldsmith's Natural History was a classic guide to the world's animals, published in 1823. A revised version for schoolchildren appeared in 1838 and it included a definition of "natural history":

> *That part of knowledge which teaches us to distinguish and describe the objects of nature; to examine their appearances, structure, properties, and uses; and to collect, preserve, and arrange them.*

Doing so in primitive areas requires skill, intelligence, determination, and luck. Thomas Nuttall had all of these qualities—especially luck. But the American west could be an inhospitable, even dangerous place, as two of his colleagues found out.

John Kirk Townsend, who accompanied Nuttall on Nathaniel Wyeth's expedition to Fort Vancouver in 1835, made an impression on Wyeth's rowdy group of fur trappers. He appeared in the field wearing oversized leather pants, a coat made from green blankets, and a "white wool hat with a round crown." Townsend bought the outfit in St. Louis before departing westward. His fellow naturalist, Thomas Nuttall, bought a matching set.

The Townsend family came from Philadelphia, where many of the family members were avid bird-watchers. Even though John became a physician, he developed a talent for bird identification and taxidermy that even impressed family friend John James Audubon. When Audubon visited Philadelphia in 1835, Townsend showed the painter a new bird species that John had discovered and preserved. Audubon formally described the bird and named it the Townsend's bunting (*Spiza townsendii*). The species was never seen again and, in fact, may have been either extremely rare or was a variant of some more common form.

Thomas Nuttall also recognized Townsend's talents in natural history, and the two men jointly collected across the western United States as the Wyeth party of 70 men and 250 horses made its way westward. Townsend typically carried a filled, two-gallon whiskey bottle that he used to preserve specimens. However, the whiskey was soon recognized for what it was, and Townsend had trouble keeping members of the party from draining all his specimen containers.

After Townsend accompanied Nuttall on the older man's first trip to Hawaii, the doctor returned to Fort Vancouver and took a position as acting surgeon, replacing a physician who had left. During the several months that he served there, Townsend shipped specimens back to Philadelphia and continued to collect new species.

Townsend sailed around the Horn and returned to the east where, in 1842, he became curator of the National Institute, which would become the precursor to the Smithsonian Institution and the National Museum in Washington, D.C. Townsend spent his days obtaining specimens for the institute and using his taxidermy skills to create realistic mounts of animals for display. He became quite well-known in natural history circles, partly because of his collecting experience in the west, and several new species were named after him, including the Townsend's warbler, Townsend's mole, Townsend's ground squirrel, Townsend's big-ear bat, and the white-tailed jackrabbit (*Lepus townsendii*).

Unfortunately, John Townsend spent almost every day working in close quarters with his taxidermy specimens and breathing too much of his special preservation powder—which contained arsenic.

John Townsend died in 1851 from chronic arsenic poisoning. He was only 42 years old.

William Gambel also met an early death while pursuing his natural history interests. As a teenager, Gambel served as one of Thomas Nuttall's assistants. Bitten by the same bug that had affected Nuttall, Townsend, and Say, Gambel headed west himself in 1843, at the age of 22. He joined a party of fur trappers that was heading to Santa Fe. There, he joined another group of trappers that traveled to California. The plants and animals that he collected, including the Gambel's quail and Gambel's oak, as well as the Nuttall woodpecker, secured his reputation as a field naturalist and led to his appointment as assistant curator at the Academy of Natural Sciences of Philadelphia.

In 1849, Gambel, like his mentor, grew restless from too much time away from the woods and fields. He joined another party heading west, this one headed by General Isaac Wistar, who liked the young naturalist but felt he had become too accustomed to the creature comforts to be engaged in travels in wild country. Gambel joined another party, but that group was delayed long enough trying to cross the Great Basin that they had to traverse the Sierra Nevadas in winter. As the Donner party, John C. Frémont, and many others later learned, the California mountains could be deadly in winter. Of this ill-fated party, only two men survived—including Gambel. The naturalist joined another group that proceeded down the Feather River to the interior foothills of California. Unfortunately, several people contracted typhoid fever and died. One of them was William Gambel, age 28.

Townsend's and Gambel's fates were tragic reminders that the pursuit of natural science always could be a risk but, as John Townsend once wrote, there are highs and lows in field collecting. The lows come from "the sorrow and grief . . . he feels when he (the naturalist) is compelled to tear himself from a spot abounding with all he has anxiously and unremittingly sought for."

Another such avid field explorer was Thomas Say. And he, also, underwent trials and tribulations during his most famous western collecting trip.

Say was selected as zoologist for the expedition led by Major Stephen Long that traveled across the Great Plains to the Rocky Mountains. It was an exciting opportunity for any naturalist, and Say's friend from Philadelphia, Thomas Nuttall, was envious. Say would be venturing into country that had never been seen by scientists—a part of the country south of the Missouri River route taken by Nuttall years before. The expedition offered countless opportunities for discovering new species of animals.

So, on the way to rendezvous with the military segment of the expedition, Say started collecting, almost from the time he left home on March 23, 1819. Weeks later, Say and some other members of the scientific party stopped in a Kansas tribal village where they purchased buffalo meat, corn, moccasins, and other supplies. Accompanied by three Kansas Indians as guides, the party made camp seven miles north of the village. While Say and a few others remained in camp with two of the guides, a party of over 100 Pawnees arrived and proceeded to steal all the horses, food, blankets, and rifles.

It was not a promising beginning to what would become one of the most difficult scientific expeditions ever undertaken in the west.

It had been more than a dozen years since the return of Lewis and Clark, Zebulon Pike, and a few other subsequent excursions into the lands of the Louisiana Purchase. Most of the territory was still completely unexplored, except for the quiet passing of individual fur trappers and native tribes.

The Long expedition had a convoluted history of starts, delays, modifications, and restarts. Even Stephen Long, the New Hampshire–born leader, had many doubts that the expedition would ever depart, but he was ready if given a chance. Stephen Long was admitted to Dartmouth at the age of 21 and, early in his collegiate career, he showed a talent for the physical sciences. Rather than biology, Long excelled in mathematics. After stints as a school teacher and school principal in Pennsylvania, Long received a commission as a second lieutenant in the U.S. Army Corps of Engineers in 1815.

He rose rapidly in rank, taught mathematics for a year at West Point, then was promoted to major in 1816. Long always had hoped to become involved in more field operations, and the corps' rapidly rising star got his chance as an officer surveying routes for the Baltimore and Ohio Railroad.

In 1817, Long was surveying in Illinois and the lower Arkansas River, then was engaged in similar work in Wisconsin and Minnesota. It was during this period that he began to design a specialized water craft that could transport men and material up the Missouri River. From most other Corps of Engineers officers, such an idea would probably have floundered in some dusty file drawer. After all, Long's experience had been as a railroad surveyor and one who had helped survey the future sites of Fort Smith, Arkansas, and Fort St. Anthony. The latter would become the future site of the cities of Minneapolis and St. Paul.

But Long was obviously intelligent, and his idea for a troop steamboat kept being circulated through the military ranks. Finally, in one of those events in history where two ideas merge at the right time, the concept came to the attention of John C. Calhoun, the secretary of war.

Calhoun had some similar plans for the upper Missouri River. He envisioned a string of army forts, staffed by American troops, that would provide ample evidence to the English and Native Americans that the United States owned the lands of the Louisiana Purchase and intended to control the fur resources and trade possibilities.

Soon, Calhoun had a plan in force to transport over 1,000 soldiers, under the command of Colonel Henry Atkinson, up the Missouri River to at least the Yellowstone River. The men would travel in five steamboats, with Long and a smaller scientific and engineering detachment traveling in a sixth steamboat. Once upriver, Long and his surveyors and naturalists would map and collect in the uncharted lands.

That was the plan. But the Atkinson expedition, commonly

known as the "Yellowstone Expedition," ended in failure. Long's design for a flat-bottomed steamboat never was implemented for the troops; the army used conventionally designed boats instead. Those unsuitable boats ran aground near the mouth of the Kansas River, and Atkinson had to march his men to temporary quarters near present-day Omaha, Nebraska. Stranded and unsure how to proceed, the Yellowstone Expedition was forced to spend the winter of 1819–1820 at their temporary fort, named Camp Missouri.

Over the winter, the situation turned even worse. Over 100 soldiers died from scurvy while awaiting orders from their superiors.

Stephen Long and his party, meanwhile, left Pittsburgh on May 3, 1819, traveling down the Ohio River in a steamboat of Long's original design, the *Western Engineer*. Long's flat-bottomed boat proved to be a more suitable craft for the Missouri River and, in September, Long and his party arrived at Camp Missouri, upriver from the location where the other boats had run aground.

Unlike the Lewis and Clark expedition, which had no trained naturalists in the company, and the Red River expedition, which had just Peter Custis, Long's group had a full complement of scientists and artists.

In the original party that prepared to head west were Titian Peale, the son of Charles Wilson Peale, who was hired as assistant naturalist. Peale ultimately served as a second artist for the expedition. The primary artist was Samuel Seymour. William Baldwin served dual roles as the expedition's physician and botanist. Augustus Jessup was the geologist, and Lieutenant James Graham and Cadet William Swift were appointed assistant topographers, to assist Major Long. Captain Thomas Biddle served as principal journalist, in charge of records and responsible for the expedition's principal journal. The most renowned member of the scientific staff, however, was Thomas Say.

Like so many nineteenth-century naturalists, Thomas Say was a native of Philadelphia. Natural history inclinations were in his blood—his great-grandfather was John Bartram, the legendary naturalist who collected and observed his way across the southeastern

United States in the 1770s. In his youth, Say was considered quite handsome and cultured, with a clump of unmanageable hair atop his head, and long, full sideburns. When not in muddy field conditions, he typically wore shirts with high, starched collars and a waistcoat. He was known for wearing a tall, gray beaver hat, which fascinated members of several Native American tribes while with the Long expedition.

His credentials as a naturalist were impressive. His original career had been pharmacy, but he soon was consumed by natural history and he became a member of the American Philosophical Society. This broad interest in science led to specific interests in invertebrates, and his mind became an open portal for information. He was a regular in the archives of the Academy of Natural Sciences, along with his friend Thomas Nuttall, and Say was a charter member of the academy. Say and Nuttall often slept amongst the stacks of books and specimens at the academy, as well as those at Peale's Museum. As Say progressed with his own taxonomic writing, he helped edit the academy's scientific journal. When Stephen Long made inquiries among Philadelphia's scientific community for recommendations for potential naturalists, the name of Thomas Say came up several times.

Unfortunately for Stephen Long, but perhaps not for American science, the original team of scientists would change somewhat. Both Say and Jessup became ill, which delayed the departure of the expedition. Once they recovered and the *Western Engineer* headed downstream from Pittsburgh, William Baldwin also became sick and had to be left behind in a small town, while the rest of the party proceeded down the Ohio River. A few days later, Baldwin died, and the Long expedition would learn later that they now lacked a physician and botanist.

Once Long and his detachment reached Camp Missouri (soon to be named Fort Atkinson, and later Fort Calhoun), they were forced to spend the winter of 1819–1820 with Atkinson's troops and witness the tragic deaths at the winter encampment. But by spring, Long was ready to depart for surveying and scientific collecting, despite his depleted command. Baldwin was now gone, and Augustus Jessup was considering retirement because of the delays in departure. In addition, Captain Biddle, a member of Philadelphia's prominent Biddle family, left to join Atkinson's command after severe personality disagreements with Major Long.

The remaining scientific team took advantage of their idle situation and did as much collecting as possible. Thomas Say, in particular, had the typical naturalist's curiosity that allowed him to realize that the nearby lands offered many opportunities for scientific discovery, even if they were not the pristine, virgin territories that the members of the team hoped to explore farther upriver.

Major Long issued orders that the "scientific gentlemen," who were still being paid $2.20 per day, should continue to collect around the winter encampment and that they be assisted by the military troops. Since Say and Peale were interested in all forms of life, the entire field of vertebrate life was an open book. Learning of a nearby stone quarry, Say visited and found a new species of bombardier beetle and several other insects. But, some large fissures in the quarry (where building stones had been removed in the past) particularly interested Say. After some crawling around and investigating further, Say found a number of snakes that had crawled inside to hibernate for the winter. In just the one day, at the single quarry, Thomas Say discovered three apparently new species of snakes: the blue racer, the red-tailed garter snake, and the western ribbon snake. After a century and a half of snake taxonomy revisions, Say's discoveries are still considered at least valid new subspecies of snakes.

By midwinter, opportunities for collecting were much reduced, so the scientists shifted their energies to making notes on the native uses of many types of plants, as well as their uses of animal parts. Say even noted that head lice were regularly eaten by Native American women, who combed the creatures from each other's hair. Say collected some specimens of the lice, but did not comment on their culinary attributes. By spring 1820, natural history collections and observations increased again, and Say and Peale recorded the timing of bird migrations, along with bird numbers and behavior. The naturalists were fascinated by the unusual sandhill cranes and recorded in their journals the total animals collected around Fort Atkinson: 144 birds, 11 amphibians, 10 reptiles, 34 mammals, and hundreds of insects.

No one was more frustrated by all the delays and the waiting than was Stephen Long. The deaths of the soldiers under Atkinson's command put a halt to further plans to create a military presence up the Missouri River. There certainly was a visible presence of nearly 1,000 men, but they were stranded well downriver and were barely noticed by the tribes and the English trappers in the principal beaver grounds up the Missouri River. The men sat and waited.

In Washington, the failure of the Yellowstone Expedition caused a political uprising in Congress. Each politician pointed an accusing finger at the others, and John C. Calhoun, the author of the Missouri River plan, was the one caught in the middle. Congress rightly questioned spending any additional funds for a mission that had been a complete failure and had cost the lives of 100 soldiers.

In the spring of 1820, Long could no longer restrain his frustration. Accompanied by Augustus Jessup, who now had decided to retire, Long traveled to Washington, D.C., and met with John C. Calhoun. At that meeting, Long proposed a grandiose plan to resurrect the scientific portion of the expedition. Long hoped that, with a successful expedition, Calhoun and the military might be able to counteract some of the bad publicity from the original Yellowstone mission. Long's plan was to take his party across the Great Lakes region to present-day Minneapolis, then up the Missouri and eventually explore the headwaters of the Red, Arkansas, and Platte Rivers. Hopefully, Long could even cross the continent to the Pacific Ocean as well.

It took five weeks for Long to get an answer from Calhoun: No. There would be no great transcontinental expedition. Congress would not authorize any additional funds for exploring trips. But the major was permitted to take his detachment of soldiers, topographers, and scientists on a modified surveying trip.

Since most of the party already was waiting in Nebraska, the new expedition could proceed, but with no additional funds. Since the previous funding and supplies were now gone, the expedition could proceed with what they could salvage at Fort Atkinson. The scientists would continue to be paid $2.20 per day, but they would have to use their personal funds to buy preserving alcohol, drying papers and presses, and other sampling equipment. Despite this unfunded mandate, Long's party was required by Calhoun to perform exemplary duty in mapping and observation, including "everything interesting in relation to soil, face of the country, water courses, and productions, whether animal, vegetable, or mineral."

To these instructions, the secretary of war attached a copy of Thomas Jefferson's instructions to Lewis and Clark as having "many valuable suggestions." In their spare time, without additional funds to accomplish their primary tasks, perhaps Long and his scientists could do these other tasks that Jefferson had suggested as well. With few supplies, the revised Stephen Long expedition had limited time to complete their mission. Accomplishing these tasks in their entirety seemed doomed from the start. Yet, Long eagerly accepted.

To replenish the party's now diminished personnel, Captain John Bell was assigned to replace Captain Biddle, and the journal responsibilities were assigned to all the members of the civilian staff. Edwin James was hired to fill the dual roles of physician and botanist. In the absence of an experienced geologist, James was given those responsibilities as well.

It would be a fortunate turn of events, because James would ultimately prove to be an extremely valuable asset to the expedition, its geological inquiries, and the completion of the final report, and his presence complemented well the original members of the group.

When Thomas Say was appointed zoologist for the original Long expedition, his good friend Thomas Nuttall had hoped to be appointed as the botanist. Nuttall was quite qualified, of course, as was budding botanist John Torrey. But Long hoped to combine the botanist position with that of medical officer. Thus, he chose Dr. William Baldwin. Long did offer Torrey the position of geologist when Augustus Jessup retired. But Torrey declined when Long was (at the time) uncertain whether the scientists would even be paid. Torrey, who would later become the dean of American botanists, would formally describe many of the plant specimens that were subsequently collected by Edwin James while in the west.

James was a native of Vermont who, after graduating from Middlebury College, studied medicine in New York. His interest in botany was sparked by reading texts by Amos Eaton. James was encouraged in his natural history interests by John Torrey and, like many physicians of the time, he had broad interests in many areas of science. At the time of the Long expedition, James was only 23, yet he had medical skills and had published scientific papers in both geology and botany. Thus, when Stephen Long was looking for replacements for his medical doctor, botanist, and geologist, James seemed to be the ideal candidate.

Titian Peale also served a dual role on the expedition. Not only was he a member of the talented Peale family of painters, but he had some natural history experience as well. He was a friend of Thomas Say and once had gone with Say and others on a collecting trip to Florida. He knew taxidermy and was an excellent marksman. His only major drawback was his age—he was only 19. Yet, he already had been a member of the Academy of Natural Sciences of Philadelphia for a year, and Say vouched for his many talents. Samuel Seymour was primarily an artist for the expedition. Yet, he often was pushed into assisting the naturalists in their collecting. Seymour was an English emigrant who eventually became part of the active group of artists in Philadelphia, and his talents caught the eye of Stephen Long.

The newly constituted Long expedition, now 22 men strong, departed Fort Atkinson on June 6, 1820, outfitted with a string of pack animals, copies of Lewis and Clark's *Journals,* a copy of Alexander von Humboldt's *Personal Narrative of Travels to the Equinoctal Regions of America,* and maps prepared by Zebulon Pike and William Clark.

The expedition stopped at a series of Pawnee villages, then

continued on to the Platte River on June 22. From there, they headed west, reaching the site of present-day Denver on July 5, 1820. Along the way, the men discovered the headwaters of the Platte, as well as Long's Peak, and a variety of new plants and animals.

At one point, the party shot several unusual foxes that would become known as swift foxes (now *Vulpes velox*). The name was suggested by Say because this fox "runs with extraordinary swiftness." The common name has endured from Say's original description, but the swift fox itself has now been extirpated from much of its original range.

The scientists were kept busy preserving and/or describing dozens of unique types of plants, yet they found time to examine huge anthills that were created by prairie mound–building ants, a species that would not be formally described until 45 years later. Numerous plant species were named for Edwin James when described by John Torrey, Asa Gray, and George Bentham in later years, and many of the names have remained valid and recognized over the subsequent years. Among them were the broad-leaved milkweed (originally *Asclepias jamesii*), the sledge (originally *Carex jamesii*), James's frankenia (*Frankenia jamesii*), galleta-grass (then *Pleuraphis jamesii*), James's prairie clover (then *Psoralea jamesii*), James's saxifrage (then *Saxifraga jamesii*), wild potato (*Solanum jamesii*), tuber starwort (*Stellaria jamesiana*), James's crestpetal (then *Cristatella jamesii*), James's rushpea (originally *Hoffmanseggia jamesii*), waxflower (*Jamesia americana*), James's evening primrose (*Oenothera jamesii*), James's nallwort (*Paronychia jamesii*), James's wild buckwheat (*Eriogonum jamesii*), and James's beard tongue (*Penstemon jamesii*).

Thomas Say formally described hundreds of species that he collected, especially in his specialties of molluscs and insects. It was improper scientific etiquette for a describer to assign a scientific name honoring himself or herself. But others describing specimens collected by Say could do so, and a bird (*Sayornis saya*) honors the zoologist.

In late July, Long and his party reached the site of present-day

Pueblo, Colorado, and the nearby Arkansas River. They traveled up the Arkansas to the impressive Royal Gorge, a steep-walled canyon that effectively stopped their upstream progress. Long's party failed to reach the headwaters of the river, as planned, so they decided to modify their itinerary and travel eastward.

Half of the party, under the command of Captain Bell, and including Say, Samuel Seymour, topographer Swift, five enlisted men, and three French guides, proceeded down the Arkansas River, along with a rich trove of specimens, journals, maps, and notes. Their half of the food and supplies would be gone within a few days.

Major Long, Titian Peale, Edwin James, and seven soldiers separated from the others and, on July 2, proceeded south to search for the headwaters of the Red River. That objective was one that had eluded the Red River expedition of Thomas Sparks and Peter Custis, as well as the exploring party headed by Zebulon Pike. If Long had accomplished that objective, he would have succeeded in most of the objectives of the revised trip. Together with the new maps and the discoveries of plants, animals, and minerals, the expedition would have become a recognized success.

Unfortunately, that didn't happen.

Food was almost gone, and hunger was accelerating the poor morale of the soldiers and civilians. Despite his positive attributes as a surveyor and steamboat designer, Stephen Long was an inconsistent leader. Like his relationship with Captain Biddle during the previous winter, Long's interactions with Captain Bell became strained and partly led to the separation of the command into two parties.

It was now the heart of the humid summer. Insects constantly plagued the travelers, and food always was scarce. The terrain was rugged and there were unfriendly encounters—but no serious incidents—with bands of Comanches and Kiowas. Even firewood and grazing grass for the animals were almost non-existent.

As the men became more and more exhausted, even Thomas Say's interest in collecting declined. Minds were too preoccupied with finding food and clean drinking water. Spending energy searching for non-edible plants and animals—even in the name of science—seemed less important.

At one point, when the shortage of food was at a critical stage, some of the men managed to shoot a young buffalo. Wounded, the animal wandered off, with the men giving chase. When they finally found the calf, it was being attacked by a pack of wolves, and the starving men had to fight off the wolves to regain their prize. One day, Long's men killed a deer, another day a wild horse. But such incidents might be days apart.

Captain Bell's group, proceeding down the Arkansas River, also was suffering. At one point, they were living on sparse game and a half cup of corn meal each day. But hunger was less serious than something else that happened—an incident that would have repercussions for the success of the overall expedition.

On the morning of August 31, Bell awoke to find that three soldiers had deserted. Along with three horses, the men had taken most of the supplies, the remaining food, and the journals, maps, scientific notes, natural history specimens, and individual daily diaries. Thomas Say alone lost five notebooks filled with details of his collections that he had entrusted to Bell's group to take downriver.

Left with only dying horses and few other possessions, the remaining members of Bell's party struggled on by foot. The group's two dogs died of starvation and exhaustion and only the generosity of a passing band of Osages, who shared their own meager food supplies, probably saved the explorers from death.

Long's group, meanwhile, was only slightly more mobile. But any pretense of optimism evaporated on September 1, when Long recorded the latitude and longitude and discovered that, instead of following the Red River to its source, as they thought they were doing, the men had actually been traveling upstream along the Canadian River, a tributary of the Arkansas River. Long and his men never had encountered the Red River.

Dejected and exhausted, the two groups inched their separate ways down the Arkansas River. Long's group reached Fort Smith,

Arkansas, on September 13, 1820, about five days after the arrival of Bell and the others.

In retrospect, the Stephen Long expedition of 1819–1820 achieved more than perhaps anyone could have predicted with the lack of financial support, erratic planning, difficult traveling conditions, and unrealistic objectives. If deserters had not stolen most of the records and specimens, the Long expedition would surely have been listed among the noteworthy expeditions of the early nineteenth century.

Despite all the problems, some positive accomplishments did emerge, and many of them were related to natural history. Even discounting the lapses in scientific collecting and the loss of a portion of the specimens, the scientific team did manage to return with the skins of more than 60 new or unusual animal species and thousands of insect specimens. Of the insects collected by Thomas Say, between 700 and 800 are thought to have been new to science. In addition, Edwin James returned with hundreds of plant specimens. Over the years, species and subspecies names and descriptions have been reevaluated, combined, and renamed. But the best estimates are that the Long expedition returned with between 140 and 500 new species of plants, which were later described in the scientific literature by James, John Torrey, Asa Gray, and several other botanical authorities.

Thomas Say was a prolific collector on the expedition, beginning in 1819, with the departure of the *Western Engineer*, and involving the extended stay at Fort Atkinson. Say is still credited with discovering 12 species of reptiles and amphibians, 13 birds, 13 mammals, and hundreds of invertebrates. The Long party was the first to see and describe the prairie gray wolf, kit fox, prairie rattlesnake, brown shrew, blue grouse, broad-tailed pigeon, blue racer, and several species of squirrels and bats, among many diverse creatures.

These numbers are only estimates, or ranges, because no one can say for certain exactly how many specimens were collected or which ones were truly unique, because almost all of the specimens were subsequently lost.

Initially, the specimens arrived safely in Philadelphia. And, years later, P. T. Barnum displayed some of the animals at his museum in New York City. But those were destroyed in a fire in 1865. The other specimens either decomposed from improper storage, or were simply misplaced or thrown away. The extraordinary efforts by Long, Say, James, Peale, and the others resulted in few lasting biological souvenirs. A handful of plants did survive at the New York Botanical Garden, and Harvard's Museum of Comparative Zoology managed to retrieve some of the animals. But most of the specimens simply disappeared, and subsequent generations are left only with the scattered notes and re-created journal entries.

The final report of the expedition was produced by re-creating the personal diaries of Stephen Long, Thomas Say, and the partial diary of Titian Peale. Edwin James's journal was not lost, and James served as the principal compiler of the records for the report. Captain Bell's diary was lost and was unavailable to James after the trip. However, Bell's original journal was rediscovered in 1932, in the possession of a family that had moved to California and was unaware of the importance of an old notebook that they had stored in their attic. The civilians who worked on the final report—namely James and Say—continued to receive their small per-diem allowances while they wrote the two volumes of *Account of an Expedition from Pittsburgh to the Rocky Mountains.* The report, issued in 1823, included illustrations by Samuel Seymour, as well as Long's maps.

At the time, the general public was largely unaware of the specifics of the expedition, the hardships that were endured, and the scientific discoveries that were made, because John C. Calhoun only authorized a few dozen copies of the final report at government expense, except for the maps. To print anything more was considered a frivolous expense. So, Long was forced to use his personal funds to publish additional copies.

Stephen Long did undertake one later surveying expedition in 1823—a six-month trip around the Great Lakes, present-day Minnesota, the Red River of the North, into Canada, back to Detroit, then to Buffalo and Rochester, New York. Again, scientific collection was an important component of the mission, and several veterans of the difficult 1819–1820 western trip signed on again, including Thomas Say and Samuel Seymour. Geologist William Keating and mapmaker James Calhoun also were members of the second expedition. Unlike the earlier trip, the final report of the second expedition was widely circulated.

Later in life, Stephen Long became a railroad surveyor, harbor engineer, and hospital architect and contractor. He wrote several books on railroad and bridge construction, and died at the age of 79.

Thomas Say's reputation as a naturalist was secured by his active participation in the two Long expeditions. Describing specimens acquired in the field kept him busy for years, and he became the nation's authority on entomology and its leading expert on molluscs, or conchology, as he preferred to classify it.

Nirvana for a naturalist would be having unlimited access to unexplored territories that were full of undescribed plants and animals. Nirvana would have the reasonable comforts of home, including an actual bed and an outhouse that didn't leak when it rained. Nirvana also would have an excellent reference library. It would be wonderful if Nirvana also had printing facilities so that scientific publications could be produced on site, rather than having to deal with the delays inherent with distant publishers.

In addition, Nirvana would provide a stipend to naturalists and other learned people so that they would not have to toil at other mundane positions in order to put food on the table. Finally, Nirvana would bring naturalists together with others in the arts, humanities, and sciences to promote an intellectually stimulating environment.

Thomas Say thought that he had found Nirvana when he became involved with the New Harmony utopian community in Indiana. New Harmony began in 1827 and, because Say and other naturalists were attracted to the community, they could find local peer reviewers for their ideas and publications. Say met his future wife, Lucy, in New Harmony, and spent many months collecting in the nearby woods and streams with Prince Maximilian, the visiting European naturalist who was heading to the upper Missouri River. It was a pleasant life, and Say received a small stipend and was able to settle into a comfortable existence in the utopian community.

It was in New Harmony's printing shop where Say printed his classic, *American Conchology*. Fellow resident and naturalist Charles Lesueur did the engravings, and Lucy Say did most of the hand watercoloring of the plates.

In 1827, Thomas and Lucy eloped to Illinois to marry prior to Say's departure on a collecting trip to Mexico. But, except for that extended trip, Say was content to spend his days researching molluscs and insects and describing new specimens that were sent to him. He assisted Charles Bonaparte with the French naturalist's revision of Alexander Wilson's *American Ornithology*—illustrated by Say's old friend, Titian Peale—and Say continued to collect in the lands near New Harmony.

Like many of the true naturalists of the period, Thomas Say lived a rather frugal life and had little regard for money. He simply worked on his science and relied on various patrons of the New Harmony community and his reputation to support his efforts.

American Conchology was issued in seven parts and became the definitive reference on the subject. Say's *American Entomology* was the first book on insects of the United States. By the time Thomas Say entered middle age, he had an international reputation. Scientists from around the world sought him out. With the possible exception of two British scientists who had access to the vast collections of the British Museum, no other person in the world discovered more species of molluscs than did Thomas Say.

If Say had any regret about his Nirvana, it might have been twofold. As he collected and re-collected in the Indiana woods and fields, the opportunities for encountering new animals decreased. Second, Say's insect collections were always being invaded by live insects that destroyed their preserved relatives. Specimens had to be continually replaced. But Nirvana did have an excellent garden, and many of the plants in Say's garden came from western seeds and cuttings, including Osage oranges and the bow-wood, *Maclura*. It was a pleasant life and, after Say's death in 1834, at the age of 47, his widow elected to remain amongst the live memorials to Say's western adventures.

Edwin James was able to list the plant varieties that were collected during the Long expedition in the *Transactions of the American Philosophical Society* in 1825. It was a lengthy list, although, over time, many of the names have been modified or combined as species became more clearly defined. James had hoped to participate in Long's second expedition to the Great Lakes and Canada, but he received an invitation too late to respond.

James was later assigned to the army medical department and was posted for three years at Fort Crawford, Wisconsin. Later, he was reassigned to several army posts in Michigan, where he studied the Ojibwa language. By 1834, James was out of the army and employed as a newspaper editor in Albany, New York. His career after that was quite varied and ranged far from his earlier interests in natural history: farmer in Iowa, Indian agent, abolitionist with the Underground Railroad. He died in October 1861, after falling from a wagon and being crushed by the wagon's wheels.

Titian Peale would continue to be active for many years in the dual natural history and art fields. Still a young man when he returned from the Long expedition, Peale served as an illustrator for several noted natural history textbooks and treatises, and he joined an expedition to Colombia in 1831, as well as the round-the-world U.S. Exploring Expedition in the 1840s. Between these trips, he served as periodic director of his father's museum in Philadelphia and later worked in the U.S. Patent Office in Washington, D.C. He remained active in natural history, however, and was one of the founders of the Washington Philosophical Society. He continued to paint, almost to the time of his death in 1885, at the age of 86.

Samuel Seymour had been hired as the lead artist of the Long expedition, and served that role in Long's second expedition as well.

His illustrations of landscapes, native tribes, and wildlife were prominent in several of the reprintings of Long's final report. Only eight of his approximately 150 paintings appeared in the original report, but more were added in subsequent versions.

Following the publication of Long's second report, many of the original Seymour paintings hung in museums. But soon thereafter, almost all of them disappeared, along with the artist.

The overall accomplishments of the Long expedition of 1819–1820 were many. The scientific accomplishments notwithstanding, Long left a legacy of maps that were noteworthy, as well as the term *Great American Desert* to characterize the Great Plains. It was Long's conclusion that the Plains were largely uninhabitable for white settlers and only fit for the vast herds of buffalo that roamed there and the Native Americans who had adapted to the terrain. As a consequence, for decades, settlers bypassed the interior of the United States, on their way to promised riches in California, prime farming soil in Oregon Territory, or the high country of the Rocky Mountains. Yet, despite its shortcomings, the Long expedition would remain a significant incursion to the western Plains and Rockies. It would be more than a decade before another group of naturalists would again visit the same ground.

Chapter 6

VISITORS FROM EUROPE

When naturalist John Kirk Townsend headed west with Thomas Nuttall in 1834 as part of Nathaniel Wyeth's expedition, he wrote about a memorable traveler whom he met en route. The man was an English officer who was traveling in North America on a great adventure.

Travelers in the remote areas of the west were not common in 1834, and Captain William Stewart was far from being common. Townsend recalled Stewart's dress in the field: a white leather jacket, wide-brimmed hat, and multicolored plaid pants. Stewart was "an English gentleman of noble family who is traveling for amusement and in search of adventure."

There was no mistaking Stewart in the field. Yet, like Thomas Nuttall, he was just one of many Europeans who were drawn to the American west in the 1820s and 1830s. Some were true naturalists. Others were curious collectors. Still others were simply hunters who looked at the rich, diverse game animals in the west in the same way that Europeans viewed the fauna of Africa.

Most of those who were strictly interested in sport in the first half of the nineteenth century were primarily interested in the thrill of the hunt. But, secondarily, some contributed to geographic discoveries and the ethnology of Native Americans. For example, Sir George Gore, a British hunter, explored parts of the Yellowstone region during his American safari, but science was never a major focus. Other European visitors did make contributions by returning with hides and skulls, and sometimes with whole animal specimens.

Spanish explorers had a long history of describing and even collecting flora and fauna of the far west that dates back to the sixteenth century. But these investigations were largely confined to the Pacific coast and southwest Spanish lands. These early scientific voyages often were combined with exploration, mapping, and descriptions of geographic features of the New World. When biological resources were noted, botany was a particular objective, especially on the voyages in the eighteenth century. Even though Spanish expeditions seldom carried artists and illustrators on board until later in the era of great sea voyages, some botanical illustrators in the eighteenth century, such as Atanasio Echeverría, were part of expeditions that explored North America north to present-day Canada. Sketch artists eventually became a regular part of ship's companies, and these illustrators drew landscapes, portraits, and representations of plants and animals.

This was just as well, because the earlier Spanish expeditions, staffed by seamen, were neither scientists nor illustrators, and their observations were intriguing but often not useful. Records from Hernando de Grijalva's expedition along the California coast in 1533 included the first sketches of the California sea lion. The animals were obviously curious-looking creatures, but Grijalva was no artist. The sea lion sketches looked more like a hybrid between a seal and a mermaid. Six years later, Francisco De Ulloa reported a colony of "a hundred thousand" sea lions, which he called *lobos marinus*, or sea wolves. Local Indians in the northern Gulf of California used sea lion stomachs as water bags, yet, to those back home in Spain and elsewhere, it was difficult to visualize such an unusual creature.

The English long included naturalists on their major sea voyages of exploration, and British naturalists with Cook, Vancouver, and others engaged in some biological collecting along the Pacific coast of North America. In 1786, a French expedition along the coast collected seeds from plants in California, and in the late 1780s, botanist Thaddeus Haenke collected specimens of the California redwood while traveling with a Spanish expedition led by Italian Alesandro Malaspina.

In 1815, a Russian expedition stopped in California and collected seeds from the California poppy, as well as a number of insect specimens. And, just a few years before the arrival of William Stewart and several other European notables, European investors sent adventurer Paolo Emilio Botta to the American west to investigate the financial possibilities of its untapped resources. Botta collected a strange "running bird"—the roadrunner—which he noted had "the ability to kill snakes for food." The roadrunner impressed Botta with its speed. "It seldom flies," he wrote, "but runs almost as fast as a horse."

William Drummond Stewart was one of the first Europeans who stayed in the west for an extended period of time, in his case some seven years. Although a hunter and adventurer and not specifically a naturalist, Stewart did make an important contribution to natural history by supporting the artistic travels of painter Alfred Jacob Miller.

Stewart was the second son of a wealthy Scottish family. Although he had funds with which to pursue his interests, Stewart was not the eldest son, so he had few prospects for inheriting the family title, its home at Murthley Castle, and most of its fortune. Instead, Stewart entered the army, fought with Wellington, and played an important role in the battle of Waterloo.

By 1833, however, Stewart was home in Scotland, married to a former servant girl, and at odds with his older brother—the family heir. Abandoning it all, he took a "leave" from the British Army and departed for North America. During the 1830s, he traveled over much of the American west, often in the company of fur trappers and, for a time, the company of Benjamin Harrison, the alcoholic son of one president and the nephew of another. The rugged fur trappers often made fun of the flamboyant Englishman, his accent, and his unusual dress, but Stewart won them over. Although noble by birth, he enjoyed the primitive conditions in the wilderness, and he was an expert marksman. He once downed a grizzly bear with a single shot, and that ability was what impressed the fur trappers the most when Stewart first made their acquaintances at the trappers' rendezvous held along the Green River.

Between 1833 and 1838, Stewart covered much of what would later become parts of the Oregon Trail, along the North Platte and Sweetwater Rivers and South Pass, as well as the Big Horn and Yellowstone Rivers, the Wind River Range, Jackson Hole, northern New Mexico, parts of Colorado, and the Columbia River west to Fort Vancouver.

Stewart returned to the west in 1843 for a final expedition into the Green River and Yellowstone country. He offered to provide transportation and pay the expenses of John James Audubon to accompany his expedition, but the painter declined. When Stewart revisited the west, he noticed a marked decline in the American fur trade. Anticipating its further demise, Stewart invested in the southern cotton market and made his fortune, not through inheritance, but by his business dealings. He even wrote at least two novels, *Edward Warren* and *Altowan,* that were based loosely on his experiences.

After the death of his older brother, Stewart eventually did return to Scotland and Murthley Castle, where he enjoyed the title of Sir William Stewart. There, he lived the life of a nobleman and appreciated the fine collection of paintings that he had commissioned from the young artist, Alfred Jacob Miller.

Stewart's contributions to natural history were more indirect than they were direct. He didn't have the professional training of a Thomas Nuttall or John Townsend, both of whom he met during his brief participation in Nathaniel Wyeth's expedition. But, in 1837, he sponsored Miller and had him accompany Stewart and paint scenes of the west: Native Americans, landscapes, endemic animals, and fur trappers. In the days before photography and at a time when few biological illustrators had visited the west, Miller's paintings provided important documentation. It was Stewart and Miller who brought back the first visual interpretations of Chimney Rock, the

Grand Tetons, and other western landmarks to be viewed by those in the east and Europe.

In many ways, another European visitor to the west in the 1830s, Prince Maximilian of Wied-Neuwied, was a clone of William Stewart. Both were of noble birth, both were wealthy and could finance trips into the west, both were military veterans, and both were accompanied by talented artists who recorded important facets of western life, flora and fauna, geographic features, and native dress and customs.

There was an important distinction, however. Prince Maximilian did have training in natural history, and his visit to the west had a scientific objective.

Wied was a small province along the Rhine River, and the prince's castle was situated along the river near Koblenz. Maximilian became a major general in the Napoleonic Wars, but his interests eventually turned to science and ethnology. Maximilian had these tendencies at an early age, and one of his teachers was J. J. Blumenbach, who also mentored naturalist Alexander von Humboldt. It was Humboldt who encouraged Maximilian to take his science training to South America. So, along with two other German naturalists, the prince traveled in eastern Brazil from 1815 to 1817. While the other naturalists studied flora and fauna, Maximilian specifically focused on native tribes in the area. He later wrote several accounts of his South American observations of plants, animals, geography, and ethnology, which were published three years after he returned.

The prince hoped to follow up his anthropological studies in Brazil with similar observations of western tribes of North America, and the opportunity came in 1832. He sailed for Boston, then traveled to Philadelphia, where he visited Peale's Museum and met with Titian Peale, the veteran of the Long expedition into the west and later a naturalist aboard the four-year U.S. Exploring Expedition that would circle the world. At the time, Titian had taken over from his father as director of the museum. Peale showed the prince specimens collected by Titian and Thomas Say during the Long expedition. Maximilian had heard of Say and also of the utopian community of New Harmony, where Say and other scientists, philosophers, writers, and artists were living in Indiana. On his way to the Missouri River, Maximilian made a point to stop in Indiana and visit Say. It was a humbling experience for the prince because he was enough of a student of the world of naturalists to know that Say was among its most prominent members.

Thomas Say was just as excited to meet Maximilian, another enthusiastic amateur. The prince arrived on October 19, 1832, accompanied by artist Karl Bodmer and hunter and taxidermist David Dreidoppel. The former had been hired to paint scenes in the west, and the latter had accompanied Maximilian during his Brazilian expedition.

The prince enjoyed his stay with Thomas Say and later wrote in his journal that he had "made the acquaintance of this interesting man . . . a celebrated writer in natural history."

Say was a hospitable host, both scientifically and socially. He showed the prince his insect and shell collections and took him on a tour of Say's garden and library. He even showed Maximilian copies of his new monograph, *American Conchology*, that was being printed at that time in the New Harmony printing shop. Say introduced the visitors to naturalist/ichthyologist Charles Lesueur, who also was a resident of the utopian community and one of those responsible for many of the plates in *American Conchology*. Lesueur was especially pleased to speak French with the visitors, and Karl Bodmer painted a watercolor of Lesueur collecting in the field. To Prince Maximilian, Lesueur was "already old" at age 54.

Lesueur was a native of France who embarked on his first expedition (to Australia) in 1800. Officially, he was a gunner's mate, but he soon found himself assisting the naturalists on board. Lesueur devoted himself to natural history because the voyage otherwise was a miserable experience. Most of the crews of the expedition's two vessels either deserted or died en route. In 1815, Lesueur came to the United States, reaching Philadelphia in 1816 in time to participate in the formation of the Academy of Natural Sciences the following year. He was a friend and colleague of not only Thomas Say and

Thomas Nuttall, but George Ord and Constantine Rafinesque, two notable eastern naturalists of the day.

Lesueur never ventured west of the Mississippi River, but he was consulted on fish specimens collected by others from the west and he was the author of *American Ichthyology, or The Natural History of the Fishes of North America*, a landmark book that, unfortunately, had little distribution beyond New Harmony, Indiana.

This might have been the end of Maximilian's interaction with Say and Lesueur, but fate intervened. The prince became quite ill and was forced to stay in bed from what many suspect was cholera.

Large-scale cholera outbreaks had been reported in Louisville and Cincinnati, among other locations near the Indiana community, but Maximilian's illness was diagnosed as some other ailment. Nevertheless, he was bedridden, then slow to recover for several weeks.

While Maximilian gained his strength, Thomas Say took the visitor on short collecting trips near New Harmony—along the Fox and Wabash Rivers—where they observed dozens of species of birds, including Carolina parakeets, mallards, wood ducks, bluebirds, and woodpeckers. Maximilian also learned to identify the local plants and recorded their descriptions in his notebooks.

The prince was particularly impressed with Say's knowledge of freshwater mussels. The mollusc expert identified 43 species from the Wabash River alone, although he would be slow to formally publish their individual discoveries. He did include them in his *American Conchology*, but only after Constantine Rafinesque and others rushed formal descriptions into print after Maximilian's visit. As a result, others, rather than Say, received much of the scientific credit for the new mussels.

By late November, Maximilian was well enough to resume his traveling, but his companion, David Dreidoppel, contracted the same disease. By the time the hunter recovered, it was well into winter, and any plans for traveling up the Missouri River had to be delayed until spring. During their five months at New Harmony, Maximilian, Dreidoppel, and Bodmer collected specimens of flora and fauna in the nearby woods and fields and paid others to collect specimens. The prince noted in his journal that he paid $2.00 for a bobcat specimen and 25 cents for a prairie hen.

The party finally left New Harmony in March 1833. On April 10, 1833, Maximilian boarded the steamboat *Yellowstone* and headed up the Missouri River. It was the same vessel that had carried painter George Catlin upriver the year before. Also in the prince's party, with Karl Bodmer and David Dreidoppel, was Toussaint Charbonneau, formerly of the Lewis and Clark expedition, who was hired as an interpreter. Maximilian would soon make his own, indirect contribution to western art and ethnology because Bodmer, in effect, became the prince's visual journal of his travels, creating some 500 paintings of Native Americans, tribal rituals, landscapes, fur trappers, and buffalo. Bodmer was a former engineer who turned to art and was able to re-create scenes and people in great detail.

Maximilian's original plan had been to cross overland to the Pacific coast. However, in St. Louis, William Clark, now a general and superintendent of Indian affairs, suggested that the party accompany a group of fur trappers with the American Fur Company. The group of armed men would provide much more protection than would a small party of naturalists and artists. Maximilian and Bodmer went 2,000 miles upriver, as far as Fort McKenzie, an outpost owned by the American Fur Company. It was in the heart of Blackfoot country, and the prince dutifully recorded everything in his journal while Bodmer painted what he saw.

Along the way, the party met William Stewart, who would later hire his own painter, Alfred Miller, to record scenes of the west.

The Maximilian party overwintered at Fort Clark, near the Mandan villages of North Dakota, re-creating some of the experiences of the Lewis and Clark expedition, which overwintered there in 1804. The following spring, 1834, the Maximilian party returned down the Missouri River, and the prince later published his journals as *Travels in the Interior of North America*.

On their return home to Europe, Maximilian and Bodmer again stopped in New Harmony, Indiana, and kept Thomas Say and the other residents entertained for days with accounts of their adventures amongst the Blackfeet and Mandan and their difficulties traveling in the upper Missouri—all illustrated by Bodmer's paintings and drawings.

Bodmer later became quite famous, but he (and Maximilian) made another important contribution that was not even realized at the time.

In 1837, a smallpox outbreak devastated the Mandan tribe in North Dakota. Only 120 survived. A similar outbreak among the Blackfeet may have reduced their numbers by half. Visual records of those tribes, their rituals, and their dress during their heyday as important Missouri River tribes only exist today through the paintings of Karl Bodmer.

On June 13, 1833, as Prince Maximilian and Karl Bodmer were traveling up the Missouri River, another naturalist found himself in serious trouble.

David Douglas, already a veteran plant collector in the Pacific northwest, was traveling with a companion in a birch-bark canoe when disaster struck. Entering Fort George Canyon, on the Fraser River of modern-day British Columbia, the canoe hit some rocks and broke apart.

Both men were thrown into the rapids, along with Douglas's dog, Billy. Caught in a whirlpool, Douglas eventually was propelled downstream for almost two hours before he could make it to shore. Amazingly, both men—and Billy—survived. But Douglas's journal, all of their food and clothing, most of their other supplies, and all of their specimens of plants were lost. It was estimated that the Fraser River consumed over 400 species of plants that David Douglas had carefully collected in the Pacific northwest.

David Douglas was Scottish, born in 1799 to stonemason John Douglas and his wife Jean. Like many naturalists, David's interests in plants and animals were formed at an early age, when he started keeping wild birds at the family home. Later, he received more formal education and support from Sir Robert Preston and, especially, Sir William Hooker. Hooker would remain a lifelong mentor and friend. It was Hooker who recommended Douglas for a job with the Horticulture Society of London in 1823, noting that his friend possessed "undaunted courage" and "energetic zeal."

At the time, Douglas was employed as head gardener for the Glasgow Botanic Garden. However, gardeners at the time were notoriously low paid, receiving less wages than any servant, so the 23-year-old Douglas leaped at the chance to become a plant collector for the society.

The Horticultural Society was formed in 1804 by eight men, including the famous Joseph Banks, William Forsyth—the royal gardener for King George III and for whom forsythia was named—and John Wedgwood, son of pottery and ceramic artist Josiah Wedgwood. The society's purpose was to promote botanic research and propagation. To do so, the society had a small garden in Kensington, but later leased a 33-acre plot west of London where the organization raised endemic and exotic species of trees, shrubs, and flowers. Successful plants were then sold to others, and the society was responsible for the worldwide spread of dozens of species of nonindigenous forms of vegetation.

To collect these exotic plants, the society employed trained plant collectors to go to the four corners of the earth and bring back seeds, cuttings, and live plants so that society members could determine whether the plants would flourish in the British Isles. When Douglas was hired, other society collectors were in Europe and Africa seeking new forms of life. Douglas was scheduled to travel to China, but an unsettled political climate there changed his destination to eastern North America. In particular, Douglas's objectives were to study fruit trees and their use in the United States. He was to bring back samples of such trees, as well as varieties of oak.

Douglas sailed for New York, traveled to Philadelphia, then collected in Pennsylvania and New York. He returned with varieties of peach and pear trees and 19 varieties of oak. Of historical note, Lewis and Clark had returned to the east with samples of the Oregon grape, and Douglas carried cuttings from those plants back to London, along with some orchids and samples of birds.

The society was pleased with Douglas's accomplishments and soon sent him to explore the American west—especially the Pacific northwest. Because of its influential standing, the society was able to secure free passage for its plant collector to the Pacific coast on one of the Hudson Bay Company's supply ships, the *William and Ann*. It was quite an economical coup for the Horticultural Society. The almost-three-year trip, including Douglas's salary, supplies, and equipment, only cost the society £400.

The *William and Ann* left London on July 25, 1824. The ship traveled around the Horn and stopped for a brief time in the Galapagos Islands—a decade before the arrival of Charles Darwin and the *Beagle*.

The plants and animals of the Galapagos were largely unfamiliar to Douglas, who noted that the birds were so unaccustomed to and unafraid of humans that they would sit on the brim of his hat or rest on the barrel of his shotgun—behavior rarely seen in modern times. Douglas collected specimens of birds, not by shooting them, but by hitting them with a stick or a rock. During his visit, he collected 45 birds of 19 genera. He prepared the skins but was unable to dry them completely. Upon leaving the Galapagos, it rained for most of the next 12 days and Douglas could only watch as the skins rotted away. Much the same thing happened to his Galapagos plant collection. Out of 175 specimens, only 40 could be saved from the effects of the tropical rains.

The *William and Ann* reached the mouth of the Columbia River on February 12, 1825, and Douglas's impression of the dangerous Columbia bar was similar to those of Lieutenant Charles Wilkes when the naval officer visited the site 15 years later. In Douglas's view, "The weather was so boisterous and frightful that it forbade everything like approaching the coast as useless."

For months, David Douglas explored the Columbia basin, venturing northward to Gray's Harbor, Washington, and south into present-day Oregon. He traveled between a string of Hudson Bay Company forts and outposts but, between these locations, he slept on beds of pine branches, all the while collecting. At times, he became so hungry and exhausted that he noted in his journal that he was relegated to crawling. "I could hardly walk."

But his efforts proved fruitful. One of the first trees that he saw upon landing in the Columbia territory was what Douglas identified as *Pinus taxifolia*, a tree originally collected by botanist Archibald Menzies, who sailed with Captain George Vancouver in 1792. Menzies's samples were used by Aylmer Bourke Lambert in his *Description of the Genus Pinus* in 1803.

We now know this common tree as the Douglas fir, *Pseudotsuga menziesii*, the scientific name attributed to original collector and its common name crediting David Douglas for bringing back samples for propagation in England.

Douglas had met with Menzies after his first trip to the west, and Douglas became familiar with some of the vegetation from the Pacific coast because of Menzies's collections. Before sailing as a naturalist with Vancouver aboard his ship, *Discovery*, between 1791 and 1795, Menzies had studied medicine and botany at the University of Edinburgh. The objective of Menzies's visit to the Pacific coast with Vancouver was to collect plants and seeds for the Kew Gardens in London and the Royal Botanical Gardens in Edinburgh. That visit would be his only exposure to the American west—and it was only along the coast. Yet, he is credited with discovering not only the Douglas fir, but the coastal sequoia redwood as well, and his collections and advice were helpful to David Douglas, Asa Gray, William Hooker, and Frederick Pursh.

David Douglas's contributions extended beyond simply plants. He collected a variety of bird species, as well as some small mammals, and he provided some of the earliest descriptions of the Native American salmon fisheries farther up the Columbia River. He noted in amusement that he could buy two fresh Pacific salmon for one half-ounce of tobacco—about a penny per fish—when a pair of less fresh Atlantic salmon would have cost £3 to £4 in England.

On November 15, 1825, Douglas returned to Fort Vancouver and, instead of returning to England as originally planned, decided to stay for the winter months. Nevertheless, he packed up 197 seed samples in a box to be shipped to the Horticultural Society on the next available ship returning to England. He also prepared a duplicate shipment that was transported overland by the Hudson Bay Company supply expedition.

Taking over 100 pounds of drying paper with him, Douglas expanded his travel to explore parts of western Canada, filling his journals with accounts of bear attacks, confrontations with hostile and friendly tribes, and extremely difficult traveling, especially in the dense forests of the Pacific coastal areas.

Evidence of civilization was extremely rare during Douglas's travels, except around outposts of the Hudson Bay Company. Most of the time, he lived off the land, shooting birds and other animals and filling his diet with fish. What he couldn't catch, he bartered from local tribes, who crushed camphor seeds into streams to stun fishes that were then readily collected. It was a fishing technique quite unlike the salmon platforms along the Columbia River, but an effective and lethal procedure that also was used by tribes in southern California and South America.

The list of Douglas's discoveries is a lengthy one, but includes at least seven species of pines, including the Lambert pine, named after Aylmer Lambert. Douglas obtained Lambert cones by knocking them out of trees with shotgun blasts. One of his most noteworthy discoveries was the sugar pine, *Pinus lambertiana*, which he collected in 1826, and also named for the pine specialist. "A new species of *Pinus*, the most princely of the genus, perhaps even the grandest specimen of vegetation," he wrote in his journal. Douglas had seen local tribes eating pine nuts from the sugar pine, and a fur trapper obtained a pine cone for the botanist, taken in the Umpqua River country of central Oregon. After considerable effort, Douglas was able to find the species in many parts of present-day Oregon.

But such efforts in unexplored, rough terrain were not without their cost. On one occasion, Douglas was following a wounded deer to the edge of a deep gully. The footing was marginal, and Douglas slipped and fell downhill. He was knocked unconscious for five hours, his face in the mud. In pain and groggy when he awoke, his life was probably saved due to a group of passing Indians who helped him back to camp.

When he wasn't cut, battered, and bruised, Douglas was wet and wind-burned by storms. "When my people in England are made acquainted with my travels, they may perhaps think I have told them nothing but my miseries. That may be very correct, but I now know that such objects as I am in quest of are not obtained without a share of labor, anxiety of mind, and sometimes risk of personal safety."

Like Thomas Nuttall and John Bradbury, who collected in the upper Missouri River in 1811, Douglas was a curiosity to the native tribes. The Chinooks thought Douglas was crazy and called him, loosely translated, "grass doctor." Even during a hostile encounter with painted, armed warriors, as happened to Douglas in Oregon, the incident was tempered by the Indians' curious fear of someone who must be crazy—or very intelligent. Local tribes always wondered why someone would risk life and limb to collect plants that had no medicinal or edible qualities. But Douglas downplayed such difficulties and once wrote in his journal that "on such occasions, I am very liable to become fretful."

After a winter of further collecting, Douglas packed up his latest seeds and specimens and accompanied the Hudson Bay Company's supply expedition (the Express) across the continent to Hudson Bay. By the time he reached ships waiting in the bay, Douglas had spent some two and a half years covering 10,000 miles, much of it on foot.

David Douglas almost didn't make it home because a huge storm came up suddenly as the men in small boats were rowing out to the waiting ships in Hudson's Bay. The dories were blown miles offshore, and the occupants of the boats were given up for dead. It took two and a half days for them to row back to shore.

Fortunately, Douglas and his specimens survived because, once he returned to London on October 11, 1827, he received a modest hero's welcome.

The Horticultural Society was ecstatic about the 210 species of plants and trees that he shipped or brought back from the Pacific northwest. Ultimately, 130 varieties found the British climate acceptable, and these were propagated and distributed around the world. Years later, an official with the society concluded that one plant alone—the flowering currant, *Rubes sangvineum*—paid for all the expenses of Douglas's multi-year endeavor, including a £5 wager that the botanist lost with a local tribal chief.

Douglas became a featured guest at parties and scientific meetings, although it took many weeks to recover his health from the hardships suffered in the west. Eventually, though, he became bored with life in London and longed to again get back into the field.

The chance came on October 31, 1829, when Douglas left London aboard the *Eagle*, another Hudson Bay Company supply vessel, ultimately bound for California.

William Hooker long had believed that California offered exceptional opportunities for plant collectors, despite a long history of visits by European vessels. The climate was quite Mediterranean in the south, moderate in the mid-coast, and damp and lush along the northern coast—comparable to the climate in parts of the United Kingdom. Hence, the reasoning was that California plants might likely survive and flourish in parts of Europe as well. William Hooker convinced the Horticultural Society of his rationale, and various groups contributed to the costs of the expedition. The Zoological Society of London even furnished Douglas with an £18 double-barreled shotgun for the trip.

Although he wasn't completely open about his plans to the financial backers, Douglas hoped to travel beyond California, to Hawaii and to Russia, and he was partially successful in these endeavors.

The *Eagle* did stop in Hawaii, or the Sandwich Islands, but only briefly, before sailing on to the mouth of the Columbia River. The company's primary mission was to supply its outposts in the Pacific northwest, and Douglas was simply a hitchhiker on that portion of the voyage. While he waited for another ship to stop on its way south to California, Douglas engaged in further collecting. For this trip, he also had received training in surveying and mapping, so he could combine his botanical wanderings with geographic contributions as well.

In late November 1830, Douglas was able to book passage on another of the Hudson Bay ships, the brig *Dryad*, which sailed to Monterey, arriving on December 22.

California was indeed a plant collector's Eden, even if there were political tensions at the time of Douglas's visit. He did discover the digger pine, *Pinus sabiniana*, named after the Horticultural Society's long-time secretary, Joseph Sabine, and Douglas did send back samples of seeds, branches, and cones, and detailed descriptions.

The Horticultural Society was not the only group interested in growing California plants. Two other collectors, Ferdinand Deppe and Thomas Coulter, were in California at the same time, securing new species of plants for others in Europe. The three botanists often joined forces and collected triplicate samples and seeds of bristlecone fir (*Abies ventusta*), Monterey pine (*Pinus radiata*), and bigcone pine (*P. coulteri*). The trio also collected some species of unusual animals and tried to secure eggs from the California condor—but were unsuccessful. Even though William Clark had shot and killed one of the giant birds soon after the Corps of Discovery's arrival on the Pacific coast, the bird always has been rare.

In August 1832, after shipping seeds and cuttings to the Horticultural Society, with a duplicate set to William Hooker (including 600 species of California annuals), David Douglas booked passage back to Hawaii. He arrived there on September 7.

It was in Hawaii that David Douglas learned that his friend Joseph Sabine had been forced to resign his post as secretary of the Horticultural Society amidst a financial scandal. Sabine's imprudent overspending left the society £3,000 in debt. The whole incident angered Douglas and, even though he had long been a member of the society, and one of its most productive plant collectors, he submitted his resignation in a letter dated September 9, 1832. He considered his employment with the society ended, and he shipped his remaining specimens back to England.

David Douglas was still a young man in age—just 37. But his body was aging rapidly. After years of hardships traveling in the American west, he was taken ill with periodic bouts of one malady after another. When he returned to Fort Vancouver, on the Columbia River, on October 14, 1832, he narrowly avoided an outbreak of fever at the fort. Only three of 140 people were left unscathed by the fever; one of the three was David Douglas. But he had several other afflictions that would have slowed most men. He suffered from rheumatism and was blind in one eye. The other eye often had blurred or double vision. He took to wearing purple-tinted dark glasses when outside.

But none of this stopped him from collecting northward to Puget Sound and—after he received an invitation from the Russian governor of Alaska—British Columbia as well.

Douglas hoped to cross overland through British Columbia on his way to Sitka, Alaska. From there, he planned to secure passage to Russia, one of his long-term goals. But, he never made it. After two and a half months and over 1,100 miles of difficult traveling, Douglas arrived at Fort St. James, exhausted and resigned to his fate that he would never reach Sitka, let alone Russia.

After he recovered, Douglas and another man, William Johnson, returned down the Fraser River, along with Douglas's terrier, Billy. On June 15, both men, Billy, and the supplies were thrown into the river in a vicious set of rapids. In another example of human achievement, the two men and dog walked some 300 miles to Fort George, where they obtained another canoe and eventually made it back to Fort Vancouver.

But the experience sapped the energy from Douglas, and he wrote in a letter to William Hooker, "This disastrous occurrence (the Fraser River accident) has much broken my strength and spirits." The "hardships and suffering" hastened his decision to seek a berth on the brig, *Dryad*, which was sailing back to Hawaii.

The ship left the mouth of the Columbia River on October 18, 1833, and the long passage and eventual pleasant climate in Hawaii seemed to rejuvenate the botanist. He still suffered from rheumatism and vision problems, but in January, he climbed Mauna Kea in four days, then did the same to the summits of Kilauea and Mauna Loa.

Still, he insisted in searching for plants in a land where vegetation was quite foreign to him. He traveled on foot around the island of Hawaii and spent the night of July 11, 1834, at the shack of a cattle trapper.

The next morning, Douglas took off, but apparently was warned about cattle traps located some two and a half miles distant where the trapper captured wild cattle, then sold their meat and hides. The trapper was the last person to see David Douglas alive.

Douglas and Billy, oblivious to everything but the flora of the island, and hampered by the botanist's poor eyesight, apparently fell into one of the cattle pits. A wild bull, also trapped in the pit, panicked at the sudden arrival of intruders and trampled David Douglas to death.

When his body was discovered, Billy was still alongside him, barking at the wild bull.

There was more than a little speculation that Douglas's death was no accident, and that there was some evidence of foul play. Several people accused the cattle trapper of murdering and robbing the botanist, but nothing was ever proven and the matter was dropped.

The list of plant and tree discoveries by David Douglas was more than impressive, but one lasting legacy never became apparent until years after his death. Of the seeds from 880 species of plants sent back to the Horticultural Society by David Douglas, 130 proved hardy in the British climate. They thrived and many eventually were distributed around the world—a significant chapter in the long

Columbian exchange of products between the New World and
Europe.

In 1841, the U.S. Exploring Expedition, under the command of Lieutenant Charles Wilkes, visited the Hawaiian Islands for an extended
stopover during its four-year, around-the-world voyage. Two members of the expedition's civilian scientific team, Charles Pickering
and William Brackenridge, visited the site of Douglas's death on the
island of Hawaii.

Pickering doubled as the ship's surgeon as well as a zoologist and
ethnologist. Brackenridge was a horticulturist. To both men, David
Douglas was a giant in the field of natural history—one who had
preceded them in Hawaii and the Pacific northwest eight years earlier. Their visit was part homage and part a connection to the next
group of naturalists who would visit the west.

Part 2

COLLECTORS AND INTERPRETERS

Chapter 7

WILKES'S "SCIENTIFICS"

Lieutenant Charles Wilkes had left a lookout at the mouth of the Columbia River. Each day, while Wilkes and the rest of his party traveled inland to Fort Vancouver, the observer would scan the horizon, looking for two ships, the sloop *Peacock* and the schooner *Flying Fish*. But day after day, week after week, there was no sign of the ships and their commander, Lieutenant William Hudson.

The U.S. Exploring Expedition was in the midst of a four-year, round-the-world cruise that was now exploring lands along the Pacific coast of North America. Wilkes and the crews of two ships, the sloop-of-war *Vincennes* and the brig *Porpoise*, left the Sandwich (Hawaiian) Islands on April 5, 1841, and sailed directly to the great Columbia River, while Hudson and the crews of the other two ships took an easterly, then northerly route to the Columbia River. Because the expedition already had lost one ship, the *Sea Gull*, with all hands, while crossing the stormy waters at the tip of South America, and because many of the original crew members who began the expedition had now been replaced en route, there was concern that the *Peacock* and the *Flying Fish* had been lost as well.

Most naturalists who ventured in the American west in the first half of the nineteenth century did so overland from cities in the east. The U.S. Exploring Expedition, however, was a novelty. On board was a team of scientists and artists, whom Wilkes called "the scientifics." They had been busy collecting and observing the natural history of South America, Antarctica, and the islands of the Pacific

Ocean, and now were exploring western North America from a watery entrance.

On July 17, 1841, three months after Wilkes and the scientifics had arrived in Oregon Territory, the lookout spotted the missing vessels arriving from the south.

Wilkes—an excellent sailor and navigator—had been alarmed when he had first seen the mouth of the Columbia River. Miles across at its mouth, the Columbia had a treacherous bar that made its entrance a formidable challenge to even experienced mariners.

"Mere description can give little idea of the terrors of the bar of the Columbia," he wrote. "All who have seen it have spoken of the wildness of the scene, and the incessant roar of the waters, representing it as one of the most fearful sites that can possibly meet the eye of a sailor."

Even with an experienced, local river pilot available to help the *Vincennes* and *Porpoise* navigate the crossing, Wilkes refused to risk it. Lieutenant Hudson—either more adventuresome, or simply newly arrived and unfamiliar with the Columbia bar, decided to take the *Flying Fish* and the *Peacock* upriver. The *Flying Fish* passed the bar without incident, but the *Peacock* was apparently caught in a crosscurrent.

It was a tragic mistake. The *Peacock* promptly ran aground and started to take on water. Waves pounded the sides of the vessel until whole sections started to break apart. Men jumped overboard and were carried along by the swift-moving waters. Fortunately, all hands were saved due to the efforts of the crew of the *Flying Fish* and local Chinook Indians. Much of the cargo, however, was lost. Thousands of entomological specimens and many of the rare and unusual plants and animals that the men had just collected in Hawaii disappeared beneath the surface.

The U.S. Exploring Expedition was a plum assignment for any navy officer and any naturalist. For the commander of the expedition, it was the opportunity to explore and map new areas of the world and to place one's name on history's honored listing of great sailors. Charles Wilkes was a rare combination of naval officer and scientist. His latter qualifications were not so much in natural history as they were in mathematics and surveying, but he had an appreciation of the sciences and welcomed the opportunity to associate his name with exploration as well as advances in science.

Born in New York City on April 3, 1798, Wilkes was urged to enter the banking profession by his parents. But, instead, he signed on as a 17-year-old cabin boy on a ship bound for France. Three years later, he was commissioned a midshipman aboard an American man-of-war and became noted as a navigator and chartmaker.

On May 18, 1836, Congress authorized expenditures for the greatest exploring expedition of the country's young history, and Lieutenant Charles Wilkes received the plum command appointment. Of 40 naval lieutenants in the U.S. Navy at the time, 38 had more sea experience than did Wilkes. Yet, either because of his scientific interests, his navigation abilities, or political favors—or some combination of the three—Wilkes was the one chosen.

The principal objectives of the expedition were to survey the southern oceans, chart potential whaling grounds, explore the icy world of Antarctica, and accurately survey the bays, lands, and the coastline of the territory between Vancouver Island and San Francisco Bay. As preparations intensified, this latter objective took on increasingly more importance. Along with these geographic objectives, the expedition's team of scientists, artists, and illustrators was to collect natural history specimens and artifacts wherever they went and to analyze and publish the results of their endeavors.

For a naturalist, the U.S. Exploring Expedition also was a prized assignment. Although the officers and crew as well as the civilians would be away from home for years, any naturalist worth his loupe and field notebook would be thrilled for the opportunity to visit exotic locales and to potentially be the first to discover hundreds, if not thousands, of new plants and animals.

Beyond the visits to exotic locations of the world, the expedition ultimately provided naturalists with access to the interior portions of the Pacific coast of North America that had been virtually unstudied previously.

Selected to accompany Wilkes were several individuals who already were well qualified for the assignment or who would make their reputations en route. Nine scientists and artists were on board. James Dana, a geologist and zoologist, was probably the best known of the group, with a book on geology already to his credit. After the completion of the round-the-world expedition, he would publish classic works on *Zoophytes* in 1846, *Geology* in 1849, and two volumes (1852 and 1853) on *Crustacea* that were collected during the voyage.

Dana was a prominent scientist before he became one of the scientifics, and his fame increased after the voyage was completed. As a professor at Yale University, many of his students went on to distinguish themselves in natural history fields, including Othniel Marsh and Clarence King. Dana published dozens of scientific papers based on his discoveries made on the U.S. Exploring Expedition, including some major work with volcanoes, and he would become an influential member of the Committee of the National Academy of Sciences.

Also aboard was Charles Pickering, the ship's physician, who doubled as a zoologist and ethnologist. Pickering had been a student of William Dandridge Peck, Thomas Nuttall's predecessor at Harvard. Pickering already had established an impressive reputation in the biological sciences by the time he joined the group of naturalists on board the *Vincennes*. His particular expertise was with mosses, but his interests were quite broad, and he was the lead social scientist on the voyage, responsible for observations of the native peoples.

Titian Peale, the artist and member of Philadelphia's Peale family of painters, served the triple role of artist, naturalist, and marksman. All of Charles Willson Peale's children had artistic talents, but Titian Peale also had a knack for natural history as well. Titian had combined his talents in art and science by being the illustrator for a bird book that was prepared by Charles Lucien Bonaparte, a nephew of Napoleon Bonaparte. Years before, he also had participated in a collecting trip to Florida and Georgia that covered much of the area traversed by naturalist John Bartram. Accompanying Peale on that southern trip were such notable figures in natural history as George Ord, Thomas Say, and William Maclure. These connections—and others—led to Peale's appointment, along with Say, on Stephen Long's expedition to the west in 1819 and 1820. Although he did some landscapes for the final reports of the expedition, his expertise was with sketches of plants and animals.

Thus, by the time that the Wilkes expedition was ready to depart, Peale was one of several experienced naturalists, including Say and botanist Asa Gray, both of whom had volunteered to join the great expedition. Say and Gray ultimately did not sail (Gray quit because of personality conflicts with Wilkes), but Peale's shooting skills proved invaluable for collecting on the naval expedition. Peale's marksmanship abilities weren't confined just to animals—he also killed several native islanders during confrontations in the South Pacific.

After the voyage returned, Peale attempted to publish a book on zoology, but it suffered from criticism from within scientific circles. Scientists were becoming quite critical of those general naturalists, like Peale or Alexander von Humboldt, who had wide-ranging interests and wrote books on subjects that some believed were best written by specialists. Peale's paintings continued to be of interest, however, and he took several landscapes prepared during the round-the-world trip and redrew them in the 1850s, 1860s, and 1870s, or prepared new oil paintings based on his earlier sketches.

The other scientists among the scientifics were Horatio Hale, William Brackenridge, William Rich, and Joseph Couthouy. Hale was a Harvard graduate and was the company's linguist, or "philologist." He would later write *Ethnography and Philology* in 1846, which examined the languages of Pacific islanders and traced linkages between dialects and vocabularies. Brackenridge was a horticulturist who would later become the appointed gardener for the Smithsonian Institution. Rich was an amateur botanist, but certainly a competent one who developed significant talents on the voyage. Couthouy was a mollusc specialist, or conchologist, who would publish a large number of molluscan papers in the years following the expedition. One of his important works, *Molluscs and Shells*, actually was completed by another scientist, A. A. Gould.

Also aboard were Andrew Agate and Joseph Drayton, excellent illustrators who produced many of the expedition's drawings of fish and mammals, as well as scenic paintings of some of the lands that were visited. Some of these were based on field sketches made by Wilkes and other officers. The narrative and scientific volumes that resulted from the expedition were enriched by the illustrations of Drayton, Agate, and Peale, particularly those made from steel engravings. Agate, in particular, was an exceptional artist who not only depicted biological specimens, but did landscapes and highly detailed portraits of native inhabitants as well. Charles Wilkes, although not in the same class as the other artists, also contributed drawings for the final reports, and later in life his oil paintings showed artistic talents.

Despite Wilkes's scientific and artistic leanings, once the expedition reached the Pacific Ocean, he began to openly despise the civilians on board, and vice versa. Whether it was a condescending attitude by the scientifics toward the officers and crew on board, jealousy by Wilkes, or some combination of factors, the friction was evident. Whatever the reasons, Wilkes felt that scientific investigations took too much time away from the surveying duties. Each time one of the scientifics wanted to collect specimens from an island, it required a small boatload of sailors to row him ashore, sometimes to stand guard (because some island inhabitants were openly hostile), and often to help look for specimens. Instead of sailing or mapping, at least one of the ships had to be anchored and waiting.

Add to this, the preservatives and the specimens themselves tended to smell—either initially or eventually. The scientifics seemed oblivious to the odors, but not Wilkes and the rest of the crew. Wilkes forbid the scientists to work on the specimens below decks. When the sailors referred to the scientifics as "clam diggers" or "bug catchers," Wilkes did nothing to stop them. It resulted in three segregated groups on board: the scientifics, the officers and crew, and Wilkes himself.

Wilkes's personality also played a role in the poor morale aboard the ships. By the time the *Vincennes* reached Oregon, the expedition had been away from home for 32 months. Nerves were stretched thin by confinement in close quarters. The crew openly despised Charles Wilkes. They called him "The Stormy Petrel" behind his back. Sometimes, the naval lieutenant would appear on deck in a captain's uniform, apparently promoting himself en route. Although Wilkes was an outstanding seaman and navigator, he lacked interpersonal skills. He was convinced that his officers were conspiring against him. He reassigned crews between ships, demoted officers, and even ordered a boat full of his most vocal detractors ashore—stranding them in Peru. Once the ships arrived in Hawaii, the enlistments of 50 men had expired. Despite being stranded in Hawaii without firm prospects for returning home, and despite Wilkes's offers of more pay, none of the men would leave paradise and sail any longer with The Stormy Petrel. Thus, by the time the ships started to explore what is today Washington, Oregon, and northern California, morale was low, ships were shorthanded, and those aboard were still many months from home.

After leaving Hampton Roads, Virginia, on August 18, 1838, the ships of the U.S. Exploring Expedition traveled along the east coast of South America, early on leaving their supply vessel, the *Relief,* behind because it was too slow. The remaining ships traveled to Antarctica, which had been partially explored by Captain James Cook, but not fully enough to determine whether the land mass was connected to other continents. With 32-foot-high waves in the polar waters, the ships eventually retreated to South America, only to have the schooner, *Sea Gull,* disappear with all hands while crossing Tierra del Fuego.

The ships explored the west coast of South America, islands in the southern and central Pacific, and Australia, before returning to Antarctica (the latter revisit minus the civilian scientifics). Wilkes's expedition was the first to prove that Antarctica was unconnected to other lands, although many English geographers refused to accept the discovery until the nineteenth century, when their own ships eventually confirmed it. Wilkes dutifully mapped some 1,500 miles of the coastline before collecting the scientifics from Australia and moving northward in the Pacific. After charting additional Pacific islands, and engaging in tragic battles with natives in the Fiji Islands and elsewhere, the ships stayed in the Sandwich Islands for three months.

Despite the extensive biological specimens collected during those three months, the Wilkes party was not the first to study the flora and fauna of the Hawaiian Islands. English naturalists accompanying Captain James Cook were familiar with some of the rich biota of the islands, and Thomas Nuttall and David Douglas had been to Hawaii some five and seven years, respectively, before the arrival of the U.S. Exploring Expedition.

Exploring, mapping, and collecting in the American west began in April 1841. Charles Wilkes was quite impressed with Puget Sound, the quiet inland waterway that had attracted settlement by the British years before.

> *Nothing can exceed the beauty of these waters, and their safety; not a shoal exists within the Straits of Juan de Fuca, Admiralty Inlet, Puget Sound or Hood's Canal, that can in any way interrupt their navigation by a seventy-four gun ship. I venture nothing in saying, there is no country in the world that assesses waters equal to these.*

The scientists thought so also. Although the British had long had a presence in the Puget Sound area, the residents of the Hudson Bay Company outpost at Nisqually were more than hospitable to the sailors and civilians. James Dana readily explored the geological features of the Pacific northwest, especially the ancient and recent volcanoes.

Charles Pickering accompanied a detachment of men under the command of Lieutenant Robert Johnson that crossed the Cascade

Mountains to explore the interior of what is today western Washington. Pickering was particularly interested in the customs of Native Americans, but his journal also included notes on Pacific salmon and tribal methods of capturing the anadromous fishes.

The *Vincennes* and *Porpoise* returned to the mouth of the Columbia River and, finding no sign of Lieutenant Hudson and his ships, took off upriver by foot and canoe to Fort Vancouver. From that post, Wilkes sent out exploring and collecting parties in all directions. One group went farther upriver to the mouth of the Snake River. Another explored Gray's Harbor, on the Washington coast, north of the Columbia River. Sometimes Wilkes himself led the survey teams. Another party, led by Lieutenant George Emmons, traveled south, up the Willamette River, in what is today Oregon. The group crossed the mountains into northern California and continued down the Sacramento River into central California.

It wasn't an easy trip for Emmons and the others. The group encountered hostile tribes and difficult traveling, but they eventually made their way to Sutter's Fort, near Sacramento, then to Mission San Jose, and finally Yerba Buena and the great bay that later would give the city its name—San Francisco. The remainder of the Wilkes expedition sailed southward, providing the first detailed maps of the northern California–southern Oregon coastline. The secretary of the navy, in studying the charts after the expedition returned, concluded that those accurate maps alone justified the expense of the entire expedition.

The scientific accomplishments also were noteworthy. Wilkes sent James Dana ashore on many occasions to study the geological features of the coastal lands. Near present-day Astoria, Oregon, on Saddle Mountain, Dana discovered a rich deposit of fossils, some of which would eventually become part of the collection of the Smithsonian Institution.

The ground and sea parties subsequently reunited in San Francisco Bay and returned home by way of Hawaii, Singapore, the Philippines, the Cape of Good Hope, and the Atlantic coast of the Western Hemisphere. The *Vincennes* arrived back at Sandy Hook,

New Jersey, on June 10, 1842, after a trip of over four years and a voyage that covered 87,780 nautical miles. Only two of the original ships and half of the original crew made it home on that date.

The geographic and scientific accomplishments of the U.S. Exploring Expedition were somewhat overlooked when Charles Wilkes and the scientifics returned. There were several reasons for this.

First, Wilkes had a strong competitor in the public eye for the honor of being a national explorer. John C. Frémont was busy mapping routes across the American west as Wilkes was off exploring. Frémont was a successful, flamboyant self-promoter who always seemed to be in the news for some great adventure or another. He also had a strong ally in Congress: his father-in-law, Senator Thomas Hart Benson. Benson eventually became Frémont's biggest supporter, and the senator attempted to publicize Frémont's accomplishments and downplay those of others. Benson and Frémont both promoted the nickname, "The Pathfinder," that became popular with Frémont's admirers among the public.

A second reason for the lack of recognition for Wilkes's accomplishments was that the disgruntled officers and crew aboard the expedition's ships complained loudly about their commanding officer. It created such a turmoil that Wilkes was brought before a court-martial. No one questioned Wilkes's seamanship or ultimate accomplishments in chartmaking, exploration, science, and completion of a difficult assignment. But his personality was put on trial. One lieutenant even testified that, "Wilkes merits hanging, only that he deserved impaling long, long ago." The navy elected to issue only a mild reprimand.

Undaunted by the adverse publicity brought about by the court-martial, Wilkes turned to the task of distributing the information obtained from the voyage. As if he were still at sea, Wilkes confiscated all diaries, personal charts, journals, and other accounts of the voyage and turned them into the official narrative of the voyage. He personally produced a book on meteorology and one on hydrology, and, logically, took the lead in preparing the atlases that proved to be exceptionally accurate.

Initially, Wilkes's plan was to produce 15 volumes. Even more resulted from the expedition. The written journal of the epic trip, *Narrative of the U.S. Exploring Expedition during the Years 1838, 1839, 1840, 1841, 1842,* appeared in five volumes, along with two atlases of maps. Yet, Congress, at Benson's urging, only authorized the printing of 100 copies of the report. Frémont's accounts of his adventures became popular among the public, but Wilkes's accounts were not widely circulated initially. The naval officer even had to use personal funds to print and distribute additional copies beyond the 100 authorized by the government. Yet, by obtaining the copyright for the narratives, Wilkes may have made his money back, and then some, because the written adventures of Americans in strange lands were quite readable and interesting to a wide audience.

This lack of initial circulation of the expedition's reports was unfortunate on several accounts. The charts of 280 Pacific islands were so accurate that they were still being used by U.S. Navy and Marine Corps forces in World War II. In addition to the islands, Wilkes and his crew surveyed 1,500 miles of Antarctic coastline, 800 miles of the Oregon Territory coastline, and 100 miles of the Columbia River, and mapped the route that Lieutenant Emmons and his party took from Oregon to San Francisco.

Natural history and ethnology Wilkes left largely to the scientifics, although he reserved overall approval of the major volumes that would be part of the expedition's records. The biological significance of the trip wasn't immediately known, as it took the scientifics and others years to catalog, identify, describe, and publish the collection of 160,000 specimens of plants and animals. It took well into the 1920s to complete the 23 volumes resulting from the expedition, including treatises on coral reefs, geology, botany, zoology, meteorology, and ethnology. Some volumes, such as those on fishes, were never fully catalogued, and most of the insect samples were lost in the bottom of the Columbia River with the wreck of the *Peacock*. With those specimens, there undoubtedly would have been even more contributions to science.

Because the publication of scientific records was such a long process, conflicts continued to exist between the scientifics and their former commander long after everyone reached dry land. Wilkes wanted accurate scientific descriptions of the material that was collected, with little personal interpretation. Some of the more progressive scientists preferred to do that, but to add their own interpretations in book-length manuscripts as to how animal grouping might be inter-related, how social groups of Pacific islanders might have developed over time, or how geological processes might have shaped geographic features.

Wilkes also wanted the major scientific work performed in the Washington, D.C., area, but many of the civilians preferred to work near the major reference collections and libraries of the day, especially those at Harvard, Yale University, and the University of Pennsylvania. James Dana refused to leave Connecticut, which put him into even more conflict with Wilkes. When Dana submitted his volume on coral reefs, Wilkes rejected it as being too much speculation and not enough description of coral collections in the Pacific Ocean. It was largely due to the influence of others that the work was ultimately published, and it became a classic in the field. It was Dana's work that helped prove the biological origins of coral atolls—something suggested by Darwin and others.

Dana did four volumes for the final report, most notably *Zoophytes*, *Crustacea*, and *Geology*. His book *On Coral Reefs* was published with private funds. Charles Pickering produced *Races of Man*, an important book in the anthropology field, but Pickering's *Geographical Distribution of Animals and Plants* also was not published at government expense. He self-published it in two parts, in 1854 and 1876.

Ultimately, the timing of this great expedition was both fortunate and unfortunate. The biological specimens and artifacts collected were so numerous that the United States did not have a proper repository for their storage, and some of the specimens deteriorated. Even John James Audubon recognized early on, in a letter to Spencer Baird in 1842, that the U.S. government was ill prepared for analyzing and publishing a massive influx of scientific survey material. On the positive side, however, it was this need for museum and archival space that eventually led to the construction of the nation's national museum—the Smithsonian Institution—as well as federal facilities for studying astronomy and botany.

Chapter 8

THE PAINTER

John James Audubon never was a rich man. His business ventures all ultimately ended in failure, and his interests in painting birds and other animals all seemed to be headed toward a dead end. But Audubon could paint. So, to support himself and his family and allow him time to paint wild creatures of North America, he did portraits of people.

For five or ten dollars—sometimes $25—a person could have John James Audubon paint a likeness of a member of the family. Often, it was in profile and quite unlike those of the birds that would make him more famous. But some portraits were frontal and showed obvious artistic talents.

One such commission was quite unusual. Audubon was traveling from village to village as an itinerant painter, and collecting and painting birds between stops. A minister's son had died shortly before Audubon passed through one town, and despite the child's death and burial, Audubon received a commission to paint a portrait of the boy. The clergyman had his son's coffin exhumed so that Audubon could draw a sketch of the dead child for a remembrance. Audubon wrote that he made "a facsimile of his face which I gave as faithfully as if he were still alive."

Pleased with the portrait, the minister returned the corpse to its casket, placed it back in the ground, and again covered it with soil.

Soon, others heard of the itinerant painter and, when a relative seemed to be on his or her deathbed, Audubon would be summoned to make a final portrait.

Fortunately for natural science, such commissions provided enough money so that Audubon could spend time painting the wild birds and mammals that he encountered or that others collected. Eventually, his talents in that area would be recognized more widely than were his rather pedestrian portraits of people—alive or dead. Audubon only made one significant trip into the west, and that was at an advanced age. But he painted and studied many bird and mammal specimens that were collected by others in the west, and his contributions are more from his illustrations of the fauna of western and eastern North America.

Audubon's prospects did not seem too promising when he was born as Jean Jacques, the illegitimate son of a sea captain in Santo Domingo, Haiti, in 1785. Fortunately, he was sent to France for schooling, where he was adopted by his natural father and the man's legal wife. There, young Audubon developed a distinctive French accent and polished manner.

In 1803, Audubon immigrated to the United States, primarily to avoid being drafted into Napoleon's army. His father convinced the boy to change his first two names to John James, and young John arrived at his father's farm at Mill Grove, Pennsylvania. From those early days in rural Pennsylvania, Audubon became fascinated by the local animals, and he filled his room with skins, taxidermy mounts, and bird eggs. Living on the farm, he became a good marksman and a competent swimmer, horseman, and dog handler. It was at this time that he made his first primitive drawings of the natural creatures that he saw.

Over the next several years, he became involved in a number of business ventures, and he married a local girl, Lucy Bakewell, who had recently emigrated from England. The marriage lasted, but his business ventures never did. At one time, however, the Audubons operated a store in Henderson, Kentucky, and owned some land and even a few slaves. But nothing seemed to last and, at one point, Audubon was even jailed for his unpaid debts and was forced to declare bankruptcy.

One of those unsuccessful ventures involved investing in a steamship, and another of the investors was George Keats, the younger brother of poet John Keats. Whether Audubon coerced the younger Keats into investing or whether it was done of Keats's own volition, the investment ultimately failed and George blamed Audubon. When the elder brother heard about it, John Keats spread the word that "I cannot help thinking Mr. Audubon is a dishonest man."

Despite these financial setbacks, Audubon continued to travel the woods trails and make the acquaintance of some of the most famous explorers and war heroes of earlier days, including George Rogers Clark and his brother, William, as well as Daniel Boone. Even though the legendary Boone was in his seventies at the time, he was still a crack shot, as Audubon found when he accompanied Boone on a hunting trip.

Audubon also enlarged his circle of naturalist acquaintances, which now included Dr. William Galt, an amateur botanist, and Alexander Wilson, the nation's leading ornithologist and a noted wildlife artist. There was some tension between the two artists when they finally met at Peale's Museum in Philadelphia. Wilson was civil, but relatively uncomplimentary of Audubon's work. Wilson's paintings were well known and the standard against which the work of all others was judged. But, certainly by the late 1820s, most impartial observers (and probably Audubon as well) considered the Frenchman as having surpassed Wilson in artistic ability.

Now in his thirties, Audubon had started to compile an impressive portfolio of birds, despite losing some 200 drawings when rats shredded his stored artwork in Kentucky. He was a failure as a businessman, so he leaped at the chance to work for Dr. Daniel Drake at his Western Museum in Cincinnati, which would allow Audubon to pursue painting *and* nature.

Drake was an unusual character who dabbled in a number of

fields, including natural history. In essence, he was an entrepreneur and showman in the mold of Charles Wilson Peale and P. T. Barnum, and he learned some of it from his mentor, Dr. William Goforth, also of Cincinnati. Goforth had discovered the Big Bone Lick fossil beds that were visited by Meriwether Lewis prior to the explorer's trip to the Pacific coast. Drake was Goforth's apprentice and was awarded a "diploma" from Goforth prior to heading to Philadelphia for additional schooling. When Drake returned, he became a part-time doctor, part-time snake-oil salesman, with an interest in botany. He later formed his own medical school, library, and museum: Drake's Western Museum.

Drake hired John James Audubon at a salary of $125 per month and had the artist create paintings of local fauna. Soon, visitors to the museum were admiring Audubon's work. Among the notables were Titian Peale—the zoologist and artist of the Long expedition (and later the Wilkes expedition) and the son of Charles Wilson Peale—and Thomas Say, the eminent invertebrate zoologist.

These contacts led to a meeting with and letter of introduction from Henry Clay to support Audubon's anticipated travels to the sparsely settled southwest. With Clay's letter in hand, the 34-year-old Audubon departed. He took a flatboat to New Orleans to embark on a collecting trip in the lower Mississippi River drainage and, he hoped, to the southwest. Audubon earned his passage downstream as a hunter of wild game, which he secured at their frequent stops on shore. The flatboat would stop, Audubon would shoot what he could for the crew's supper, and (if birds were included) do sketches of the animals. Some of Audubon's "new" birds turned out to be errors on his part, such as naming a juvenile bald eagle as a new species. But the trip did allow Audubon to compile a more extensive portfolio of species. He also did portraits by commission—enough to keep him in supplies. In those long weeks in and around New Orleans, he often accompanied Charles Bonaparte—Napoleon's nephew—who was attempting to update Alexander Wilson's *Ornithology* using Titian Peale as the illustrator.

All of these experiences led to Audubon's emerging reputation as a painter and naturalist. In 1824, he attempted to interest publishers in New York and elsewhere in publishing a compilation of his bird paintings. But no printer or engraver seemed receptive. So, in April 1826, Audubon sailed for England, hoping publishers there might have an interest in his proposed *The Birds of America*. As he envisioned the work, there would be engravings of hundreds of species of birds, together with accompanying text. Audubon was then 41 years old and at an age when he felt that time was running out on producing a major ornithological work—something that would secure his reputation and make money in the process.

With $1,600 in life savings and letters of introduction from Henry Clay, DeWitt Clinton, and naturalist Vincent Nolte, Audubon made the rounds of British engravers and publishers. He was a popular guest in homes and at parties, and he became a fellow of several British scientific and artistic societies. With his long hair and French accent, Audubon was considered by many to be the epitome of a "frontiersman" and definitely a romantic character: rough around the edges, but clearly educated and artistic. To the English, he was a Renaissance man who had returned from the wilds of Kentucky.

But publishers were not as enthused or curious. Audubon always carried his drawings in a large portfolio, trusting it to no one else. And, when he would open it and spread the paintings out on a table for others to see, viewers always were impressed, but they recognized how costly a folio of engravings would be. To do the paintings justice, it would take an excellent engraver—equally as talented as the original artist—to create a beautiful facsimile of the painting. Audubon thought that he had found one such man in Scotland, William Lizars, and Lizars was enthusiastic as well.

The original plan was to produce 400 oversized paintings (29 inches x 39 inches sheet size), showing birds life-size, with five plates per folio, and each folio costing about $12 U.S. Rather than a large print run, the number of folio sets would be restricted to the number of subscribers. To do this, Audubon almost literally went from door to door, trying to convince individuals in England, France, and later the United States to commit to as much as $1,000 for a complete set of *The Birds of America.*

Even when William Lizars had to back out because of rising costs, Audubon was able to interest another engraver—Robert Havell—to take over, and he continued to solicit subscribers and to fill in his missing bird species with additional excursions in the United States. King George IV became a subscriber and helped sponsor the folio. In the United States, Daniel Webster signed up, as did the U.S. House of Representatives. Eventually, Audubon and his publishers had 100 subscribers from England and 75 in the United States.

In 1829, Audubon was back in the United States, painting more birds and sending the completed works to the engraver in London. He wrote the text that would accompany the folios, calling it *Ornithological Biography*, and traveled to the southern part of the country, as well as to Labrador in search of missing bird species. Thomas Nuttall gave him some bird specimens, loaned him others, and sold Audubon some 100 specimens from the northeast and the west. The painter traveled to Texas—his first foray into the west, where he met Sam Houston, but added few birds to his list. Yet, his Texas specimens, along with Nuttall's contributions, enabled Audubon to add 81 new species to his overall compilation.

Every time he thought he had a firm number of birds for his listing, a new one would appear—and he had yet to scour much of western North America. He was reluctant to keep adding plates and folios—and charging subscribers *ad infinitum*—so he finally settled on 489 species, appearing on 435 prints, placing more than one species on some of the engraver's plates. The folios were issued in four volumes between 1826 and 1838.

When the complete *The Birds of America* was issued, Audubon grossed about $175,000. After expenses, his profit was minimal. A later reissue of *Birds*, with lithographs rather than engravings, was issued in a smaller format and in seven volumes between 1840 and

1844. It was more affordable to ordinary people and did provide Audubon with some profit as well as an obvious boost to his reputation. After his death, several other versions of *Birds* were issued, each more affordable and more widely available. But, even as his name became synonymous with birds and nature, he already was thinking of a new project that would take him into the heart of the west.

Audubon envisioned another folio of paintings, accompanied by text, entitled the *Viviparous Quadrupeds of North America*—a treatment of North American mammals. To complete the work, he needed to fund an expedition into the Rocky Mountains, where many of the continent's mammals were found. So, hoping to secure funding—or at least support—he traveled to Washington, D.C., where he secured letters of support from John Tyler, Secretary of War John Spencer, General Winfield Scott, Daniel Webster, and others, but few subscribers. Eventually, though, Audubon, his friend Edward Harris, and a small entourage raised sufficient funds to outfit themselves. Several members of the party paid their own way for the chance to undertake a great adventure. Along with the generosity of others, they were able to plan an extended, if frugal expedition. The group purchased several "6-barrelled revolving pistols," blankets, bullet molds, clothing, mosquito netting, knives, life preservers, food, and—in the case of illness—a supply of the all-purpose "James's Pills."

William Stewart, the Scottish adventurer, heard of Audubon's plans and offered to take the painter along with his small party that was preparing for another of Stewart's trips up the Missouri River. Just as he had done with Alfred Jacob Miller on his first such trip to the west, Stewart hoped to have a talented painter accompany him upriver, but Audubon declined. When the two men actually met face-to-face in St. Louis, Stewart tried again to convince Audubon to join forces, even offering the painter and his friends the use of five mules and a wagon. But Audubon wasn't taken with Stewart's manner, noting, "He is a rather tall, very slender person and talks with the lisping humbug of some of the English nobles." In his journal, Audubon noted that Stewart was "a very curious character." Audubon also was concerned with Stewart's rather cavalier planning for the trip—electing to take only 16 days provisions, then live off the land after that. Audubon was more concerned about difficulties upriver and, not having been in the wilds of the upper Missouri before, he was reluctant to leave too much to fate.

In this way, Audubon was more like Spencer Baird's mother. Baird, the young naturalist and correspondent with Audubon, hoped to accompany Audubon on this great adventure, but Baird's mother would hear none of it. Her son was barely out of his teens and many years removed from his career with the Smithsonian Institution, and Mrs. Baird had heard too many stories of dangerous river travel, hostile tribes, ferocious grizzly bears, and severe weather in the west. Even though the young naturalist was not able to go on the trip, Audubon did encounter a new bird species that he named for his friend, Baird's sparrow.

Fortunately for the cash-strapped Audubon party, the St. Louis Fur Company offered the painter and his companions free passage as far upriver as Fort Union, in the Dakotas.

Sailing aboard the steamer, *Omega*, in 1843, the 58-year-old Audubon was hoping to go even farther upriver, to the Yellowstone River and several hundred miles into the mountains from there. But that part of the trip never materialized.

Audubon, Harris, and several others, along with about 100 fur trappers, headed up the Missouri in the spring. The *Omega* was stocked with 500 dozen eggs, 15 dozen bottles of alcohol, and enough other supplies for the Fur Company to last for weeks, and even months. The painter, with his relatively high level of schooling and refinement (he often traveled with his flute and violin, as well as his paints) was shocked by the trappers. They knew little of arts and literature and could recognize few of the animals of the country, except those that they might trap or eat. The behavior and identification of most bird species was a mystery to those men who lived much of their lives in the wild environment. And, perhaps more surprising to Audubon, the trappers had little interest in learning about such matters.

It took 48 days—until mid-June—for the flat-bottomed *Omega* to reach Fort Union, near the mouth of the Yellowstone River. The passengers disembarked and the *Omega* was loaded with 25 packs of buffalo tongues, 30 packs of beaver hides, and 100 packs of buffalo hides for the vessel's return trip to St. Louis. Each pack was a pressed and tied bundle of a particular weight—usually 50 pounds—that was usually covered in deerskin or some other material to protect the pelts.

For two months, Audubon and his party wandered near Fort Union, collecting (especially mammals) and engaging in at least one bizarre activity.

Local custom among native peoples was to place their dead on platforms or in trees, exposed to the elements. One of these bodies belonged to a chief, White Cow, who had died some three years earlier. Anxious to obtain a souvenir, Audubon and another man went to the "grave" site, equipped with instruments that could be used to sever the chief's skull from the rest of his body. The corpse was found in a coffin that was nestled in the branches of a tree. Opening the box, the men found that they didn't need the instruments after all—a simple twisting movement separated the skull from the rest of the skeleton. Despite the callous disregard for the dead, the incident does illustrate how conventional mores did not always apply when it came to Native Americans. To Audubon, White Cow's skull was just another specimen that could be collected, like a bird egg from a nest. No white person questioned his actions.

Another incident also illustrates a widespread attitude that almost led to the demise of the American buffalo, although Audubon's party did suffer some pangs of regret for their actions. Audubon described in detail a buffalo hunt that the white travelers were able to undertake at a time when buffalo seemed so vast in number that the killing of one, or even a hundred, seemed quite insignificant.

Thomas Nuttall, taken later in life, before his return to England.
(Gray Herbarium Archives, Harvard University)

Asa Gray (kneeling at lower left, holding plant press), while on a collecting trip in Colorado in 1877. Also present are Mrs. Gray (seated at table, center) and botanist Joseph Hooker (seated behind Gray).
(Gray Herbarium Archives, Harvard University)

Spencer Fullerton Baird.
(Smithsonian Institution, Record Unit 95, Box 2,
Negative 46853)

Robert Kennicott.
(Smithsonian Institution, Record Unit 95, Box 14,
Negative 43604)

John Wesley Powell (right), paleontologist, geologist, and explorer, with Paiute chief, Tau-Gu.
(Photograph by John Hillers. National Archives and Records Administration & U.S. Geological Survey)

Cholla cactus, Arizona.
(John Moring)

Grasshopper on corn stalk,
Oregon.
(John Moring)

Cook Inlet, Alaska.
(John Moring)

Saguaro National Monument, Arizona.
(John Moring)

Martha Maxwell with her collection of taxidermy mounts.
(Colorado Historical Society, Negative F33,373)

John Muir as a young man.
*(State Historical Society of
Wisconsin, Negative WHi(X3)5766)*

Paleontologist Joseph
Leidy, with fossil tibia of
Hadrosaurus, taken
in 1858.
*(Ewell Sale Stewart Library,
Academy of Natural Sciences of
Philadelphia)*

Othniel C. Marsh (center, back row), with a group of colleagues and students at Yale University, preparing to go to the West in 1872.
(Peabody Museum of Natural History, Yale University)

Florence Merriam Bailey, from her class photo at Smith College in 1886.
(Smith College Archives)

Audubon found it nearly impossible to describe the numbers of buffalo that roamed the plains, noting that "the buffalo's bellowing could be heard for miles." At age 58, Audubon himself was not as active as were some other members of his party, so he observed the hunt from a high point of land:

As they (the buffalo) discovered what we were at, with the quickness of thought they wheeled, and with the most surprising speed for an animal apparently so clumsy and awkward, flew before us. I could hardly imagine that these enormous animals could move so quickly, or realize that their speed was as great as it proved to be, and I doubt if in this country one horse in ten could be found that will keep up with them.

Most of the men in Audubon's party killed buffalo. The carcasses were skinned and the meat loaded into carts, which were then hauled back to the fort. On the way, the group passed another, smaller herd of buffalo. Even though the carts were full, and the trappers at Fort Union had no need of further meat, the Audubon party stopped to slaughter several more buffalo. The hunters kept the buffalo tails as souvenirs and removed the tongues, but the carcasses were left where they fell.

A fur trapper once told Audubon that he had once seen a buffalo herd so large that he was delayed for six days while he waited for the herd to pass. An exaggeration—perhaps. But not much of an exaggeration. Enough confirmed incidents exist of huge herds that extended for miles that the gist of the trappers' tale probably had a ring of truth. The moral was that most people thought that the buffalo herds were so vast and inexhaustible that they would last forever. They were as many as the blades of grass on the great prairies, and few gave them much thought.

Even decades later, buffalo seemed to be inexhaustible. In January 1872, Grand Duke Alexis and his party took a train to North Platte, Nebraska, where they were joined by their guides, including Buffalo Bill Cody. On January 15, in Colorado, the 21-year-old duke's party, including George Armstrong Custer, killed 56 buffalo. Six days later, the party killed 50 more of the animals. It was all wonderful sport.

Edward Harris did exhibit some apparent pangs of guilt after the slaughter of the bison in the smaller herd. That evening, he wrote,

> We now regretted having destroyed these noble beasts for no earthly reason but to gratify a sanguinary disposition which appears to be inherent in our natures. We had no means of carrying home the meat and after cutting out the tongues we wended our way back to camp, completely disgusted with ourselves and with the conduct of all white men who come to this country.

Despite these written words of remorse, the next time Harris was invited to go on a buffalo hunt, he accepted immediately and found himself attempting to gratify that same animal disposition found in humans. He would go on several more hunts that summer.

In August, Audubon and his party built a small boat to take the men and their bird and mammal specimens downriver. It was not a pleasant trip, as the weather turned cold and rainy, and the wind blew, but the group finally reached St. Louis on October 20, 1843.

It would be Audubon's first major expedition into the American west, and his last.

He eventually published *The Viviparous Quadrupeds of North America* with the assistance of his two sons (John W. and Victor) and their father-in-law and close Audubon friend, John Bachman. But admirers of Audubon's earlier work with birds noticed a decline in his artistic talents—although the renderings were clearly in the same distinctive Audubon style. Audubon's national and international reputation, however, remained intact, right up to the time of his death on January 21, 1851, when he was 65 years old.

The number of birds and mammals named by and for Audubon is lengthy, and included such diverse creatures as Audubon's oriole and the desert cottontail rabbit, named by Spencer Baird as *Sylvilagus auduboni*. Like botanists Asa Gray and John Torrey, there is a mountain peak in Colorado that is named for the artist. And there today exists a large conservation organization, the Audubon Society, that was founded long after the painter's death, that functions as a proactive advocate of birds and other inhabitants of nature.

In *Quadrupeds*, Audubon predicted that the buffalo was "perhaps sooner to be lost than is generally supposed." He was close to being correct, of course. The buffalo almost was lost. The vast herds that he witnessed in 1843 and those that had been recorded by William Clark in 1806 were gone forever. But Audubon's personal glimpses of birds and animals, many of which were recorded in his *Ornithological Biography*, signaled the beginning of a new approach to natural history that would dominate in the late nineteenth century.

Chapter 9

IN THE FIELD BEFORE
THE GREAT WAR

Captain John Feilner's mind was drifting. As he stopped his horse alongside a small stream near the Missouri River, he was thinking of many things: the Civil War in the east that Feilner had recently left; his young wife, who was expecting a child; and . . . birds.

John Feilner was a battle-hardened army veteran. But he also was an amateur naturalist who noticed the natural world around him. Dismounting from his horse, he might have been distracted by a bird that flew overhead, or a snake that slithered into some rocks.

He failed to notice that three Sioux warriors were hiding in the bushes nearby.

Surprised, Feilner was shot and mortally wounded. His budding career as a naturalist ended abruptly alongside a stream in the Dakotas, far from home.

In the early decades of the nineteenth century, naturalists were few in number and often forced to accompany large groups of armed men when traveling in the unsettled country. Nuttall, Bradbury, Townsend, Maximilian, and others all did this, at least from time to time. Those who took off on their own, like Nuttall and Douglas, were simply lucky that they survived. It was a dangerous time and a dangerous land.

To the established experts in natural science in the east, the situation was quite frustrating. Sending someone into western North America (or going themselves) required considerable planning and finances. Government-sponsored exploring trips, led by Lewis and Clark, Pike, Wilkes, Long, and others, were few and far between. Even John C. Frémont, who made several trips west and caught the eye of the public with almost everything he did, contributed only a little to natural history. He personally had an interest in new flora and fauna, but not the training or burning passion. Nonetheless, he did collect plants for botanist Asa Gray and had plants named for him, such as *Fremontia vermicularis*, native to coastal California and Oregon.

Frémont had an unfortunate legacy of disastrous expeditions, usually due to his own quest for public acclaim and his poor judgment with winter travel. Several men died during Frémont's forays, and many others narrowly escaped drowning or hypothermia. One of them was a naturalist, Frederick Creutzfeldt. A botanist by specialty, Creutzfeldt almost froze to death during Frémont's fourth expedition in 1848. He escaped a snowy death in the San Juan Mountains of Colorado only to meet a different fate in another part of Colorado. Assigned to a railroad survey team led by Captain John Gunnison, the party was attacked at dawn by a band of Paiutes. Their chief's father had recently been killed by whites, and the Paiutes were seeking revenge. Unfortunately, the naturalist and the survey team were easy prey, and Creutzfeldt, Gunnison, and several others were killed near Sever Lake. The loss of life was tragic enough, but natural science suffered as well. Creutzfeldt was more than a competent botanist, and even Gunnison had interests in science. At least one plant and one animal were named for him.

It wasn't until the late 1840s and into the 1850s that the situation changed for natural history scientists. First, the government sponsored many more surveying expeditions—for boundary mapping and proposed railroad routes—and numerous naturalists and collectors were employed to obtain specimens and to write up the scientific results in conjunction with the topographic results.

Second, more and more people were moving into the American west. Some of these new residents had interests in plants and animals but, more commonly, these were military men who now found themselves stationed at remote outposts and forts. They had time on their hands and opportunities to observe and collect new species of plants and animals. Some did so simply because of personal interests—natural history was an avocation. Others were pleased (and often paid) to be collecting for the Smithsonian Institution or other eminent eastern facilities.

One of these military collectors was John Feilner, an emigrant from Europe who joined the army as a private in 1856. While assigned to Fort Cook, California, Feilner started collecting local birds and their eggs. Soon, he had a personal collection of over 300 skins and almost as many eggs.

It was difficult for an enlisted man to possess and transport too much personal property, with limited space in quarters and periodic reassignments. Feilner didn't quite know what to do, as his hobby was getting out of hand. He didn't want to discard the specimens. Fortunately, in 1859, he met another soldier, John Xantus, a Hungarian immigrant who arrived in the United States in 1851, and had been a regular collector for Spencer Baird at the Smithsonian Institution. Xantus provided the eastern scientist and the Smithsonian with thousands of bird samples from areas near army posts, along with hundreds of mammals, reptiles, fishes, and insects. It was Baird who arranged for Xantus to be assigned for two years at Fort Tejon, near present-day Bakersfield, California, and later for another two years at Cabo San Lucas, in Baja California. The latter assignment was with the U.S. Coastal Survey.

To Baird, Tejon and Cabo San Lucas were prime locations for scientific collecting. Xantus responded with crate loads of specimens to the Smithsonian, the National Museum of Hungary, and the Academy of Natural Sciences of Philadelphia. But, despite Baird's opinion of the scientific attributes of the two locations, life in the hot, oppressive environments was miserable for humans. "There is not a blade of grass in the country," wrote Xantus before he finally left.

John Xantus became one of Spencer Baird's most prolific collectors in the west. He discovered an estimated 300 new species of animals and several hundred plants, and more than 50 are named for him. Xantus himself published just two scientific papers, but became relatively well known for two books of his adventures and travels in North America. As popular as the books were, however, they were highly embellished with incidents that happened to others or included stories that were complete fabrications.

Xantus suggested that John Feilner write to Baird and explain what he had in the way of specimens. Soon, Feilner was a member of Baird's growing group of collectors in the west. The scientist provided shot, several gallons of alcohol, five pounds of arsenic for preserving skins, ornithology manuals, and continual encouragement and support.

Partly because the Smithsonian was an agency of the federal government, it was highly influential in Washington. As a result, Feilner and other members of the military were actually encouraged to support the sciences, especially on non-army time. Baird even arranged for Feilner's commanding officer to allow his soldier to make collecting trips to other parts of northern California and southern Oregon.

On one such excursion, in May 1860, Feilner and a companion were attacked by a band of Modocs who chased the pair for six miles before the soldiers took refuge in a cabin. After two days of attacks, Feilner killed the Modoc chief and the Indians departed.

Despite this incident, Feilner continued to send bird specimens to Spencer Baird on a regular basis, even after he was promoted to sergeant. When Feilner was being considered for an officer's commission, it was Baird who wrote a letter of recommendation. Despite Feilner's lack of formal education and limited use of the English language, Baird pointed to John's bravery in the incident with the Modocs, his valuable assistance to the Smithsonian, and his enthusiasm and dedication to natural sciences.

Baird's support was justified. Feilner received his commission and, when the Civil War erupted, he was assigned to an infantry unit in Virginia. His bravery on the battlefield was recognized by the army, and he was elevated in rank on up to captain before Spencer Baird again intervened on his behalf.

To Baird, Captain John Feilner was one of his most valuable assets: a knowledgeable and enthusiastic field collector who could obtain specimens, classify them in at least gross terms, preserve them, and ship them to Washington along with documentation— and do it at regular intervals. And when Feilner was assigned to western posts, he was able to travel under the protection of armed troops. It cost the Smithsonian only a few bottles of alcohol and some arsenic.

So, Baird arranged for the army to reassign Feilner to the west. Captain Feilner had mixed feelings about this. He was glad to be away from the bloody battles of the Civil War, but he was recently married and his wife was expecting a child. Assigned to the west, he would be even farther away from his New York home.

But the positive aspects of the duty seemed to tip the scales: a chance to travel in the upper Missouri River country and new opportunities for scientific collecting. Feilner was assigned to an engineering detachment with a unit being organized by General Alfred Sully that was being sent to the Dakotas to quell Sioux activity. With many army troops recalled to the east to fight in the war, numerous areas of the west became quite dangerous for white settlers, miners, and travelers. During the 1860s, Apaches became more aggressive and active in the southwest. The same thing was happening with the Sioux on the Great Plains.

Feilner left his home in April 1864. Sully's command gathered in Iowa before disembarking, but was delayed in its departure for the Dakotas. So Feilner tried to do some local collecting, much as Thomas Say had done while waiting for the Stephen Long expedition to depart some 45 years before. Feilner wrote to Baird that birds were scarce in Iowa: "Little is in this section of the country at present." He only was able to shoot 12 birds, and he sent them to the Smithsonian on June 3. Soon thereafter, Feilner was ambushed and killed along the Missouri River.

General Sully wrote of his captain, "It was hard that he should lose his life in this way. It was allowing to his enthusiastic desire to collect as many specimens as possible for the Smithsonian Institute."

Baird continued to correspond with and assist Feilner's widow for years after her husband's death, but Baird's corps of western collectors scarcely missed a beat. Feilner had recruited several assistants from the enlisted ranks, and one of them, Sigmund Rothhammer, stepped in to continue collecting for Baird.

Although Baird had many collectors among western military men, few were as productive as John Feilner. An exception was someone who also was a hero at the Battle of Gettysburg, Gouverneur Warren. His military and leadership qualifications aside (he ranked second in his class at West Point in 1850), Warren became an enthusiastic collector for Spencer Baird after meeting the scientist in 1854. The two men remained friends until Warren's death in 1882.

Because of his military rank and position, Warren was able to make more than simply personal contributions to collecting. An experienced mapmaker, Warren led several expeditions that, under another's direction, might have left their legacies to just geographical exploration. Instead, Warren readily encouraged scientific objectives in his travels. Ferdinand Hayden was part of his expedition into the Powder River and Yellowstone country, and Warren and Hayden oversaw the collection of some 1,500 plants, 65 molluscs, 186 birds, 28 reptiles, 47 mammals, and 391 fossils that were listed in Warren's *Preliminary Report of Explorations in Nebraska and Dakota, in the Years 1855–56–57.* Baird and the Smithsonian were the recipients of those collections.

Another of Warren's legacies was his collection of Native American artifacts that was shipped to Washington and included numerous rare items. He started this when he was part of a detachment assigned to Colonel William Harney that engaged Sioux forces at the Battle of Blue Water Creek. It was actually a massacre more than a battle; 87 Sioux were killed and another 70 were captured in retaliation for the earlier massacre of 32 soldiers near Fort Laramie.

After the battle, Warren collected native weapons, clothing, and other artifacts that were strewn about the battleground and shipped them to Spencer Baird in Washington. There, they became part of the collection of the newly named Museum of Natural History.

In the early part of the nineteenth century, Benjamin Smith Barton was probably the principal recipient of biological samples collected in the west. In the middle part of the century, three men—botanists John Torrey and Asa Gray, and zoologist Spencer Baird—were the principal overseers of eastern collections. When a government-sponsored expedition returned, it often was pre-arranged that experts in the field who may have accompanied the expedition would work on the results, or the specimens would be sent to eastern authorities. Vertebrate fossils were routinely sent to Joseph Leidy, and later to Othniel Marsh or Edward Cope. Plants went to Benjamin Barton, and later to John Torrey and Asa Gray. Animals would go to a number of individuals, including Thomas Say, then Louis Agassiz or Spencer Baird.

Like so many early naturalists, John Torrey had a medical degree, but he switched from medicine to botany while in his twenties.

Born in 1796, Torrey practiced medicine in New York City until he was exposed to botany by a prison inmate, Amos Eaton, the author of *Manual of Botany for the Northern States*. Eaton (and his writings) would later inspire Asa Gray as well as botanist and physician Edwin James. Originally trained in the law, Eaton was convicted of forgery and spent four years in prison, where he met Torrey, the son of a prison official. Eventually, Eaton was pardoned by Governor DeWitt Clinton, and the botanist went on to a highly successful career as a professor at Williams College.

Thus inspired by Eaton, 31-year-old John Torrey shifted to botany and became a professor at Columbia University in 1827. Later, he also became a professor at Princeton and for years actually held joint appointments at both colleges. In the years after the death of Benjamin Smith Barton, it was John Torrey who assumed the mantle of leading botanist in the country. He was not a collector of western flora, but he became an authority of flora of the west that was collected by a number of others. Torrey described some of the plant specimens brought back by the Charles Wilkes expedition and collaborated with his colleague and former assistant, Asa Gray, on the botany volume that resulted from the expedition. Torrey was the recipient of John C. Frémont's plant specimens, and Torrey worked on the botany collection from the six-year Mexican Boundary Survey that was directed by Lieutenant William Emory—a volume that was highly praised by Gray and others.

Torrey finally made it to the west in 1877, at the age of 76, when he visited Colorado. Two mountain peaks had recently been named for Torrey and Gray, but Torrey, who visited Mount Torrey several weeks after Gray's visit, was physically unable to climb this geographic monument to his notoriety.

Torrey died in 1873, but his botanical legacy was astounding. Among the many plants and trees named for him are the Torrey pine, *Pinus torreyana*, and the yew, *Torreya*. The Torrey Botanical Club, one of the country's oldest devoted to the subject, was organized by his friends in Torrey's later years.

Unlike active field collectors, such as Thomas Nuttall and David Douglas, John Torrey and Asa Gray seldom wandered far from their eastern herbariums. Gray, in fact, was a schoolteacher in New York when he became preoccupied with botany after reading Amos Eaton's textbook on the subject. At the age of 22, Gray quit his job and became John Torrey's assistant in 1832. The two botanists became fast friends and co-authored the book *Flora of North America*.

Gray became a successor to Thomas Nuttall at Harvard and even lived in Nuttall's old quarters on campus. He arrived there in 1842, as the new Fisher Professor of Natural History. Prior to Nuttall's return to England, Gray met the man who had become known as the leading botanist of his day, but the two did not depart cordially. Asa Gray was another of what Nuttall called "closet collectors" and did not visit the west until 1872, when he hiked some of California's mountains with John Muir. Gray was back in Colorado and the Sierra Nevadas in 1877, accompanied by his wife and British botanist

Sir Joseph Hooker of the Royal Horticultural Society, as well as an entourage of botanists and assistants. By that timer, Gray was 67 and not as active as he would have liked. Yet, he again visited with John Muir, and the two engaged in more botanical collecting.

Despite his limited field collecting in the west, Gray (and his wife) did make several collecting trips to other parts of the United States and received numerous awards and tributes, including honorary degrees from Oxford, Cambridge, and the University of Edinburgh. Like John Torrey, Gray was an extremely prolific writer, with many descriptions of new genera and species of plants as well as his *Manual of Botany*, a principal guide to northeastern plants. He, too, had a genus named for him: *Grayia*. And he also became somewhat embroiled in the controversies surrounding Darwin's theories on evolution and selectivity. Gray looked at Darwin's evidence and reasoning and spoke favorably of Darwin's conclusions, even though this seemingly conflicted with his own deeply religious beliefs and the opinions of many notable scientists. In 1864, Gray offered his extensive personal collection of plants to Harvard University on the condition that the school build a suitable building to house and preserve the specimens and other archive material. Eventually, Harvard was able to do so, and the Gray Herbarium continues in a modernized existence today.

The other major recipient of western collections was Spencer Fullerton Baird. Baird was probably the most influential person in the field of natural history in the country. Although his personal field collecting experience was limited, he left his mark on almost every naturalist of the mid- and late nineteenth century.

A case could be made that Baird also was a closet collector, as most of his career he was the recipient (at least on behalf of the Smithsonian Institution and other agencies) of collections derived from the labors of others. But that label would be unfair. In his younger days, growing up around Carlisle, Pennsylvania, Baird was an avid collector. In 1842 alone, he reportedly traveled over 2,000 miles in pursuit of specimens; he shot over 650 birds.

Baird began corresponding with John James Audubon and even

furnished the artist and naturalist with specimens of mammals from Pennsylvania. Audubon recommended that the young collector preserve his specimens in "common Rum," rather than whiskey or brandy. Probably, most people would have thought this a waste of good spirits, although Baird presumably used the most inexpensive rum that he could find. Although none of the drinkable whiskeys has sufficient alcohol content for proper long-term preservation of specimens (85 percent alcohol is best), the darker brandy or whiskey tends to dull the true colors of animals. Thus, such samples are less useful to painters, like Audubon, who are trying to re-create the live appearance of animals in nature.

This correspondence with and assistance to Audubon would ultimately prove valuable because, after 19-year-old Baird visited Washington, D.C., in 1842 and became acquainted with a number of naturalists, including James Dana of the Wilkes expedition, he secured a teaching position at Dickinson College. Natural history and regular field trips became an important component of his classes. Four years after the founding of the Smithsonian Institution, in 1850, the position of assistant secretary became available, and Spencer Baird applied. Many of his naturalist colleagues wrote letters of recommendation, but the one from John James Audubon—arguably the most famous wildlife artist of his time—was the most influential.

Baird was offered the position.

Spencer Baird was paid $1,500 per year initially, and he would remain in that position for 28 years before becoming secretary for another nine years.

It is Baird who is most credited with expanding the Smithsonian's collection of natural history specimens from approximately 6,000 when he arrived in 1850 to close to 100,000 by 1860. Baird alone brought two boxcar loads of personal specimens when he arrived in Washington, and the institution regularly received hundreds of shipments each year from dozens of collectors and donors.

Although Baird's personal field collecting slowed dramatically once he arrived in the nation's capital, categorizing him with the same brushstroke as a Benjamin Smith Barton or John Torrey—in terms of being describers rather than collectors—would not do Baird justice. As he aged, Baird had heart problems, which prevented him from pursuing exhaustive field surveys. Instead, he worked long hours, even including holidays, to arrange collections from others. He directed the description, classification, and publication of those samples by the authorities of the day, such as Gray, Torrey, and Joseph Leidy.

Baird himself was no amateur zoologist, especially with birds and fishes. But he also had an excellent working knowledge of mammals and a sufficient broader background to discuss other subjects in the biological sciences as well. He personally wrote hundreds of scientific manuscripts and edited hundreds of other publications by others. Baird wrote the fishes material obtained by Lorenzo Sitgreaves's expedition of 1851 to the southwest, and the zoology samples from the Ives expedition of that same year. When the extensive pre–Civil War Pacific Railroad Reports were prepared, Baird was responsible for three volumes himself. In addition to the many animals named by Baird, a glacier in Alaska and several mammals, birds, and fishes are named for him, including Baird's sandpiper, *Calidris bairdii*, and Baird's sparrow, *Ammodramus bairdii*.

These accomplishments alone would have secured Baird a significant place in the history of natural sciences in the United States. But where Baird left his legacy was in establishing a network of collectors across the west. He was a prolific correspondent who wrote thousands of letters (3,050 in 1860 alone) to naturalists and others. By the post–Civil War era, Baird had over 1,000 collectors in his realm—amateur and professional, military and civilian—on the lookout for specimens for the Smithsonian Institution. Baird offered encouragement in his letters and often furnished preserving and collecting supplies (e.g., alcohol, drying papers, shot, powder, arsenic, identification guides, and even shotguns). The logistical complexity of keeping in contact with these field collectors, outfitting them, arranging for shipments, cataloging, storing, and describing the specimens, and keeping the collectors informed, required energy that only a Spencer Baird could provide.

Others in Baird's stable of collectors were John Newberry, an eastern surgeon who concentrated on birds during his many travels, and John Le Conte, the son of a wealthy family. Le Conte's father also was fascinated with natural history, and young John was soon following his father across meadows and through woods near their home. While the elder Le Conte's particular interests were reptiles, birds, insects, and plants, the son was pursuing his own directions. In 1843, Le Conte followed the Santa Fe Trail to California and discovered several new species of plants and animals. That was the positive aspect of the trip. The rest of the traveling was far from pleasant. Along the Gila River, Indians stole Le Conte's horses, forcing him to walk for 30 miles across the desert to the nearest settlement.

Both Le Contes, father and son, became quite active in the Entomological Society of America and, after serving in the Civil War, John signed on as a naturalist with the ongoing Pacific Railroad Surveys. He collected flora and fauna in Kansas and New Mexico and subsequently wrote an important monograph on the beetles of the west, based on his own collections and specimens purchased from one of Spencer Baird's other collectors, John Xantus. Le Conte personally described over 5,000 species of beetles, many of which ultimately were deposited in one of Harvard's museums.

Le Conte later explored North Africa and parts of Europe and became one of the notable names in American science. He was one of the founders of the National Academy of Sciences and served as president of the American Association for the Advancement of Science. He published scientific papers for over 40 years, and among the many animals named for him was Le Conte's thrasher. And, like so many naturalists of the era, Le Conte had a connection with Spencer Baird, but in this case, it was two connections. Le Conte collected specimens for Baird and he also was a distant relative of the Smithsonian representative.

Farther to the south, Gideon Lincecum pursued his interest in southern Texas. Lincecum only had a few months of formal schooling. Yet, he considered it enough to proclaim himself a doctor. Despite his limited medical training, people in rural Texas, along the Mexican border, were happy to have him. As a teenager, Lincecum applied a form of local folk medicine that he learned from various Native American tribes, including the Comanches, with whom he involuntarily spent time. He had a reputation, he once noted, of being a "sure-cure Indian doctor." Later, he became much more confident in his own healing powers and applied treatments that he later admitted probably killed many of his patients. Eventually, as his knowledge of botany improved, he became a practitioner of natural botanical cures—which actually seemed to do some good.

Lincecum married young ("I was utterly incompetent to the duties and responsibilities of domestic life"), and his wife bore him 13 children. Ten of them survived to adulthood, even with Gideon Lincecum as their family doctor. As Lincecum matured, he became more fascinated with natural science and started to correspond with such notables as Charles Darwin, Spencer Baird, paleontologist Joseph Leidy, oceanographer Matthew Fontaine Maury, Joseph Henry—secretary of the Smithsonian—botanist Asa Gray, paleontologist Edward Cope, zoologist Elliott Coues, and Robert Fitzroy, the commanding officer of the *H.M.S. Beagle*.

Lincecum passed on many of his specimens to Charles Darwin and Elliott Coues, and his papers and articles were published in such diverse outlets as *The Journal of the Linnaean Society of Zoology*, *The Southern Cultivator*, *The Zoologist*, *Proceedings of the Academy of Natural Sciences*, *Prairie Farmer*, and *The Practical Entomologist*. Although he ultimately specialized in beetles, he wrote widely on the geology of Texas and countless other topics.

A little farther north, another prolific collector of the era also was pursuing his natural history avocation. Samuel Woodhouse was born in Philadelphia in 1821 and, like so many naturalists, he could trace his interests in plants and animals to his youth. Unlike others who initially pursued science independently, Woodhouse had access to the Academy of Natural Sciences, its collections, and its library. Regular visits to the academy also allowed him to meet such prominent naturalists as Thomas Nuttall, John Townsend, Samuel Morton, and Paul Goddard. Woodhouse became a regular face around the building and even helped move the collections and books to its new location in 1840. That same year, one of the birds that he collected in Pennsylvania was dutifully logged into the academy's records and, a year later, he was elected a member of the academy.

Despite the personal satisfaction of pursuing natural history, it was obvious to Woodhouse that pursuing a career in the field would never reap much in terms of financial rewards. He took to farming and collected only in his spare time. Yet he continued to correspond with another Pennsylvania boy, Spencer Baird, who was then only 19 years old. The two continued to exchange specimens and give each other advice on collecting locations and species.

Unfortunately, Samuel Woodhouse suffered health problems and, eventually, the strenuous daily work involved with farming became too much. His farming career ended and a new career began. Partly due to the suggestion and encouragement of an uncle, who had been a professor at the University of Pennsylvania, Woodhouse entered the university in hopes of becoming a physician. It turned out to be an excellent career choice, and he received his medical degree in 1847. Soon thereafter, he obtained a position as assistant resident physician at the Philadelphia Hospital.

Despite this change in vocation, his avocation continued to be natural history—as it was with so many physicians in the nineteenth century. So, in 1849, on the basis of recommendations from prominent academics, Woodhouse received an appointment as physician and naturalist with the Creek Boundary Survey that was heading to the Indian territory of present-day Oklahoma.

As with so many survey expeditions, it was a prudent appointment to find a medical practitioner who also was a competent naturalist. The position could then be combined—as it was with Edwin James—with more efficient use of the person's time and salary.

Although this was Woodhouse's first professional employment as a naturalist, he performed admirably and was selected for a similar position on another survey, the Sitgreaves expedition along the Zuni and Colorado rivers.

At the time, this area of the southwest was still quite remote, unexplored, and dangerous to cross. The terrain was rugged, the desert heat oppressive, and some of the southwestern tribes quite hostile to intruders. Yet, the expedition led by Lorenzo Sitgreaves would ultimately become noteworthy, from both its topographic contributions as well as Woodhouse's biological contributions.

Samuel Woodhouse traveled westward from Texas to Santa Fe, collecting specimens as he went, to join the military and topographic detachment. The expedition left Santa Fe on August 13, 1851, in the heat of the summer. After traveling along the Zuni River, the party reached the Zuni Pueblo in early September. Unfortunately for Woodhouse, his curiosity as a naturalist got him into severe trouble.

Spotting a rattlesnake that he hoped to collect as a specimen, Woodhouse smashed the snake's back, seemingly killing it. Unfortunately, it would take more than a stunning blow to kill the snake.

Reaching down to grab the serpent, the snake bit Woodhouse on his left index finger. Almost immediately, he felt severe pain and, for days, the expedition's surgeon and natural history expert was in agony. Few of the soldiers could relate to a man who attempted to pick up a poisonous snake. To most veterans of the frontier, proper behavior was to kill any rattlesnake and perhaps cut its head off, but not to keep the serpent as a souvenir for science. But Woodhouse was a naturalist in the tradition of Thomas Nuttall and even Meriwether Lewis. Sometimes, they learned through their mistakes. It took days of alternately opening the wound and sucking out the blood and poison and irrigating the puncture with a mixture of ammonia and water. Using all his medical skills, Woodhouse applied a poultice of flax seed meal, and he drank large quantities of brandy and whiskey. Even drunk, he was in pain for weeks and had to have others do his collecting. No other collector was particularly interested in searching for more rattlesnakes.

The survey party reached the Little Colorado River, then traveled through the San Francisco Mountains. Like many early naturalists and explorers, Samuel Woodhouse had a geographic landmark named for him, in this case a mesa northeast of present-day Flagstaff, near what later would become Wupatki National Monument.

The Sitgreaves party continued through the mountains, reaching the Colorado River, which the group followed downstream. By then, drinkable fresh water was becoming scarce, even with the huge quantities of silt-laden Colorado River water churning nearby. There were increasing encounters with hostile tribes and some of the soldiers as well as civilians were killed. Pack mules started to die, food ran out, and the men were forced to eat some of the dying mules.

During one encounter with a party of Mojaves on November 9, Woodhouse was shot in the leg with an arrow. Exhausted and hungry, the Sitgreaves survivors finally arrived at a remote outpost near the Gila River. There, they rested before continuing across the desert to San Diego. They arrived a week before Christmas 1851. Despite all the difficulties, Woodhouse managed to keep a number of specimens intact, along with his journal.

After a sea voyage north to San Francisco, which was in its Gold Rush heyday, part of the survey party (including Sitgreaves) sailed for Panama. There, they crossed the isthmus along with hundreds of disappointed gold seekers also returning from California. Woodhouse and some others attempted to return to the east via Mexico, but they had difficulties trying to locate a large enough party going that way. So, eventually the rest of the survey party also sailed for Central America and crossed the isthmus through Nicaragua.

When Sitgreaves compiled his report of the southwestern exploration, *Report of an Expedition down the Zuni and Colorado Rivers*, Samuel Woodhouse wrote the natural history appendix section, as well as a medical report of the company's ailments and treatments.

This initial accounting of specimens in the final report led to a series of scientific papers on birds and mammals that appeared in the *Proceedings of the Academy of Natural Science of Philadelphia*. But Woodhouse's collections from Oklahoma, New Mexico, and Arizona were more extensive than one person could describe, so he sent specimens to others who had specialized expertise. One of those was Woodhouse's boyhood friend, Spencer Baird, who was now with the Smithsonian. Baird and Charles Girard were talented ichthyologists and handled the fish specimens. John Le Conte was the beetle expert and received the bulk of those specimens. Edward Hallowell described Woodhouse's reptiles, John Torrey and Asa Gray received the plants, and Woodhouse retained many of the birds and mammals. In addition, Woodhouse authored a paper on his geological observations in the southwest.

Despite being a relative novice in taxonomic description, Woodhouse did formally describe a number of seemingly new species, and several of these have remained so over the passage of time. Most of the animals that have retained Woodhouse's original scientific names were mammals, particularly rodents, but a form of desert coyote continues to be distinctive as a subspecies. In return, Woodhouse was honored by having several species and subspecies of animals named for him by others who formally described specimens that Woodhouse had collected. Woodhouse's jay and several other animals have since lost their Woodhouse-honored scientific names because the animals were later considered synonymous with previously described forms.

Taxonomy and nomenclature is a fluid, continuously evolving field. As species are more clearly defined, through new molecular and meristic evidence, some longstanding scientific names are reconsidered. Scientific boards and committees are continually re-examining the nomenclature of plants and (especially) animals. A consensus by such groups can change a species to a subspecies of another form, or several families can be grouped into one. Or a longstanding scientific name can be replaced by another name that was properly proposed earlier.

Changes continue to occur in scientific nomenclature every year. The name of the rainbow trout, *Salmo gairdneri*, honored Dr. Meredith Gairdner, a naturalist with the Hudson Bay Company. The scientific name stood for more than a century and a half. It was described from a specimen collected near Fort Vancouver, along the Columbia River, in 1836, 32 years after the fish was seen by Lewis and Clark. In 1989, taxonomists concluded that the fish was more closely related to the Pacific salmon, *Oncorhynchus* spp., than it was to the "true" trouts, such as the brown trout and Atlantic salmon. And, at the same time, taxonomists reached a consensus that the trout was actually the same species as one described in Kamchatka in 1792, *Salmo mykiss*. Because of that, the previous name, *mykiss*, took precedent and thus deserved the honor of initial naming. As a consequence of those decisions, *Salmo gairdneri* became universally known as *Oncorhynchus mykiss*, a name change made after 155 years.

Unfortunately, many species named for Samuel Woodhouse have disappeared over the years. Even plants named for Woodhouse by Asa Gray and John Torrey have been modified over time.

Fame is sometimes fleeting.

Samuel Woodhouse, however, retains an important niche in early natural history. He later accompanied an expedition to Central America (in 1853) that surveyed a potential railroad route through Honduras. While the topographers concentrated on surveying, Woodhouse collected plants and animals, some of which appeared in Ephraim Squier's report of the survey, *Notes on Central America*, which was issued in 1855. Woodhouse was later elected to the Academy of Natural Sciences and, in 1903, he was named a fellow of the American Ornithologists Union. Although his western field collecting ended with the Sitgreaves expedition, he continued to participate in meetings of scientific societies, even at the age of 83—just a month before his death.

Despite the thousands of specimens supplied by Baird's many

collectors, his most prolific field operative was a man whose life was quite brief. Robert Kennicott was a frail youth growing up in northern Illinois. Because of his poor health, he only had a few years of formal schooling. Yet, he had a keen mind and was the epitome of an overachiever.

His interest in natural history led to collecting trips near his home and correspondence with Spencer Baird at the Smithsonian Institution. By the age of 18, Kennicott already was part of Baird's collecting network and, a year later, the two finally met in Washington, D.C.

Baird took an immediate shine to young Kennicott, who would become one of the founders of the Chicago Academy of Sciences in 1856—despite Kennicott's young age. He was just 21 years old. Soon thereafter, Kennicott would become one of the driving forces behind the creation of a natural history museum at Northwestern University.

It was Baird who proposed that Kennicott undertake a three-year collecting expedition into Canada and the far north. Robert immediately accepted.

At the time, the flora and fauna of Alaska, the Arctic, and the Canadian north were still very much unknown, despite some collections by early naturalist Georg Steller in the eighteenth century; John Richardson, who was with Sir John Franklin's arctic explorations in the 1820s; and other periodic visitors to the boreal north. To Spencer Baird, this part of North America offered the greatest opportunities for collecting and discovering new species in the mid-nineteenth century. But financial support for such a long endeavor was not easily obtained. So, while Baird worked out a complex arrangement involving private and academic donors, Robert Kennicott embarked on his first lengthy expedition—a four-month collecting trip up the Red River of the north, and into Canada as far as Lake Winnipeg.

Kennicott was a valuable asset for such a journey: energetic, enthusiastic, and tireless. His collection of specimens was impressive, and he spent the winter of 1857–1858 at the Smithsonian, living in rooms reserved for the institution's resident researchers.

By 1859, funding was in place to send Kennicott to the far north. Baird insisted that the Smithsonian receive examples of all the species collected, and Kennicott insisted on the same arrangement for the Chicago Academy of Sciences. Other specimens were divided among the sponsors of the trip—each of them receiving a pro-rated quantity that was apportioned according to their investments. For example, the University of Michigan donated $250 toward Kennicott's expenses and, in return, Spencer Baird divided the collections in Washington and shipped the university's share to Ann Arbor.

Like David Douglas, who collected plants in the Pacific northwest decades before, Kennicott relied on the generosity and assistance of the Hudson Bay Company and its employees. Several of the Hudson Bay people actually served as Kennicott's assistants. Some were paid in cash, whiskey, or (in one case) an accordion. Others participated solely in the interest of science. As added incentive, Spencer Baird wrote each of Kennicott's assistants to thank them for their efforts.

Local Indians also collected for Kennicott and were paid with sewing needles, bolts of cloth, shotguns, and other trade goods.

Kennicott's travels took him north in May 1859, to Manitoba and Saskatchewan, then to Fort Yukon. Much of the way, he traveled in a party of French-Canadian trappers and Iroquois who paddled large birch-bark canoes. Animal life was quite rich in the Yukon drainage, but other parts of the Canadian north were relatively barren except for ferocious mosquitoes that drew blood from humans and destroyed many of the collected bird skins and eggs.

"If it were not for the fine insects I'm getting, I should be quite discouraged," Kennicott wrote in a letter to Baird.

Plant life was quite varied and undoubtedly included many undescribed species. But Kennicott's priorities were the animals. He had a plant press and drying paper and offered to collect plants as he traveled, but none of the financial sponsors seemed interested in flora, at least according to Baird's responses to Kennicott. Instead, Spencer encouraged Kennicott to obtain more bird eggs (many had been damaged in shipment back to Washington). Also, he particularly wanted skulls of mammals. "Can't have too many," Baird urged.

The arduous expedition reaped considerable riches. After some three years of field collecting, in largely uncharted territories, Robert Kennicott sent back (by his reckoning) over 10,000 specimens.

After a period back at the Smithsonian to work on cataloging his arctic specimens and to recover his health that had suffered in the rugged north, Kennicott was hired to be one of six naturalists with the Western Union Telegraph Expedition in 1865. The survey, much like the railroad surveys across the continental west, was designed to plot a route for a telegraph line across arctic lands. Like the railroad surveys, the natural history of the lands surrounding the route would be canvassed as well.

Among the naturalists was William Dall, who would later become a major presence in North American science. But, at the time of the survey, he was green and relatively inexperienced. Upon Baird's recommendation, Kennicott hired Dall at a salary of $30 per month.

The telegraph survey was plagued by problems from the start. Some were logistical, but many were primarily personnel conflicts. Some of the scientists balked at the Western Union policy that required all of its employees to wear uniforms, even in the field. The company operated in a semi-military fashion—an arrangement that historically seemed to bring out conflicts between civilian scientists and military men in many of the great surveys. Whether these were factors or whether it harkened back to Robert Kennicott's poor health as a youth, it was an extremely stressful time. On the morning of May 13, 1866, co-workers found Kennicott's body, the victim of an apparent heart attack. He was only 30 years old.

Despite his limited time in the field, Robert Kennicott ultimately was the Smithsonian Institute's most productive individual collector. He discovered and named Baird's sandpiper along the shore of Great Slave Lake, and he had at least five species and subspecies of animals named for him, including a wasp and several birds.

William Healey Dall, who was shocked by Robert Kennicott's sudden death, was appointed as lead naturalist for the telegraph survey to replace Robert. It was a post that would lead to a fruitful career in natural history. At one time, Dall was collecting simultaneously for Spencer Baird at the Smithsonian, and Asa Gray and Louis Agassiz at Harvard.

Fifteen years after the Western Union survey, Dall was appointed honorary curator of the U.S. National Museum (Smithsonian), and he worked tirelessly on the mollusc collection, eventually producing hundreds of scientific papers, along with the book *Alaska and Its Resources*. His contributions to natural history were numerous and even included a study of the effects of temperature on oyster growth—one of the earliest such investigations on the role of temperature. In his honor, the Dall sheep was named for him, along with several other animals from the west.

In addition to Baird's network of private collectors, the Smithsonian was involved, in one way or another, in most of the surveys of the west that included some natural history investigation. One of the most important pre-war surveys was led by Lieutenant William Emory, a red-haired topographic specialist who was recommended for admission to West Point by John C. Frémont. Emory first gained notice during the Mexican War in 1846, where he led the topographical detachment assigned to General Stephen Kearny's Army of the West as it traveled to Santa Fe, then on to California. It was a difficult journey, with the desert heat, hostile Mexican troops, hostile tribes, rugged terrain, and hand-to-hand combat at the Battle of San Pascual. Despite the difficulties, Emory and his men mapped the route and recorded weather conditions. Despite its lengthy title, his subsequent report, *Notes of a Military Re Conaissance from Fort Leavenworth in Missouri to San Diego in California, Including Parts of the Arkansas, Del Norte, and Gila Rivers*, was noticed by Emory's military superiors when it was issued in 1848.

Following the Mexican War, Emory appeared to be the ideal candidate to map the relatively new U.S.-Mexico boundary. The assignment ultimately took six years, 1849 to 1855, beginning just before Spencer Baird was appointed deputy secretary of the Smithsonian. This arduous expedition thoroughly mapped the 1,800-mile border and also gathered a huge quantity of information on plants and animals of the borderlands. Emory (now a major and later a general) was responsible for preparing the three-volume final report, *Report on the United States and Mexican Boundary Survey*, that was issued in stages between 1856 and 1859.

One of those volumes—on zoology—contained a description of a snake that was named for the expedition's leader, *Scotephis emoryi*. John Torrey prepared the botanical volume, and John Clark— another Baird protégé—was the principal naturalist of the survey. In total, members of Emory's boundary survey collected over 2,600 plants and hundreds of specimens of animals.

While these major survey efforts were under way, other expeditions crisscrossed the west along proposed railroad routes. Most of these included a natural history component, and many southwestern surveys were influenced by the science interests of William Emory. One of these surveys, the Whipple expedition of 1853–1854, included a scientific team that was chosen by Spencer Baird and the Smithsonian Institution. John Bigelow, a medical doctor, doubled as botanist, and Caleb B. R. Kennerley—another physician— doubled as the expedition's zoologist. Both had connections with the Smithsonian, and Kennerley, especially, had worked closely with Baird in the past. Also part of the survey team was artist Balduin Möllhauson, who was assigned his own tent to use as a studio to produce paintings and drawings for the final reports.

As the Mexican Boundary Survey reports were being issued and the Arctic Telegraph Survey was under way, and Baird's collectors across the west were dutifully shipping specimens back to the east, another set of important surveys also was in progress. In the pre–Civil War years, there was considerable interest in surveying possible routes for railroad lines across the west—primarily those that would result in transcontinental links to the Pacific coast. As survey crews mapped the many possibilities across the plains, naturalists were employed to scour the nearby woods and fields and to collect and describe a broad path westward and south. These collections in turn were compiled in a series of *Pacific Railroad Reports* that proved to be invaluable inventories of western flora and fauna.

Many individuals were connected with the railroad surveys. John C. Frémont's disastrous fourth expedition was supposedly designed to survey a possible, ill-conceived railroad route along the 38th parallel. Captain John Gunnison's survey team, which included botanist Frederick Creutzfeldt, was ambushed while surveying for the Pacific Railroad Survey, and Captain William Warner was ambushed by Pit River Indians while surveying a possible railroad route along the upper Sacramento River, in California. John Le Conte, John Clark, and many others were employed by the surveys at one time or another, and some of the surveys continued after the Civil War. Spencer Baird, James Hall, and many eastern scientists participated in the publication of the reports. The result was one of the most extensive collections of plants, animals, and fossils ever compiled. The principal reports were issued in 13 volumes between 1855 and 1860, and these publications served as definitive field guides to western flora and fauna for decades following the Civil War.

Chapter 10

COLLECTING THE WEST

An obituary for Charles Bendire in 1898 noted, "It is probable that while stationed at Fort Lapwai, Idaho, from 1868 to 1871, Major Bendire first began the systematic study and collection of objects of natural history, and that he was led thereto by his fondness for hunting and interest in the haunts and habits of game mammals and birds."

A surprising number of post–Civil War naturalists were like Bendire (born Karl Emil Bender)—army officers and non-commissioned officers who found themselves stationed at western forts. They had time on their hands, interest in the flora and fauna around them, and scientific intelligence and curiosity.

Unlike many of these men, who were collectors for scientists in the east, Bendire would go on to achieve noteworthy accomplishments in many fields of zoology, even though, as one colleague noted, "He never allowed his interest in birds to interfere in the least with the strict performance of [army] duty, and more than one anecdote is related of his losing valuable specimens through his unwillingness to delay his command for a few minutes."

Karl Bender was born in Germany in 1836 and, after being dismissed abruptly from school because of a now long-forgotten infraction, he sailed for New York with his younger brother, Wilhelm, in 1853. The following year, Karl enlisted in the U.S. Army, changing his name to Charles Bendire at the same time. He rose through the enlisted ranks until he was commissioned a second lieutenant in 1864 as a reward for "gallant and meritorious service in the Battle of Trevillion Station, Virginia." He rose to first lieutenant, then captain in 1873, and finally to major in 1890 for "gallant services in action against Indians at Canyon Creek, Montana" back in 1877.

Although stationed all over the country, including many parts of the west, it was in Idaho during the 1868–1871 period that Bendire first started passionate collecting. He reported the northern range extension of several Mexican bird species and discovered new species and subspecies; three were named for him: *Harporhynchus bendirei, Megascops asio bendirei,* and *Loxia curvirostra bendirei,* as well as fish, fossils, and mammals that were named for him by such scientific notables as Lesquereux, Brewster, Ridgway, Coues, Merriam, and Bean.

Initially, he was most fascinated by bird eggs and became an early expert on the eggs of western species. It was this expertise with bird eggs that first caught the eye of Spencer Baird at the Smithsonian Institution. Soon, Bendire was a regular collector for Baird, not just of birds but animals in several other fields of zoology as well.

In 1883, Baird arranged for Bendire to be assigned to Washington as "Honorary Curator of the Department of Oölogy of the National Museum." Bendire organized the bird and bird egg collection, donated his personal collection of some 8,000 specimens, and encouraged friends to contribute specimens as well—all of which formed an outstanding reference collection in Washington.

Before his death in 1897, Bendire prepared a two-volume set of *Life Histories of North American Birds,* an outstanding contribution to the field of ornithology. He also was one of the founders of the American Ornithologists Union, and he made his mark in the military as well as in natural history.

Charles Bendire was not an atypical naturalist in the post-war era. There were many officers and enlisted men stationed at western posts, as well as civilians who collected for eastern museums and eastern scientists, as they had in the years prior to the Civil War, and the ranks of these experienced field collectors included William

Hammond, Edward Greene, and Edward Palmer. Hammond was an army surgeon and part-time ornithologist and herpetologist who collected for Spencer Baird. He became John Xantus's mentor and later rose to the rank of surgeon general of the United States. Unfortunately, he was court-martialed for a political/personal conflict, but was reinstated by an act of Congress, and went on to a distinguished medical career. Greene collected plants for Asa Gray in 1870 and later published botanical papers under his own name, and Palmer became a noted botanical collector.

Edward Palmer was an English-born army doctor who became interested in plants, particularly those used by Native Americans. He collected plants in California and Arizona, including Palmer's saltgrass, *Distichilis palmeri*, which he found being harvested by the Cocopa tribe around the mouth of the Colorado River in 1889. Palmer first started collecting for the Smithsonian Institution while on a trip to Paraguay. Later, while stationed at army posts in the west, he sold specimens to eastern collectors and naturalists before the war and was a regular collector for Spencer Baird, Asa Gray, and John Torrey in the years following the Civil War. In 1865, Palmer teamed up with Elliott Coues on a collecting trip and, soon, Palmer was busy shipping southwestern plants to Gray, Torrey, and Baird, as well as the Kew Gardens in London, the New York Botanical Garden, and the U.S. National Herbarium. Edward Palmer was such a prolific field collector that he, reportedly, collected over 100,000 plants during his career. In addition to the saltgrass, which was named for Palmer by George Vasey, the genus *Palmerella* was proposed by Gray, and several animals, such as Palmer's chipmunk, were named for him by his friends Elliott Coues and C. Hart Merriam.

Farther to the north, Edward Nelson became one of the Smithsonian Institution's most prolific collectors once he was assigned to Alaska in 1877. Nelson was a meteorologist with the U.S. Army Signal Service along the coast of the Bering Sea—one of the few areas of the west than remained relatively uncollected late in the nineteenth century.

In his spare time, Nelson roamed parts of the Yukon River valley and Norton Sound, collecting biological samples and artifacts from native tribes. He is credited with collecting over 2,000 bird skins and over 1,500 bird eggs. A government report on the natural history of Alaska in 1887, which included illustrations by ornithologist Robert Ridgway, relied heavily on Nelson's collections. Yet he remained much more than just a collector. He spent so much time among native peoples of the far north that he compiled these observations in a book, *The Eskimo about Bering Strait*, in 1899—one of the earliest careful treatises on the indigenous peoples of Alaska.

Nelson was a native of New Hampshire and worked for Edward Cope in the Rocky Mountains and was a friend of Spencer Baird and ornithologist Robert Ridgway. Before Nelson went on to become the chief of the U.S. Biological Survey in 1916, he had become so renowned as an expert on Alaskan fauna that naturalist John Muir sought him out for advice. In the summer of 1881, Muir accompanied Nelson on an Alaskan expedition aboard the cutter *Thomas Corwin*.

In addition to all this experience, Edward Nelson spent 15 years living in Mexico, where he was credited with discovering numerous species new to science, including Nelson's wood rat, *Neotoma nelsoni*. His tenure with the U.S. Biological Survey lasted 12 years, until it was merged with the United States Bureau of Fisheries, to become the U.S. Fish Commission. Over the years, species of mammals, fish, reptiles, and butterflies were named for Nelson, along with one genus and numerous geographical landmarks.

There were many such private collectors in the 1860s and 1870s, but this era of western discovery will be remembered most as the era of the great surveys. Unlike the railroad surveys of mid-century, there were several major survey teams that emerged in the years when the military and civilian funding could concentrate, not on battles, but on exploration and mapping. During overlapping years, the major surveys were led by John Wesley Powell, Clarence King, Ferdinand Hayden, and George Wheeler. Each survey had a specific set of marching orders and geographic boundaries. But, once the teams were in the field, their actual explorations sometimes over-lapped and their specific objectives eventually became blurred. Overall, the different surveys were assigned to map portions of the United States west of the Mississippi River. But they all competed for funding from Congress. Each group tried to outshine the others, and their competition sometimes became bitter, especially between the Hayden and Wheeler teams.

The situation came to a head in July 1873, when the Hayden and Wheeler survey parties actually camped near each other in Colorado. Charges of "invading" each other's territory were exchanged, and Congress began to question the apparent duplicate efforts of the various survey groups. There was certainly evidence that some money had been ill spent and it is known that some areas of the west were mapped twice, with one survey covering the same ground as another. But this controversy and bickering marked the beginning of the end for the multiple surveys. By 1879, the independent surveys were combined under a single agency, the U.S. Geological Survey, which was first led by Clarence King, then by John Wesley Powell.

The primary focus of all the surveys was mapping and geology. But each had some level of collecting of flora and fauna as well. Powell and Hayden had personal interests in fossils, and Hayden encouraged natural history collecting for the Smithsonian Institution by hiring ornithologists, zoologists, and botanists as part of his survey's explorations.

Of the major surveys, however, perhaps George Wheeler's group involved biological scientists the most—although it was a strained relationship.

A native of Massachusetts, Lieutenant George Wheeler was an 1866 graduate of West Point who missed the opportunity for battle-field glory in the Civil War. He was trained as a topographer, so instead of military action, he hoped to become a latter-day John C. Frémont by making his mark as an explorer. He somewhat had his chance in 1867 when he was assigned to survey parts of the Great Basin south of where Clarence King's team was surveying. Through much of the following decade, Wheeler and his U.S. Geographical

Surveys West of the 100th Meridian covered much of the American southwest. His most famous excursion was in the Great Basin and across Death Valley, where he almost lost three men to thirst and the desert heat. His party then took boats up the Colorado River as far as the Grand Canyon—just two years after John Wesley Powell's pioneering trip down the river.

Like Clarence King, Wheeler saw the value of photographic records of his travels, and he employed photographers Timothy O'Sullivan, who apprenticed with Matthew Brady during the Civil War, and William Bell to record the travels of the Wheeler survey.

Despite these significant surveys in inhospitable environments, Wheeler had hoped to survey the entire west, even though much of the land had been covered by others. In so doing, his team duplicated some of the efforts made by surveys by the Powell, King, and Hayden teams (as did Ferdinand Hayden to the others), and this caused all manner of conflict in the increasingly bitter political rivalry among the military, politicians, and survey team members.

These criticisms aside, Wheeler's topographic and biological accomplishments were significant. At one time or another, paleontologist Edward Cope, botanist and acting assistant surgeon Joseph Bothrock, ornithologist Henry Henshaw, and army surgeon and zoologist/ornithologist Henry C. Yarrow were all members of the Wheeler survey. Cope, Fielding Meek, and Charles White wrote most of the extensive paleontological reports of the survey.

Cope and his rival, Othniel Marsh, would later dominate the field of vertebrate paleontology in the latter part of the nineteenth century. Bothrock became one of the early leaders in the country's conservation movement, and Henshaw would later direct the Biological Survey of the U.S. Department of Agriculture.

By most accounts, Wheeler was a hard taskmaster and strict military man—an attitude that sometimes came into conflict with civilian scientists. But he grasped the added significance of his survey's natural history, geological, and ethnological discoveries—to himself and to science—and he encouraged and supported the publication of the scientific results. He forbid the personal biases and personality attacks between Marsh and Cope from creeping into the scientific reports, and insisted that the publications adhere strictly to the science—much to the displeasure of these two feuding paleontologists.

The demise of the survey era, when extensive collections were not only lethal, but accepted practices as well, also signaled the decline of such practices among naturalists. New naturalists were appearing who were writing about what they saw and what they experienced as part of nature.

Perhaps no naturalist of the nineteenth century bridged this transition period between the survey/collection era and the new approach to natural science as did Elliott Coues. He had connections, directly and indirectly, to the Lewis and Clark expedition, the great surveys of mid-century, the budding museum and exhibition field that would become more prevalent in the latter quarter century of the 1800s, and the new wave of nature writers who emerged in the latter part of the century.

Coues was active as a field biologist in the 1860s and 1870s and later became a senior statesman of the broad field of natural history. His particular expertise was birds, and, like Charles Bendire, he was one of the founders of the American Ornithologists Union. But Coues had wide interests and knowledge and could converse easily with ichthyologists, botanists, and mammalogists as well as he could with bird specialists.

In 1872, Coues was in the Dakotas and Montana, collecting birds, insects, fishes, and mammals, and he later became a naturalist with the U.S. Geological Survey. His publications were extensive, but his earliest books, *Birds of the Northwest*, published in 1874, and *Birds of the Colorado Valley* (1878), were especially praised.

His practical and personal experience with flora and fauna of the upper Missouri River landed him the assignment of editing the first unabridged version of Lewis and Clark's journals in 1893. With decades of improved knowledge of western flora and fauna since the two explorers returned to St. Louis in 1806, it was much easier for Coues to use hindsight to interpret what Lewis and Clark were describing in their scientific journals. Coues's annotations to the journals proved invaluable and strengthened the positive perception of Lewis and Clark as important (although amateur) naturalists, even if such recognition did not come until almost the twentieth century.

Editing the original journals of Lewis and Clark was a mammoth task, and the result originally appeared in four volumes. Yet Coues took the job quite seriously and consulted dozens of experts on flora and fauna, a veritable who's who of late-nineteenth-century nature science: Andrew Allen, G. Brown Goode, Theodore Gill, Edward Cope, Barton Evermann, John Wesley Powell, and many others. The original title of his annotated Lewis and Clark journals was the lengthy *History of the Expedition under the Command of Lewis and Clark to the Sources of the Missouri River, Thence across the Rocky Mountains and Down the Columbia River to the Pacific Ocean, Performed during the Years 1804-5-6, by Order of the Government of the United States.* Most readers shortened the title for everyday conversations.

Coues also edited Zebulon Pike's records of flora and fauna in a three-volume record with a title that was much easier to remember: *The Expeditions of Zebulon Montgomery Pike* (1895). And Coues interspersed his academic pursuits with field collections in the southwest. Among his many accomplishments: he described six new genera of birds, four genera of mammals, and numerous new species of animals. Yet it was his encouragement of other naturalists—professional and amateur alike—that earned him the most admirers.

One such collector, a woman from Colorado, was gaining notice for her taxidermy skills. She earned special praise from Coues. When a collection of Martha Maxwell's mounted animals was exhibited in Washington, D.C., Coues was a frequent visitor. Having just returned from a collecting trip to the Rockies, he was especially delighted to see the wide variety of animals and to see such lifelike renderings amongst natural settings. He made sure to write Martha and tell her how much her exhibit had "afforded me pleasure and instruction."

Part 3

THE NEW NATURALISTS

Chapter 11

MARTHA MAXWELL AND
HER MUSEUM

When Martha Maxwell went collecting, she slipped on bloomers, or "Turkish trousers," as she called them. She added a medium-length dress, jacket, and long, hobnailed boots. She wore a wide-brimmed hat and carried a mesh game bag, ammunition, and a shotgun. Usually, her faithful water spaniel accompanied her. Off they went, looking for unusual birds or small mammals. She was a deadly shot and had a keen eye for nature.

Her hunting costume, as she called it, was of strong material, with a brown-and-white checked color to blend in with the woods, one of "neutral tint and firm texture." It was a practical design for walking in the woods, but raised some eyebrows among those fashion-conscious members of society who felt that it was too daring and almost too masculine. Fortunately, attitudes toward such clothing for women were more liberal in nineteenth-century Colorado. For Martha Maxwell, the outfit was comfortable and practical for her purpose, which was to secure specimens for public display.

Most biological specimens collected in the first half of the nine-teenth century were destined for dusty laboratories or cupboards and drawers at museums, universities, or government archives. There, they were carefully studied, sketched, or (later) pho-tographed. Sometimes, they were described by the original col-lector, or an assistant, or someone who had purchased the specimens. Sometimes, the specimens—preserved or pressed onto drying paper—were filed away for "science" or "reference." Perhaps they remained that way for decades, or the specimens deteriorated and were lost forever.

In any case, new or strange creatures from the American west generally were seen only by scientists who frequented those halls of research. The public often was unable to see these new inhabitants of the west, unless they were put on display.

Americans always have been fascinated by unusual animals and "living curiosities." That is why an African lion was such a popular attraction when it was displayed in the east in 1716. The first elephant appeared in 1796 and was even more impressive. Giraffes were not displayed in the United States until 1837. The first museum to exhibit live and preserved animals for display was Peale's Museum in Philadelphia, beginning in 1786. When Lewis and Clark sent back hides and skeletons of a pronghorn antelope and a bighorn sheep, it was Peale's Museum that prepared the full-size taxidermy mounts and put the strange creatures out for public display. Other parts of Peale's collection would later include specimens brought back by Zebulon Pike and other early explorers. The live, black-tailed prairie dog (Lewis's "barking squirrel") that was sent to President Jefferson in 1805 was a featured attraction at Peale's for months.

Charles Wilson Peale, the founder of the museum, was an exceptional painter, as were many members of the Peale family in the nineteenth century. Charles Peale's portraits of Meriwether Lewis and William Clark are today our best representations of the actual explorers. But Peale concentrated on science at the museum, and his collection was truly inspiring to Thomas Nuttall and Thomas Say, among others. Peale also was part showman. He recognized early on that curiosities—whatever the type—attracted paying customers. Not only did he relish displaying the live barking squirrel, but the museum exhibited albinos and other unusual human "freaks" as well.

Peale always professed a higher purpose—unusual animals were preferable to unusual-looking humans, or "nature's mistakes," he often said. But that seemed to be more the philosophy of the Philadelphia Museum. When another Peale's Museum opened in New York, human oddities were a staple. Martha Ann Honeywell, a limbless woman, sat on display in New York and two "cannibals" from the South Pacific were popular attractions in 1831.

The initial exhibits at Peale's Philadelphia Museum were fossil bones collected from Big Bone Lick. The site had been excavated since at least 1762. Benjamin Franklin received bones from there; so, too, did Thomas Jefferson, courtesy of Meriwether Lewis. John Adams saw some of the bones that were displayed in Philadelphia, and many other visitors to the city became fascinated with dinosaur bones. Peale, who was strictly a painter at the time, displayed some of the Big Bone Lick bones in his studio, and the relics created quite a stir—more so than did Peale's paintings.

The studio soon became a rudimentary museum and, by 1787, part of Peale's house was turned into a larger museum—the American Museum—that displayed all manner of natural curiosities and specimens. Crowds gathered every day, each person happily paying a 25-cent admission fee.

One of the early highlights at the museum was a 15-foot-long mastodon skeleton. Later, Peale helped to excavate a larger mastodon, some 30 feet in length, that was billed as "The Ninth Wonder of the World," and encouraged Peale to raise his admission fee to 50 cents. Peale found what others would soon learn: that the American public was fascinated by things that they had never seen.

Thus, throughout the nineteenth century, easterners at least had some opportunity to see live and preserved animals from Africa and Asia and the American west, although it might require a trip to Philadelphia, New York, or Washington, D.C. Eventually, most major cities of the east had some type of museum that exhibited natural history items—at least at some level. Most were modest collections, but one museum stood out: the Smithsonian Institution.

No such national repository and exhibit hall existed when Charles Wilkes and his U.S. Exploring Expedition returned in 1842. Even with the loss of the *Peacock*, which sank with most of the entomological specimens, the Wilkes expedition brought back some 4,000 specimens of animals, which included nearly 2,000 new species from around the world. Half of these animals were birds. Even more impressive was the collection of 50,000 plants. These included some 10,000 species. The live specimens were so impressive that they formed the basis for the new U.S. Botanic Garden.

The massive volume of biological specimens, along with native artifacts, fossils, and rocks, had no suitable place to display and study what was undoubtedly the single largest contribution to the natural sciences. For a time, the Wilkes collection was the property of the National Institute for the Promotion of Science, housed in Washington, D.C.'s Patent Office Building. Until his death, John Townsend—Thomas Nuttall's fellow collector and colleague—did his utmost to study, preserve, and display the animals in the limited display facilities. But it was not until James Smithson donated $500,000 to the United States that there was finally adequate room to display what would become the nation's National Collection. Eventually, the Wilkes material and what remained from earlier collections formed the basis of the large displays available to the public.

Smithson never specified that his donated funds were to be used to create a museum. He left the disposition open to the wishes of the government, as long as the ultimate use was for "the increase and diffusion of knowledge among men."

Politicians, scientists, and laypersons alike debated the intent of those instructions, and among the many suggestions for using the money were a national library, a university, and an observatory. Seventeen years after Smithson's death, in 1846, Congress finally established the Smithsonian Institution.

At first, the Smithsonian's secretary, Joseph Henry, refused to accept the Wilkes collection, believing that the museum should be "a momento of the science and energy of our navy," that would support the ongoing collection of new species. That was his view in 1848. Eventually, he relented and, in 1857, the Wilkes material—or what was left of it—was turned over to the Smithsonian. The museum took formal possession the following year, and during the

1850s, the Smithsonian's biological specimens increased twelvefold. This proliferation largely was due to the plethora of government-sponsored expeditions and railroad surveys in the west and the personal involvement of the institution's assistant secretary (and later secretary), Spencer Baird.

But the Smithsonian Institution was in Washington, D.C. There were few opportunities for westerners to view the rich flora and fauna of their own region.

One such opportunity was Martha Maxwell's Rocky Mountain Museum, located first in Boulder, Colorado, and later in Denver. But Martha's path to museum exhibition was a circuitous one and certainly an unusual journey for a woman in the mid-nineteenth century.

Born in 1831, Martha Dartt lived in Pennsylvania until she moved as a 16-year-old with her family to Baraboo, Wisconsin. Early on, she became aware of coeducational Oberlin College, in Ohio, and in 1851 the family borrowed tuition money from an uncle and sent their daughter off to college. Martha traveled by stagecoach to Milwaukee, then by steamship across Lake Michigan, then by train to Detroit, and another steamship across Lake Erie to Cleveland. From there, she booked passage by train to Wellington, Ohio, and finally traveled by another stage to Oberlin.

Although tuition was only $12 per year, there only was money for one year. But, during that time, Martha took two classes each morning and two in the afternoon, interspersed with daily prayer meetings and life in a local boardinghouse. One of those classes was natural history.

When the money ran out, Martha returned to Wisconsin and began teaching at a local schoolhouse, two miles from home. A local widower, James Maxwell, sent his two oldest children to the newly opened Lawrence University, in Appleton, Wisconsin—some 80 miles away—and he asked Martha to accompany the children in exchange for tuition and living expenses to continue her education.

Martha readily agreed and found that women students in the more progressive Appleton were now wearing a new type of clothing that was much more comfortable for active women. These "bloomers" consisted of a skirt, over baggy trousers, topped by a jacket. It was an outfit that Martha would later adapt for her hunting and collecting trips in the field.

When James Maxwell's wife died, he was left with six children and, although he was almost twenty years older than Martha, he eventually asked his children's chaperone to marry him. By all accounts, James was a decent, enterprising man who was also wealthy—and there were few such prospects in the Baraboo area. The two married on March 30, 1854, when Martha was 23 years old.

Unfortunately, by the time their daughter, Mabel, was born, James lost most of his fortune in the financial crash of 1857. In March 1860, James and Martha, accompanied by James's son, Jim, and four other Baraboo men, loaded a wagon and headed west, seeking another fortune. They left Mabel and other members of the family with relatives and traveled along the increasingly popular trail near the Platte River. At Shinn's Ferry, the group joined with other wagons for the remainder of the trip to Colorado. There were now about 20 men in the party. Martha Maxwell was the only woman. At one point, a passing band of Indians spotted Martha and offered three horses for her. The men were amused by the offer, but declined. Martha was not amused.

In early May 1860, the party arrived in Denver, after a journey of two months. James did some mining in a small Colorado town, Mountain City, and the Maxwells ran a boardinghouse. Later, they moved to Nevadaville and operated another boardinghouse and, in several of the camps, they bought up old mining claims and staked squatter's claims on other sites. The boardinghouse burned down at one point, and James returned to Wisconsin to bring back more family members. Over the next several months, the family moved between mining camps and a ranch near Denver.

The time spent at the ranch, however, turned out to be eventful in one respect. At one of the Maxwell's properties, Martha had a confrontation with a squatter—a gruff German immigrant who, coincidentally, excelled at the unusual avocation of taxidermy. The man refused to teach Martha the secrets of preparing realistic bird and mammal mounts, apparently fearing that he might create competition for the limited earnings that he derived from preparing taxidermy mounts for others. Undaunted, Martha confiscated a number of the specimens, arguing that they were due the Maxwells for unpaid rent.

Whatever the legalities, Martha kept the specimens and carefully studied the skins and forms and, after returning to Wisconsin to visit her mother and daughter, she became even more experienced in the craft. She read everything she could on taxidermy and learned through experience by helping a local professor stuff birds for his collection. What distinguished Martha from other taxidermists of the day was that Martha Maxwell always attempted to place stuffed animals in natural poses and amongst natural surroundings. This talent was what would separate her work from others and make her animals so popular with exhibitors and viewers alike.

While James and Jim Maxwell were building sawmills, Martha, Mabel, and Martha's sister, Mary, joined the family in Boulder, Colorado. It was while in Boulder that Martha's talents as a taxidermist improved substantially, and her collection of specimens increased by leaps and bounds. She developed a special pickling solution for soaking hides. Not only did this mixture of water, salt, arsenic powder, and soda soften and preserve the hides, it also killed destructive insects as well—long a problem with museum specimens.

But Martha Maxwell was more than just a taxidermist. Although not a professionally trained naturalist, she tried to learn as much as she could about the animals that she was preserving and displaying. She wrote to scientists at the Smithsonian Institution, sending them unusual specimens. In return, naturalists recommended textbooks and other publications that would be useful to her.

This exchange was mutually important, as Martha learned more about biology and scientific observations, while the Smithsonian scientists obtained new specimens and heretofore unknown observations of animal behavior. When Martha collected and mounted a new variety of gray owl, ornithologist Robert Ridgway determined it to be a new subspecies, which he named Mrs. Maxwell's owl, *Scops asio maxwelliae*. She also was credited with capturing the first specimens of the rare black-footed ferret. She actually obtained three of the ferrets, and sent one of them to the Smithsonian. This was noteworthy, because the ferret had once been observed by John James Audubon, but the painter/naturalist had been unable to capture one. As a consequence, most eastern scientists had been skeptical that such a creature actually existed—until Martha Maxwell's specimen arrived in a shipping crate.

Oftentimes, when James would haul a load of lumber in one of his wagons, Martha would don her hunting outfit and ride along, looking for new specimens. Soon, their house was filled with all manner of stuffed birds and mammals.

When it was announced that there would be a fair in Denver in late September–early October 1868, Martha gathered together her nearly 600 mounted specimens, loaded them into three lumber wagons, and drove with the family to Denver. Her exhibit at the Third Annual Exposition of the Colorado Agricultural Society was far from the usual type of display. Nothing of that type or magnitude had been seen before in the Rocky Mountain west, and the governor of Colorado personally awarded her a prize.

The *Rocky Mountain News* announced that "the largest collection of Colorado birds we have ever seen is now on exhibition at the Fair Grounds. They were picked up by Mrs. Maxwell, of Boulder, within six months, count over one hundred different kinds, and are arranged in two large shrubs of cottonwood with a great deal of taste."

The collection was so impressive that the governor asked that Martha represent the territory at the St. Louis Fair the following year. Martha was torn, however, because an exhibitor from Shaw's Gardens (now the Missouri Botanical Gardens) offered to buy Martha's entire collection. Shaw's was an impressive facility that was roughly designed to imitate London's Kew Gardens. If she sold the collection, there would be no specimens for the St. Louis exhibit.

However, the money was attractive to the cash-starved Maxwells, and Martha felt confident that she could collect and stuff most of the species again before she needed them for the fair.

She sold the collection for $600 and, with part of the money, the Maxwells built a cabin with an attached shed that could be used exclusively for taxidermy. Her collection at Shaw's Gardens would remain on display until 1889. By that time, the mounts had started to deteriorate and, after a period of storage, the specimens were eventually discarded.

Over the following months, Martha collected in earnest and kept live squirrels, prairie dogs, raccoons, ferrets, rabbits, and owls, and even rattlesnakes and bear cubs at the cabin so she could observe their behavior. This also allowed her to create more realistic-looking mounts. With more space and the time to spend on her nature activities, Martha developed several new taxidermy techniques. Of particular note was her creation of plaster body molds for large and small mammals—a technique that is still used in modern times, except for the development of newer mold material.

This new approach allowed the taxidermist to re-create a full body skeleton and musculature and to shape the animal in a realistic pose, without the need for the original bones and skulls and padding—all of which tended to sag over time. Taxidermy was now Martha's full-time profession. She did custom taxidermy for clients and was still able to replace her entire previous species list.

When the St. Louis Fair ended, Martha Maxwell moved on to her next project: the development of a museum that could exhibit not only her collection of Colorado animals, but other curiosities as well. This endeavor would result in the opening of her Rocky Mountain Museum—the first of its kind in the interior west and the first opportunity for many westerners to view curiosities in a venue similar to that experienced by easterners.

To expand the museum's focus, Maxwell scoured Colorado for samples of rocks and minerals, fossils, and native crafts—anything that would add variety to the new museum. After exhausting her possibilities in Colorado, she traveled alone to California for additional acquisitions. Like the lessons learned by Charles Peale, she realized that casual visitors might become repeat customers if the displays offered variety. So, in California, she bought and bartered natural history items, along with items not associated with science: kimonos, Japanese swords, Asian art, and artifacts from Pacific coastal tribes. While in California, she lived in a small room and skipped as many meals as possible in order to save expenses. When she returned to Boulder, she rode in a railroad car, along with her acquisitions.

Martha Maxwell's Rocky Mountain Museum opened on June 4, 1874. The Maxwells rented three upstairs rooms in a building at the corner of Pearl and 12th streets for $25 per month, and they charged visitors 25 cents admission to see Martha's animals and display cabinets that held her rocks, artifacts, and art pieces.

A brass band and a string band marched outside for the opening, and flags fluttered along the rooftops. Most people in Boulder eventually toured the museum at one time or another—but this was part of the problem. A museum has a limited visitor base, and this is especially so if it exists in a small town—as Boulder was at the time. The population in 1873 was estimated to be just over 1,100, and Colorado suffered from a poor economy along with the rest of the country in those years. Repeat admissions were not common unless exhibits kept changing to spur visitors's interests.

Martha tried to do this by bringing in displays of monkeys engaged in human settings, as well as bringing in live birds, squirrels, rattlesnakes, and two orphaned bear cubs. But it didn't help.

By the fall of 1875, the museum was undergoing financial problems, in spite of a positive review in the *New York Independent* by author Helen Hunt Jackson and the enthusiastic visit by explorer and scientist Ferdinand V. Hayden—then of the Hayden survey team. Hayden reported that the collection at the museum "excelled every other in the West." He even sent several of his exploration reports to Martha to use in the small reading room that was attached to the exhibit rooms.

The Maxwells's finances became so severe that Martha tried to sell part of the collection, but she found no takers. Fortunately, fate smiled on the fledgling museum in the form of a sponsor, John H. Pickel, who offered to pay the first year's rent if the museum would relocate to Denver where there was more of a visitor base—from residents as well as tourists.

The museum survived, but Martha Maxwell's talents in taxidermy, science, and museum exhibition remained largely known only regionally until 1876 when the state of Colorado asked her to create a large display of Colorado fauna (and flora) for the Centennial Exposition in Philadelphia. The centennial commissioners from Colorado offered to pay the railroad transportation expenses for Martha and her specimens, and she traveled to the east with some 400 birds and 200 other animals.

The exhibition, a celebration of the nation's first 100 years, was the idea of Professor J. L. Campbell of Wabash College of Indiana, who suggested it in a letter to Philadelphia's mayor in 1866. Almost a decade later, the exposition opened on May 10, 1876, ran for 159 days, and closed on November 10, 1876. It included 30,864 exhibitors from 50 countries, and attracted almost 9.8 million visitors—the largest attendance of any international exposition ever, eclipsing the Paris Exposition of 1867, which ran for 217 days.

Each building at the exposition seemed to be more magnificent than the next, and 10,217 of the exhibits were agricultural in nature. As such, the horticultural building itself was especially impressive: of a Moorish-style construction, it was 383 feet long, 193 feet wide, and 72 feet high. It cost $251,937 to construct. There would be no way for an individual visitor to take in everything at the centennial. Every country had a sampling of its arts, agricultural products, and technology. Visitors were amazed by the U.S. displays of ice crushers, electric burglar alarms, steam engines, police and firefighting equipment, magnetic printing telegraph instruments, Gatling guns, and countless other displays.

The Kansas-Colorado Building was the largest structure on the fairgrounds. Constructed in the shape of a giant Maltese Cross, each arm was 132 feet by 46 feet, and the structure was housed under a semi-hexagonal roof and a huge dome. The Colorado portion occupied the west wing of the pavilion, and it took Martha two weeks of effort to construct the various display groups of animals, each placed within simulated habitat that included running water and actual Colorado trees and shrubs.

During those two weeks, visitors often viewed the progress and marveled at the animals, wondering aloud whether it was really a *Mister* Maxwell who had done the actual hunting and specimen preparation. To most people, it was inconceivable that a woman could have been the creator—even when Martha put up a sign that read, "Woman's Work."

Maxwell's exhibit occupied an entire wall of one of the wings of the building, which centennial chronicler J. S. Ingram described in 1876:

> *The most striking feature of the Colorado exhibit was a sanded, tin representation of a Rocky Mountain peak. . . . The mountain was thickly covered with pines and cedars, and with stuffed specimens of the principal wild animals and other game of Colorado.*

There were at least two other displays of stuffed animals among the 8,175 U.S. exhibits at the exposition. In the main building was an "elegant kiosk" that was filled with stuffed birds from Missouri that were collected by Captain W. W. Judy and preserved by taxidermist Rudolph Boercher. Three stuffed whooping cranes were the most popular representatives.

In the government building was an impressive collection of stuffed animals that included a polar bear, grizzly and black bears, deer, pronghorn antelope, bighorn sheep, pumas, beaver, mink, sea otters, buffalo, and numerous other creatures. And there was a popular fish display that had been prepared under the direction of Spencer Baird and G. Brown Goode, of the U.S. Fish Commission and the Smithsonian Institution. The display featured small commercial fishing dories and equipment, photographs, pressed and framed seaweeds, fresh fish specimens preserved on ice, and impressive plaster casts of fishes that were hand painted by Smithsonian artist J. H. Richmond.

In addition to these displays of American animals, other countries had small collections of, especially, birds. The British Colonial exhibit had such a bird exhibit, along with a display of furs. But all of the displays paled in comparison to Martha Maxwell's exhibit. As J. S. Ingram noted in his centennial compilation, published a few months after the close of the exposition, the exhibit by "Mrs. M. A. Maxwell . . . was beyond all comparison one of the most effectively arranged displays of the whole exhibition." So appreciative were the Colorado and Kansas commissioners of Martha's efforts that they presented her with a beautiful Evans rifle as a token of admiration.

After the Centennial Exposition closed, Martha remained in the east, separated even more months from her husband James. Their marriage had been deteriorating for years, and the frequent long separations did not help matters. A book written by Martha's sister, *On the Plains and among the Peaks, or How Mrs. Maxwell Made Her Natural History Collection*, in 1878 brought Martha to the attention of easterners.

So, too, did her collection of animals, with which she toured in the late 1870s. Martha signed a contract with two businessmen, John Gardiner and Alvin Buck, to exhibit the collection on Pennsylvania Avenue in Washington, D.C., until February 1, 1878. She was to have been paid $100 per month, but "Mrs. Maxwell's Centennial Exhibit" attracted sparse crowds. Ultimately, Martha failed to receive all the money due her. The collection was next exhibited back in Philadelphia, as part of the "permanent exhibit" that was housed in the old main building that remained from the exposition. But, again, Martha suffered financial setbacks. The building closed in the winter, and officials in Colorado had still not paid her for all of her costs associated with the original centennial display—over $700. The Maxwells's debts, in the east and back in Colorado, were accumulating rapidly.

The Rocky Mountain Museum, in Boulder and then in Denver, and the impressive display at the Centennial Exposition were undoubtedly Martha Maxwell's legacy from a broader geographic perspective. Her scientific contributions, however, were less familiar and only became known after her death.

Elliott Coues, the famous ornithologist and naturalist who would edit the natural history collections and notes of Lewis and Clark at the end of the nineteenth century, had corresponded with Martha Maxwell during her Colorado years. He also visited the Centennial Exposition and was obviously impressed. During the winter of 1876–1877, he had the opportunity to inspect the collection even closer when it was on display in Washington, D.C.

Martha's taxidermy, he noted, was "far superior to ordinary museum work." He added,

> *While the collection embraced several specimens of high scientific interest, I regarded it as one of the most valuable single collections I had seen—far beyond the scientific value which any collection of the animals of a locality may possess, it represented a means of popularizing Natural History, and making the subject attractive to the public.*

With Martha's permission, Elliott Coues cataloged the mammals, with annotations, so that scientists could have a greater appreciation for her talents and natural history contributions. Among the many animals displayed, including eight species of squirrels, were species first described by Coues, as well as Rafinesque, Say, Woodhouse, Baird, and Audubon.

One of Martha's more frequent correspondents, and another visitor to the Philadelphia exposition, was ornithologist Robert Ridgway, who cataloged Martha's bird specimens. He was equally impressed: "The collection consists of excellently mounted specimens," which had been prepared by the "enthusiastic and intelligent efforts of a woman naturalist!"

Martha collected several species of birds from Colorado that were previously unknown. Although not academically trained as a naturalist, Martha's contributions also attracted the attention of

Spencer Baird, who noted her "most excellent knowledge of natural history" and "extremely well prepared" specimens. She also impressed naturalist Joel Allen, who wrote that Martha Maxwell was "something more than a successful and enthusiastic taxidermist; she is an ardent and thorough student of nature."

Martha Maxwell once wrote to P. T. Barnum for advice on exhibiting her collection of animals. Barnum, who also had visited the Centennial Exposition, suggested connecting the collection to a business or a university. Martha also wrote to Julia Ward Howe, the composer of *The Battle Hymn of the Republic* and an early advocate of women's rights. Howe suggested that Martha might take her collection on tour. This she did, hoping to find a permanent home where the specimens could be protected and finances would never again be an issue.

It never happened as she had hoped. Martha Maxwell died in Rockaway Beach, New York, on May 30, 1881, not quite reaching her 50th birthday. In desperate financial straits, Martha was offered a teaching position on a reservation back home in Colorado. The pay was $700 per year, but she declined. Instead, she hoped to exhibit her collection at a beachfront hotel and tourist attraction at Rockaway Beach—the Rocky Mountain House. The plans never quite materialized, and after her health deteriorated, she simply remained in Rockaway Beach until her death.

The legacy of Martha Maxwell's museum extends, in subtle ways, beyond the scientific and beyond the novelty of museum displays. Maxwell developed several innovative taxidermy techniques that advanced the art beyond what was commonly practiced. And her presentation style—with family groupings amongst natural habitat—was innovative for the time, yet would become a common practice by later exhibitors. William T. Hornaday is often credited with developing the "natural" habitat groupings that came into vogue in the late 1870s and early 1880s. Some point to exhibits created by Frederic Webster in the 1860s. But, whoever might receive the proper credit, both men publicly downplayed the contributions of Martha Maxwell to this new museum philosophy. Hornaday, at least, later did acknowledge that a visit to Martha's centennial collection in Philadelphia in 1876 did influence his thinking on the matter.

It is fortunate that Elliott Coues and Robert Ridgway cataloged Maxwell's specimens prior to her death, because afterward, the preserved animals were stored in a barn in Saratoga, New York. Eventually, as with any taxidermy mounts left to exposure and destruction by insects, the specimens deteriorated and were lost. The catalogs and photographs are all that remain of one of the west's most impressive museums, yet one that only had a relatively brief tenure.

Chapter 12

JOHN MUIR AND
THE NEW NATURALISTS

The earliest naturalists collected specimens of plants and animals and, when possible, arranged for talented illustrators to draw accurate representations of the new species. Usually, these were line drawings, but some were more colorful and realistic. As talented artists, such as Bodmer and Audubon, ventured into the west, paintings became popular.

After the Civil War, black-and-white photography became more common and reliable. Specimens could be photographed and reproduced in scientific journals, field guides, and books. Eventually, exhibitions of taxidermy mounts allowed the general public to see nature up close and in three dimensions. It was Martha Maxwell and some of her contemporaries who transformed the taxidermy art form into a scientific representation of form that could be placed amid natural-looking surroundings.

The next logical step for bringing nature to the masses was to exhibit live animals—first in cages, then in pens and aquaria—the exhibit zoos that remain popular today. Even zoos have evolved, from those that exhibited animals that were confined to claustrophobic cells, to the display of animals in more natural settings or botanical gardens.

As this display of nature evolved over time, so too did the attitudes toward nature. Shooting a bird, and perhaps sending its skin to a scientist who might later describe the animal in scientific terms, evolved into displays of live birds, then studies of bird behavior in the wild. Instead of merely collecting a plant or animal for later study, naturalists of the late nineteenth century would sit for hours watching a bird construct a nest. Or naturalists would observe how species interacted—perhaps a predator and its prey—or document the reaction of a territorial animal to an intruder. At the end of the day, these naturalists might return home with nothing more in their game bags than a notebook filled with words. In the late nineteenth century, those who could write about nature became increasingly more popular and influential.

In the latter third of the nineteenth century, two men in particular became known for their nature writings. John Burroughs became associated with New York and the wilds of the northern forest, although he did make some trips to the west. John Muir became associated with the west, although his roots were elsewhere.

Muir once wrote that "Yosemite Park is a place of rest, a refuge from the roar and dust and weary, nervous, wasting work of the lowlands, in which one gains the advantages of both solitude and society. . . . Its natural beauty cleanses and warms like fire and you will be willing to stay forever in one place like a tree."

No one has ever become more associated with Yosemite and the Sierra Nevada range than has John Muir.

Muir was born in Dunbar, Scotland, on April 21, 1838, the oldest son of a deeply religious family. The Muirs lived over the family store and Johnnie—as he was known at the time—would disappear to the nearby woods or the seashore whenever he had the opportunity. Unfortunately, that sometimes meant on Sunday—a day when any such activity was strictly prohibited in the Muir household. The elder Muir insisted on keeping the Sabbath sacred and Johnnie was told, "I must play at home in the garden and back yard lest I should learn to think bad thoughts."

A visit to the seashore on the day of rest brought an immediate whipping. Such punishments would continue for a number of religious transgressions well into Muir's teenaged years, and they tended to shape aspects of his adult life. Religion was paramount, and the Muirs learned to live a frugal life of hard work and Bible study.

In February 1849, John, his younger brother David, sister Sarah, and their father endured a six-week voyage across the Atlantic Ocean to the United States to start a new life. From New York City, the group went up the Hudson River, across the Great Lakes, and eventually to the upper Midwest, where they built a cabin near the Fox River in Wisconsin. Eventually, the rest of the family joined them from Scotland, and the Muirs scratched out a meager living as farmers.

When Muir was 13, the soil played out and the family moved to another small farm, which they named Hickory Hill Farm. John's father essentially quit working as a farmer, leaving the continual chores to his sons. The elder Muir joined one fringe fundamentalist religious sect after another, never quite finding one to suit his tastes. He spent his days reading the Bible and, according to John's recollections, beat his oldest son almost every evening. Sometimes it was for no particular reason, only for transgressions that the father felt might have occurred but were unseen. Everyone was a sinner in his mind, and some sins are not always obvious.

John Muir always felt inadequate about expressing his feelings about nature in words. He wanted people to come to know everything about nature the way he knew it. But he wasn't sure that he was the one who could express those feelings.

Muir escaped the world of beatings and Bibles by entering the world of nature. He could describe in detail the seasonal arrivals and departures of all the bird species near the family farm, and he was able to note which birds remained through the winter. He spent hours observing animals, including lowly insects, and he wrote it all down in his journals—something he would continue to do for the rest of his life.

For decades, John Muir entered random thoughts into his journals, but he always doubted his own influence. For many years, Muir never believed mere words on a page could do justice to a subject that he held so precious. He once told a friend that he wanted "to get these glorious words of God into yourself—that's the thing; not to write about them (words about Nature)."

Muir also was a clever and resourceful inventor who could fashion almost anything for any purpose—especially inventions carved or fashioned from wood. In September 1860, with several of these inventions in his knapsack and $15 in his pocket, Muir departed the family farm and enrolled at the University of Wisconsin in Madison. There, he spent three years, living as frugally as any college student ever has.

He was able to reduce his living expenses to 50 cents per week by living on baked potatoes, bread and molasses, tea, and graham mush. Muir's father once sent his son $10 for college expenses, but warned him not to spend the money frivolously, and to remember those who were truly destitute.

At the end of three years, Muir left the university without a degree, and none in sight. He had not followed any particular list of degree requirements during his college days, but only took classes that he found interesting. He had some vague ideas about enrolling at the University of Michigan and working toward a medical degree, but this was probably quite unrealistic. Instead, when it appeared that he might be called into the Union Army during the peak of the Civil War, Muir left for Canada where he helped to invent various types of machine parts for a factory.

Nature was then only part of his life. He did collect plants in his spare time, but that was infrequent. He spent little on himself, so almost everything that he earned, he saved. When the factory burned to the ground on March 1, 1866, he left for Indianapolis, another manufacturing center.

Muir's later life might be traced to some point during those days in Indiana. It was then that John Muir decided, rather impulsively, to hike to the Gulf of Mexico. This decision was likely influenced by a factory accident where Muir was almost blinded. After he recovered, further work in factories seemed to pale in comparison to life outdoors reflecting on nature.

This thousand-mile trip would effectively shape the course of

Muir's future activities because he kept careful journal entries of the places that he visited, the people who he met, and his thoughts about nature. These accounts were never published until after his death, in a book entitled *A Thousand Mile Walk to the Gulf*. But this was not unlike many of Muir's books; they would appear late in life (or posthumously) after others convinced him of the importance of and interest in his writings.

Muir had no specific agenda or route for his trip to the gulf, quite like his later wanderings in the mountains of California. He only intended to travel "in a general southward direction," and do so on the less-traveled trails and roads.

Even after being slowed by a bout of malaria, Muir reached the Gulf of Mexico, and in January 1868, he sailed on the schooner *Island Belle* to Cuba. The ship was anchored for weeks in Havana Harbor, and Muir spent his nights sleeping on deck. His days were spent collecting plants ashore.

One of his lifelong goals was to travel up the Amazon River, but he was unable to book passage to Brazil from Havana. Instead, he sailed on the *Island Belle*, through winter storms, to New York City. In the spring of 1868, Muir found himself crammed into the steerage section of another ship filled with immigrants bound for California. After weeks at sea, the ship finally arrived in San Francisco Bay and Muir was ready for quieter environments.

He stopped a passerby and asked for directions out of town. When asked where he wanted to go, Muir replied, "Any place that is wild."

The man pointed to the Oakland ferry as Muir's first step. Eventually, Muir and a fellow passenger from the ship made their way to the foothills, then on to the Sierra Nevadas.

At Pacheco Pass, he overlooked the vast Central Valley of California and marveled at the splendor of the expanses of wildflowers. The sight was "like a lake of pure sunshine, forty or fifty miles wide, five hundred miles long, one rich furred garden of yellow compositae."

Muir's initial visit to California's mountains would include one and a half weeks in Yosemite Valley. It was an experience that would shape the remainder of his life. He would later travel to Alaska on several occasions, visit his birthplace in Scotland, and even visit the Amazon River late in life, at the age of 73, but in most of his remaining years, he would never be absent for long from Yosemite or the Sierra Nevada.

Initially, Muir worked odd jobs in the foothills, herding and shearing sheep, breaking horses, sawing lumber. In his spare time, he wandered in the mountains, writing his thoughts in his journal, and spending hours observing a single animal or the changing light patterns of the afternoon sun. A highlight of Muir's second summer in the Sierras was the visit of 68-year-old Ralph Waldo Emerson and his entourage of New England friends.

Muir was 35 years Emerson's junior. But he was in awe of the older man and tried to instill in Emerson some of California's wilderness experience. But it was difficult. Emerson and his party wanted to enjoy a camping trip and see the famous natural features, but without the inconveniences of the wilderness. Muir tried to rid the others of their "house habit," but he was largely unsuccessful. Few people were like John Muir: sleeping under the stars, walking for hours, eating almost nothing. Yet, Emerson's visit was one of the highlights of Muir's early years in California. He enjoyed Emerson's eloquence and simplicity of thought upon viewing the giant sequoias for the first time:

"Those trees have a monstrous talent for being tall!"

Muir also was impressed by the giant redwoods. On a trip to the Kern Basin in the 1870s, Muir traveled some 200 miles through groves of sequoias, finally stopping at what he felt was the largest tree in the woods—one that had finally succumbed to damage from some long-ago fire. Muir spent most of one day measuring the tree and counting its growth rings. He estimated the diameter of what remained to be at least 35 feet. He spent hours counting the tree rings—some 4,000 in all. In its last 1,672 years, the tree diameter increased by ten feet.

As a naturalist, John Muir had broad interests. He collected plants and always was looking for new varieties. He particularly was fascinated by trees and once accompanied a U.S. Coast and Geodetic Survey team into Nevada partly because it allowed him to study the nut pine. Muir was appalled at what he saw in areas near human populations where whole tracts of forests were cut.

"Any fool can destroy a tree," he was fond of saying.

He also had a keen interest in geology and advanced the theory (in an article, "Yosemite Glaciers: The Ice Streams of the Great Valley," in 1874) that Yosemite Valley was created by the effects of receding glaciers. This proposal was strongly opposed by several imminent geologists of the day, particularly Clarence King—later to become the first director of the U.S. Geological Survey—and Josiah Whitney, former Harvard professor and then California state geologist. Whitney considered the unique Yosemite Valley to have been formed from the sinking of the earth's crust. Whitney called Muir "a mere sheepherder," in reference to his occasional occupation in the mountains, and "an ignoramus," someone who obviously lacked the proper credentials for making such a geological observation. "A more absurd theory was never advanced," concluded Whitney. In response, Muir continued to scour the valley's nooks and crannies, locating the origins of its streams, discovering evidence of scouring, and locating moraines and deposits of glacial rock flour. Over time, the glacial theory became the accepted interpretation among most scientists, although other processes aided in the creation of the valley.

Muir also was the first to discover an active glacier in the Sierra Nevada, and he went to Alaska's Glacier Bay on several occasions to study the massive glaciers there. One of the huge ice rivers there was discovered by Muir, and it is still known as Muir Glacier.

Muir began to leave Yosemite Valley after 1874, expanding his explorations south and north in the Sierra Nevada range, with occasional—but brief—visits to Oakland and San Francisco. When in the mountains, Muir traveled light. He once described the process quite simply. He would "throw some tea and bread in an old sack and jump over the back fence."

Quit literally, that was almost all that he would take, except for his ever present journal. He never carried a gun and had little respect for those who hunted because they failed to recognize "the rights of animals and their kinship to ourselves."

He ate little and was notorious for disregarding the need for food—a practice honed during his college years. While his hiking companions would spend considerable energy worrying about their growling stomachs, Muir seemed oblivious to such needs. Tea or coffee, and hard-crust bread were sufficient for his needs. If others caught a trout, or offered him venison, he would take it, but he wasn't much interested in spending valuable time cooking and eating. He didn't carry a sleeping bag, but gathered together a bed of pine needles and slept under the stars. During his years of wandering in the mountains in the early 1870s, he was able to keep his living expenses to about $3.00 per month—mostly for tea, coffee, and bread.

Despite all the months and years of traveling over difficult terrain, Muir suffered only one serious fall. It happened in the winter of 1872. Muir lost his footing and almost tumbled over the edge of a precipice. Fortunately for him, and for the American conservation movement, his body became wedged between some small live oaks that were clinging to the edge of the cliff. He was knocked unconscious, and later "felt degraded and worthless," for letting himself come so close to senseless death.

Muir certainly had other close calls. In April 1875, he led a U.S. Coast and Geodetic Survey team to the top of Mount Shasta, then returned two days later, accompanied by a friend, to scale the mountain again. This time, his casual approach to traveling in the mountains almost caught up with him. A storm came up and, during their descent, the temperature dropped to 22°F. The wind howled and the men were pelted with hail. At one point, they stretched out on the mountainside and let the wind blow over them. By the time they reached the bottom of the mountain, their feet were frozen and painful to thaw.

"How beautiful seemed the golden sunbeams streaming through

the woods between the warm brown holes of the Cedars and Pines," he wrote in his journal, once he could again move his fingers.

Despite his limited requirements, even John Muir needed some spending money. He earned extra money working as a guide in Yosemite Valley, or as an occasional sheepherder and part-time newspaper correspondent. It was the latter activity that elevated John Muir from being the solitary man of the mountains to someone with a broader audience of newspaper readers in California and beyond.

Although Muir always felt inadequate about writing anything that would be viewed by others, he always had written copiously for himself. Eventually, he was convinced to turn some of his observations and adventures into newspaper articles for the San Francisco *Daily Evening Bulletin*. Later, his articles appeared in *Harper's, The Atlantic, Scribner's Monthly,* and the *Overland Monthly*.

The result was that a national audience began to know about John Muir, about Yosemite, about nature, and about the processes that intertwined humans and natural history.

John Muir authored many books, but they all appeared late in life, or were issued posthumously. His first book wasn't published until he was 56 years old. His second, an autobiography, appeared at age 70. He never used a typewriter, always writing in longhand. When ink was in short supply or too expensive to purchase, he used the fluid from sequoias to provide an effective substitute.

Over the years, many Muir books resulted from the efforts of others, who compiled collections of Muir's writings, journal entries, or newspaper stories. *The Story of My Boyhood and Youth* only appeared through the efforts of E. H. Harriman, who arranged for a stenographer to follow Muir around when the naturalist visited Harriman's lodge at Klamath Lake, Oregon, in 1908. Muir talked about growing up in Scotland and Wisconsin, and the notes later became a very readable book.

Our National Parks appeared in 1901. *My First Summer in the Sierras* was published when Muir was 71—over 40 years after the events occurred.

Although Muir's writings would not become widely read until the early part of the twentieth century, they made a considerable impact on a public that was ready to embark on a new conservation movement. Muir served as president of the Sierra Club and became a nationally recognized voice for nature preservation and conservation. Noted easterners sought him out when they visited the Sierra Nevada. In 1903, Theodore Roosevelt spent three days in the mountains with John Muir as his guide. Botanists Asa Gray and Joseph Hooker joined Muir to hike Mount Shasta and collect unusual plants.

Despite the perception of Muir as a recluse who was only happy when in the embrace of Mother Nature, he did enjoy human company. He liked to talk and could entertain people for hours with stories of his adventures. Each year at Christmas, when he lived in central California, he would go to the bank and withdraw a handful of five-dollar gold pieces. These he would distribute to the neighborhood children as presents. When asked for donations to religious organizations and causes, Muir gave readily, although his father's experiences with religious groups had soured the son on belonging to any particular church. It was the organized dogma and rituals of the religious organizations that bothered Muir, not the belief in God. He always remained firmly in awe of God's creations, especially in the mountains of California.

But, despite his love of nature, it surprised many people when John Muir married Wanda Strenzel on April 14, 1880, and settled into a rather ordinary life raising grapes on a farm in Martinez, California. Muir, as usual, was frugal, and saved almost every penny he made. At the end of ten years, he reportedly had accumulated $100,000. It was a huge nest egg for most people. For John Muir, a man with simple needs, it was more money than he would ever need in his lifetime.

What the money brought, however, was Muir's ability to travel beyond California. He visited his birthplace in Scotland, finally made it to the Amazon River, and traveled to New York and Arizona. He went to Alaska on five occasions between 1879 and 1899, primarily to study the massive glaciers. But he also collected specimens of flora and fauna. In 1881, he ventured north aboard the cutter *Thomas Corwin*, where he explored Wrangell Island and visited Lawrence Island, where 1,500 people had died of starvation just two years earlier. Also on the trip was Edward Nelson, who was collecting specimens for the Smithsonian Institution. One of the plants that Muir brought back from Alaska was sent to Asa Gray, who named the new species for Muir.

In 1899, John Muir was invited to go to Alaska as part of the Harriman Expedition, organized by E. H. Harriman. Also invited was the other major nature writer of the generation, John Burroughs. Muir and Burroughs became fast friends, and they shared an overall vision of nature and the involvement of humans. In retrospect, naturalists from any era would have been thrilled to have been part of the expedition and interact with the two noted chroniclers of nature at the end of the nineteenth century.

Burroughs was born in 1837, just a year prior to John Muir, and the two men had other similarities beyond age. Both were influenced by Ralph Waldo Emerson. Both reflected at great length on the connections between humans and nature. Both influenced thousands through their essays and philosophies. Both were sought after by notables of the day to be guides on wilderness and rural trips (Emerson, Roosevelt, Gray, Hooker, C. Hart Merriam to Muir; Thomas Edison, Henry Ford to Burroughs), and both were keen proponents of a simple, rural life.

Of the two, Burroughs was probably the more adamant about the virtues of the country and the evils of the city. The movement of people to the city he called a "spiritual catastrophe." Whereas Burroughs preferred quiet and was not overly outgoing, Muir loved to talk. Burroughs was comfortable with his writing, and he produced over two dozen books of essays in his lifetime. Muir always felt inadequate with his writing, and most of his writing was not published until late in life. Neither man was relaxed in front of audiences. Yet, they remained friends, despite Burroughs's occasional need for solitude.

"He is very entertaining," Burroughs once said of Muir. "But he sometimes talks when I want to be let alone; at least he did up in Alaska."

Ten years after the Harriman Expedition ended, Burroughs and Muir arranged to meet in the west, prior to Burroughs's visit to Hawaii. The two rendezvoused in the little town of Adamana, Arizona, and the friends were truly excited about spending time together. So, too, were Burroughs's traveling companions, who were in awe of not only being around Burroughs, but to have John Muir as their guide. The next day, Muir took his visitors out to some of the petrified forests in the vicinity. There were five in all, and Muir and his daughter had been the first to discover one of them when they were exploring the desert a few years earlier.

Muir kept the visitors entertained with a continual monologue of his adventures, quotations, scientific facts, and theories. Burroughs was in awe of almost everything that he saw, especially after a long train trip on the Santa Fe across what he considered to be monotonous and boring stretches of flat Kansas.

The Grand Canyon thoroughly amazed John Burroughs, who called the sight the "Divine Abyss." Even after the party departed the canyon for camping in the Mojave Desert, and the relative civilization of San Bernardino, Riverside, and Pasadena, in California, Burroughs's thoughts were back at the Grand Canyon. Later, Muir guided his visitors to his favorite places in Yosemite, and Burroughs could appreciate why the valley held such a fascination for John Muir.

Although both men were in their seventies, Muir still had little time for food or rest. Burroughs required just the opposite, and he was continually teased by his friend, who told him, "You can sleep when you get back home, or, at least in the grave." It was somewhat like the advice that Muir gave Ralph Waldo Emerson and his friends when they visited the Sierra Nevada more than 38 years earlier.

Despite the good-natured teasing, the two naturalists of the new order did enjoy each other's company. When Muir was in New York City, and kept postponing a visit to Burroughs's home in the

Catskills two years later, Burroughs became frustrated. He was anxious to see his soul mate and show him Burroughs's own familiar part of nature. Yet, money and fame meant little to either man. Muir eventually would receive honorary degrees from Yale, Harvard, the University of California at Berkeley, and his old alma mater, the University of Wisconsin at Madison. Burroughs routinely turned down such offers if they proved to be inconvenient. Burroughs died in 1921, seven years after Muir, the other major nature writer of the time.

Before his death, however, Muir had other uses for his nest egg, accumulated from his sales of grapes. He involved himself in issues relating to conservation, the creation of national parks and wilderness areas, and other efforts "to entice people to look at Nature's loveliness." It took years of effort, but Muir is generally credited with being the prime force behind the creation of Yosemite National Park. His efforts and philosophies also influenced the eventual preservation of the Grand Canyon and Petrified Forest in Arizona, and the Kings Canyon and Sequoia tracts in California.

Muir had his share of plants and animals named for him, including a rock rabbit from Yosemite and a butterfly from the Sierras, *Thecla muiri*. He also discovered several new species of plants and butterflies. But it was his conservation legacy—largely the result of his writings—that provided the lasting legacy. Even a century later, his name is attached to lakes, trails, parks, campsites, mountains, and towns in at least three states.

One of the joys of John Muir's teenaged years on the family farm in Wisconsin was the arrival of passenger pigeons:

> *It was a great memorable day when the first flock of passenger pigeons came to our farm. . . . [O]f all God's feathered people that sailed the Wisconsin sky, no other bird seemed to us so wonderful. The beautiful wanderers flew like the winds in flocks of millions from climate to climate in accord with the weather, finding their food—acorns, beechnuts, pine-nuts, cranberries, strawberries, huckleberries, juniper berries, hackberries, buckwheat, rice, wheat,*

oats, corn—in fields and forests thousands of miles apart. I have seen flocks streaming south in the fall so large that they were flowing over from horizon to horizon in an almost continuous stream all day long, at the rate of forty or fifty miles an hour, like a mighty river in the sky, widening, contracting, descending like falls and cataracts, and rising suddenly here and there in huge ragged masses like high-splashing spray.

The last passenger pigeon on earth died, alone and caged, in a zoo in Cincinnati on September 1, 1914. It was the same year that John Muir died. The year marked the extinction of a species and the loss of someone who fought to save species of plants and animals. Muir would be the first to mourn the passing of the passenger pigeon, but his efforts at conservation, nature writing, and preservation surely saved countless other plants and animals from similar tragic fates.

Chapter 13

DIGGING UP BONES

Sitting in a classroom at Yale University, Othniel Marsh and Clarence King became very familiar with Charles Wilkes's U.S. Exploring Expedition and the scientists on board. One of the "scientifics" on the expedition was their professor, James Dwight Dana.

Any type of science, when presented in a classroom setting and in an eastern university, could easily become boring and uninspiring. At Yale, however, Dana told stories about naturalists sailing among monstrous Antarctic icebergs, battling Fiji natives, hiking to the top of Mauna Loa—the active Hawaiian volcano—and discovering a deposit of fossils on a mountain of coastal Oregon. Dana's firsthand experiences with the four-year-long Exploring Expedition whetted the appetites of not only Marsh and King, but of dozens of prospective naturalists as well.

Unfortunately for students at Yale in the 1850s and 1860s, the days of virgin collecting in the American west were long gone. No longer could a Thomas Nuttall stroll along a beach in San Diego, as he did in 1836, bend over and discover 15 new species of crustaceans and 21 new molluscs just while he awaited the departure of his ship.

By the late nineteenth century, most of the west had been visited by at least one professional naturalist at some time or another. This is not to say that there were no new species of plants or animals to discover. Far from it. With patience, an observant field biologist could still find biological variations. Such discoveries continue to be made into modern times. But, the common forms of life in the west—those abundant or easily accessible—had long since been poked, prodded, and described.

One area of natural history, however, was still in its infancy in the west: paleontology and the discovery of ancient fossils and bones—particularly those of dinosaurs.

Most naturalists collected some fossils in the course of their travels. But this often was related more to their personal curiosities about natural subjects rather than specialized knowledge on the subject. Lewis and Clark found fossils on their epic trip westward, and Meriwether Lewis visited Big Bone Lick, the dinosaur bone deposit near Cincinnati, with a local paleontologist in 1803. But most fossil collectors were amateurs. Thomas Say was an exception. A talented zoologist and entomologist, he also was a fossil expert in the early part of the nineteenth century, and others often brought him their specimens for identification or description. But dinosaur bones and their pursuers were another story entirely.

Paleontology is essentially a marriage between the biological and the physical worlds. Competent paleontologists must have more than a working knowledge of geology because identifying the age of geologic deposits can aid in dating the fossils of plants and animals that are trapped within. In many ways, paleontology is like a giant puzzle. Scientists uncover the partial remains of creatures that no longer exist and often bare little resemblance to modern animals. Paleontologists must then place these strange forms in some sort of classification, and this may be based on only a portion of the skeleton. To become such an expert requires a special kind of person, with extensive experience and access to a diverse reference collection.

Many of the great surveys in the west following the Civil War had a strong geology/paleontology focus. Those who were especially keen on the subject attracted the attentions of the public, and soon "bone picking" became as competitive and highly charged as any natural history pursuit.

All of the students at Yale's Sheffield Scientific School took an ample sampling of liberal arts classes along with their science subjects. But even in science, students such as Othniel Marsh and Clarence King followed the lead of professors James Dana and Benjamin Silliman. Faculty whetted the appetites of students in many fields, and students often found they had wide interests by the time their studies were completed.

Clarence King was a native of Newport, Rhode Island, who graduated from Yale in 1862, a member of the first class to receive bachelor of science degrees from the new Sheffield School. Although King retained a general curiosity about fossils, his interests shifted more toward geology. So, after some brief study of glacial geology under Alexander Agassiz, King joined his boyhood friend, James Terry Gardner, and headed to California.

While King attended Yale, Gardner had studied at what is today Rensselaer Polytechnic Institute in New York. Gardner's health was frail, and both young men reasoned that the climate in California would be much more conducive to improving Gardner's condition. It took some convincing of family members, but with the Civil War in full force, their sons avoiding the conflict seemed prudent to both families. The trip to California was an adventure in itself, dodging battlegrounds in the east, then traveling by horseback with a wagon train heading west.

King and Gardner spent four years with the California Geological Survey, led by Josiah Whitney, the brother of one of King's teachers at Yale, William Whitney. In California, King earned his reputation as a geologist and surveyor and James Gardner became a renowned mapmaker.

Back in Washington, D.C., Clarence King used his Yale contacts and other recommendations to organize the Fortieth Parallel Expedition—one of the more important western surveys that would include, among other things, paleontological collections. This experience, in turn, led to King's appointment as the first director of the U.S. Geological Survey when the agency was created in 1879. Recommendations for his appointment were provided by James Dana, Spencer Baird, and many other notable scientists of the day.

King only lasted in the post for a year before he retired and turned the agency over to explorer and geologist John Wesley Powell. But King's long interest in fossils would lead to increasing emphasis in the field by federal and private collectors in the last third of the nineteenth century. Fortunately for the field of paleontology, Powell also had a lifelong interest in fossils, and he continued to support such endeavors by U.S. Geological Survey crews. Powell, in fact, included an amateur geologist and paleontologist, John Stewart, on Powell's second expedition down the Colorado River. Powell and Stewart had met while both men were searching for fossils in Union earthworks prior to the battle of Vicksburg during the Civil War.

From the early days when Thomas Say and a few other scientists developed reputations as paleontologists of one type or another, the field developed rapidly in the middle of the century. Part of this was due to the strong interest in fossils by Ferdinand Hayden. Hayden was already teaching schoolchildren when he was only 16 years old, and collecting rocks, fossils, and other curiosities in his spare time. At age 18, he enrolled in Oberlin College and, after graduating, entered Albany Medical School. There, he made friends with Dr. John Newberry, a part-time geologist, and James Hall, a paleontologist, both of whom had connections with Spencer Baird and the Smithsonian Institution. Newberry and Hall would both leave their marks in fields of natural history, and they sparked interest in the physical sciences for young Hayden as well. After receiving his M.D. in 1853, Hayden took off to the White River area of South Dakota's Badlands, accompanied by another paleontologist, Fielding Meek.

In the 1850s, there were few nationally renowned authorities in paleontology, but one certainly was Leo Lesquereux, a Swiss immigrant who became a specialist in mosses. He developed a solid reputation as a paleobotanist. He was 40 years old when he immigrated to the United States, and he was completely deaf. Despite his handicap, Lesquereux worked closely with botanist Asa Gray for many years, and also was quite knowledgeable about invertebrate fossils. But his particular interest was plants. In 1876, he responded to a question about why he considered such work important: "Vegetation is in absolute relation with atmospheric circumstances, the fossil plants are, indeed, the written records of the atmospheric and physical conditions of our earth."

Lesquereux was routinely contacted when many of the great post-war surveys returned from their topography and natural history expeditions in the west. Spencer Baird often relied on the paleobotanist to describe the fossil plants, and Lesquereux was still producing important monographs long after the many surveys were combined into the U.S. Geological Survey. Clarence King, during his brief tenure as director, and John Wesley Powell turned to naturalist authorities to produce scientific monographs for the survey. In the late nineteenth century, John Newberry (fossil fishes), Charles Wolcott (fossils), Othniel Marsh (fossil vertebrates), and Samuel Scudder (insects) all produced monographs for the government that sold for $1.00 to $8.40 each (the latter was for a 775-page publication, plus appendices). Leo Lesquereux's monograph on *The Flora of the Dakotas Group* was published posthumously in 1891. U.S. Geological Society bulletins were shorter, and sold for 5 to 25 cents each and included natural history papers by Scudder, Wolcott, Charles White, John H. Clarke, William Dall, and others.

In his preface to Lesquereux's *Flora* monograph, F. H. Knowlton called Lesquereux America's "most distinguished vegetable paleontologist ... [and] her foremost bryologist ... as well as a genial companion, a kindly critic, and a sympathetic friend." Lesquereux's publications were too numerous to count, yet he was a very modest man, who once remarked in a letter in 1884 that, of his publications, "I have forgotten many and many are not worth much."

The other principal authority on fossils of the time was Joseph Leidy, of the University of Pennsylvania and (later) Swarthmore College. Leidy was the undisputed expert on vertebrate paleontology and, when Hayden and Meek returned with bones that they excavated in the Dakotas, they shipped the specimens to Leidy.

Leidy was the prototype, old-time scientist who had developed a reputation over the years in his specialty—something at the time considerably less glamorous than those involving live plants and animals. His reputation was secured by his discovery of the remains of the unusual-looking duckbilled dinosaur (*Hadrosaurus*) in 1858. By the time his career ended, Leidy was credited with describing 130 new genera and over 300 new species of fossil vertebrates.

As Hayden and Meek continued their surveys prior to and after the Civil War, they continued to send specimens to Lesquereux and Leidy—especially in the 1850s and 1860s. So many arrived in Pennsylvania that Leidy was able to publish his classic text, *The Ancient Fauna of Nebraska*. In it, and in separate papers, Leidy discussed the discovery of bones from ancient horses and his theories on the evolution of the horse. This not only had ramifications for Charles Darwin's theories on evolution, but it indicated that horses as well as camels and other creatures had been part of the North American landscape long before the arrival of the Spanish in the fifteenth century.

Ferdinand Hayden's contributions to natural history and paleontology are probably less widely known than are his contributions to geology and geography. But his interests in all branches of science were reflected in the operations of his many surveys. He always kept an eye open for the unusual, and so too did those who worked for him. He sent numerous specimens of insects and fossils to Spencer Baird at the Smithsonian Institution and even arranged for a specimen of the rare black-footed ferret to be sent to Baird in 1868.

It was in 1867 and 1868 that Hayden and Meek explored what is today Agate Fossil Beds National Monument in Nebraska. In 1871 and 1872, Hayden led the first scientific parties into the Yellowstone region, and it was partly through his efforts that the unusual geological area eventually was protected as Yellowstone National Park. Hayden became a professor at the University of Pennsylvania in 1872, and the remnants of his survey organization were merged with other such surveys into the U.S. Geological Survey in 1879.

Hayden and King and several others involved with post–Civil War surveys were instrumental in promoting the discovery, description, and classification of fossils. But, by the early 1870s, Joseph

Leidy had become less of a factor in the emerging field of dinosaur bones.

There were several reasons for this. First, government agencies and expeditions were now funding many of the excavations, and specimens were being turned over to a new group of paleontologists, especially those associated with the Smithsonian Institution. Joseph Leidy found that funding was becoming more difficult to obtain.

Second, and more important, the field of vertebrate paleontology was now being dominated by two men: Edward Drinker Cope of Philadelphia, and Othniel Charles Marsh of Yale University. Both men were independently wealthy and relentless collectors who considered any bones to be personal property—no matter where they might be buried.

And Cope and Marsh hated each other.

Both men were talented in their field and both considered keeping the other from discoveries to be almost as important as the discoveries themselves. Their petty bickering and jealousy alienated the entire community of bone pickers. But, at the same time, intense competition led to economic opportunities for amateur paleontologists. If Cope wasn't interested in buying a dinosaur bone, than Marsh probably was—even if it was only to keep it away from Cope. Science, ethics, property rights, and even cultural sympathies for Native Americans were tossed aside in the rush to gain notoriety.

It was partly this intense rivalry between Cope and Marsh and their questionable collection techniques that led to Joseph Leidy's virtual disappearance from national prominence in paleontology. Leidy was at least a little jealous of the unlimited personal finances available to the other two scientists. He certainly couldn't compete with the others in terms of financial resources. But he also openly questioned their collection techniques. How much his retreat from active field work was due to the former and how much to the latter is unknown. Whatever the reasons, Leidy's scientific ethics were never questioned.

The two men who did emerge as the leading figures in vertebrate paleontology were both flamboyant and extremely competent. They both gained experience working for others in the worlds of geology and paleontology, fossil collection, and western surveys, but they came from very different backgrounds.

Edward Cope was nine years younger than his rival, born in 1840 in Philadelphia. Even at the age of six he could recite the names of dinosaurs, and the subject remained his passion throughout his life. The son of wealthy Quaker parents, he could afford to pursue paleontology, even if the financial rewards of the profession were far from being lucrative.

After a year of study under Joseph Leidy at the University of Pennsylvania, and time with Spencer Baird, Cope entered a near 10-year association as a paleontologist with the Hayden survey (1870–1879), with one year (1874) working for the competing Wheeler survey. By 1889, Cope had become a professor at the University of Pennsylvania, following in the footsteps of other naturalists, such as Benjamin Smith Barton, Leidy, and Hayden.

Othniel Marsh, meanwhile, also came from a prominent and wealthy eastern family. His uncle, George Peabody, would found Yale's Peabody Museum. Even as a boy, O. C. Marsh was fascinated by fossils and bones. Growing up in upstate New York, he often followed after workmen who were excavating parts of the Erie Canal. Marsh would sift through the tailings to look for fossils.

Further inspired by James Dana and his other professors at Yale, he studied in Europe during much of the Civil War and returned to be appointed a professor of paleontology at Yale—the first such professorship in the United States. Marsh's explorations in the west began in 1869 when he was 37 years old, and they came about almost by accident.

Even today, field trips associated with scientific meetings are relatively common. In 1868, the Union Pacific Railroad offered attendees at the annual meeting of the American Association for the Advancement of Science in Chicago a chance to ride the railroad to its (then) westernmost point. Marsh decided to take advantage of the offer and rode the train to the end of the tracks, some 60 miles west of Benton, Wyoming.

Marsh was immediately transfixed by the beautiful country and its potential Garden of Eden possibilities for deposits of ancient bones. As he crossed the plains, he noted, "There must be the remains of many strange animals new to science." This initial trip in 1868 marked the beginning of an almost 30-year period of collecting by Marsh, his students, and his teams of professional diggers.

Marsh tried to organize a trip to the west in 1869, but hostile tribes kept him away. The following year, however, Marsh was back, accompanied by a team of Yale graduate students—all of them armed to the teeth with all manner of weapons. The group left June 30, 1870, and traveled by train across Nebraska to Fort McPherson, near the North Platte River. There, they picked up an armed escort, two Pawnee scouts, Buffalo Bill Cody, and several other experienced western hands.

The party spent weeks crisscrossing the North Platte country, eventually excavating numerous fossils in a large, ancient bed along the Loup Fork. Among the prizes were primitive horses, camels, and a mastodon.

From Fort McPherson, they traveled to Fort Russell in Wyoming, and then found a Miocene-era formation in northern Colorado. Finally, they traveled to the site of Ferdinand Hayden and Fielding Meek's discoveries along the White River in South Dakota. There, they found remains of birds, early turtles, primitive rodents, and a horned creature that had a jaw that alone measured four feet in length.

Before returning to Yale, Marsh treated his students to a trip to Salt Lake City, where Marsh discussed his fossil horse discoveries with Brigham Young. Young was fascinated with the subject, not only because of his own curiosity, but also because he felt that the remains tended to support Church beliefs about the origins of the Mormon people and the significance of their return to "The Promised Land" of Utah. Obviously, the inland region had been the site of abundant life long ago.

After a final side trip to Yosemite National Park, the paleontologists returned east by way of Kansas. There they were escorted by armed cavalry troops because of hostile Cheyenne bands in the area. Despite the obvious danger, the scientists kept their eyes peeled downward and uncovered the bones of giant monosaurs—35-foot-long sea creatures from millions of years ago.

When the party returned to New Haven, Connecticut, it returned with 35 boxes of bones and a lifetime of adventures.

This would be the pattern of subsequent Yale expeditions to the west. Marsh and his students traveled west in 1871, 1872, 1873, and 1874, each time by train as close as possible to new and previously discovered fossil beds. They always arranged for a military escort, a favor from Marsh's government and military contacts. Each trip was largely financed by Marsh's personal funds, and he retained control and credit for all discoveries.

On each trip to the west, Marsh would enlist new collectors to search in the months that he was absent, especially in Wyoming and Colorado. Edward Cope did the same, and the two men were always hiring field collectors away from each other. The network of bone collectors would contact Marsh or Cope in the east, and one or the other often purchased specimens. Unfortunately, much of the scientific evidence was lost in such excavations. Instead of slowly extracting a skeleton, bone-by-bone, while mapping and drawing each step, the bone collectors were primarily interested in the end product: a fossil bone that could be exchanged for money or at least some share in the notoriety of the discovery. Excavations often were made quickly and with resultant destruction to the surrounding fossil beds.

Marsh, too, engaged in such practices when he was in the field. His objective was to extract the bones quickly and ship them back to Yale where, he reasoned, he could examine them at his leisure.

Two of the knowledgeable collectors who were hired by Marsh and Cope were Benjamin Franklin Mudge—later a professor at the University of Kansas—and Arthur Lakes—a longtime professor at the Colorado School of Mines. Mudge was born in Maine and became a lawyer in Massachusetts and mayor of the town of Lynn. During the Civil War, he moved to Kansas and became the state's first state geologist in 1864. Long interested in fossils, he helped to organize the Kansas Natural History Society. When he lost his faculty position at the State Agricultural College, he was hired by O. C. Marsh to collect fossils in Kansas and Colorado. Later, he accepted a position at the University of Kansas. Many of Marsh's collections of fish, reptile, and bird fossils from Kansas were collected by Mudge and his assistants.

Arthur Lakes was born in Martock, Somerset, England, in 1844 and was educated for two years at Queen's College at Oxford University. He left school before graduation and immigrated to the United States. There, he taught writing and drawing at Jarvis Hall, a preparatory school in Golden, Colorado, that eventually would become the Colorado School of Mines.

Geology and paleontology were always Lakes's hobbies, and in his spare time, he wandered the mountains of Colorado, looking for unusual outcroppings. He was an active collector of fossils for Leo Lesquereux, some of which ended up being described in annual reports for the Hayden survey.

While in Colorado, Lakes became an Episcopal minister, traveling between mining camps. The travel allowed him even more time to study geology and fossils in the mountains. Lakes knew of both Cope and Marsh from their publications and, at various times, both men would employ him as a collector. This was fortunate, because Lakes supported himself through teaching, his traveling ministry, and bone digging.

While Lakes pursued his interests in the mountains of Colorado, the rivalry between Marsh and Cope intensified, as did their incessant desire to uncover more bones. Marsh's most notorious episode occurred in 1874. Many of the best fossil beds in South Dakota also happened to be located on Indian lands, especially in the Black Hills and the Badlands. But such designations meant little to Marsh, who could be ruthless in his collecting. Private property ownership and treaty reservations meant nothing if there were fossils buried there.

At the Red Cloud Indian Agency on November 4, 1874, Marsh and his team arrived ready to dig, only to find that the Lakota had refused to give him permission to excavate fossils from a bed that was located on tribal land. Despite his military connections, Marsh was rebuffed because of cultural and other tribal concerns.

Undaunted, Marsh waited until after midnight before traveling to the fossil beds under cover of darkness. There, Marsh and his team hurriedly excavated the grounds using the light from oil lanterns. By morning, they had filled several wagons with fossil bones. The Lakota noticed the diggings the next day, and the scientists exited from the area just ahead of an irate war party.

Later, Marsh would make some amends by helping tribes during a government scandal involving cheating Indian agents, but his callous attitude in collecting was not atypical.

Edward Cope was not above such practices himself, and the intense rivalry between the two men reached its pinnacle in 1877 when two sets of collectors, working independently of each other in Colorado, made important discoveries at sites just 100 miles apart. One collector contacted Cope and the other contacted Marsh, and the competition was on. Science suffered as each group tried to steal, destroy, and hide bones collected by the other. The two sites, at Morrison and Cañon City, became the scenes of frantic excavations, theft, betrayal, bribes, and outright destruction of specimens—all to keep Cope or Marsh from getting the notoriety of the discoveries.

The amateur collector who discovered the Morrison site was Arthur Lakes, the part-time teacher and minister. In March 1877, Lakes had completed his Sunday preaching in one of the mountain mining camps, and had agreed to go collecting with Henry C. Beckwith, a retired navy captain, at a promising site. Encouraged by what they saw, they returned the next day and encountered something unusual at a site three miles south of Morrison. Lakes recounted the moment in his journal:

"Here then was the cast of a very large bone belonging to some gigantic animal. . . . We soon traced the loose slab to the parent rock of brown sandstone from which it had slipped and as I jumped on top of the ledge there at my feet lay a monstrous vertebra carved, as it were, in bas relief on a flat slab of sandstone."

The large bone was 33 inches in circumference.

"We stood for a moment without speaking, gazing in astonishment at this prodigy and threw our hats in the air and hurrahed."

Within a week, Lakes wrote to O. C. Marsh at Yale University and sent some bone samples to whet the paleontologist's interests in buying the larger bones. But Marsh didn't reply immediately, so Lakes wrote to his competitor, Edward Cope, and sent some other samples. But, before Cope could reply, Marsh announced that the bones were from a new dinosaur species and offered to hire Lakes at $100 per month to do more excavations. He even promised a raise in salary to $125 if the find was productive.

It was an attractive offer, especially when Jarvis Hall burned down and Lakes temporarily lost his teaching income. Throwing themselves into their work, Lakes and Beckwith soon shipped almost a ton of bones back east to Marsh. Lakes spent the winter of 1878–1879 at Yale, studying his finds and increasing his own knowledge of paleontology by working with Marsh. The following year, Lakes moved to Como Bluff, Wyoming, another famous deposit, where he learned from another pioneer paleontologist, William Harlow Reed—although the two men disliked each other intensely—along with paleontologist Benjamin Mudge and entomologist Samuel Scudder.

This practical experience with some of the leading field scientists at two of the most important fossil sites in the west led to Lake's appointment in 1880 at the newly reconstructed Colorado School of Mines in Golden. He later worked for the U.S. Geological Survey, was western editor for *Mines and Minerals*, and published numerous scientific papers—all due to his chance discovery at Morrison and the evolving competition between Cope and Marsh.

This competition had been brewing since the days when Cope and Marsh were part of the Wheeler and Hayden surveys. Cope included disparaging remarks about Marsh in his reports for the Wheeler survey, only to have Lieutenant George M. Wheeler, the survey leader, edit the comments out of the scientific summaries. Marsh, in turn, complained to Wheeler about Cope, and soon everyone involved in geology or paleontology seemed to be involved in scientific politics. Wheeler directed Cope to send some specimens to Marsh, but the Yale scientist complained that Cope intentionally sent only worthless fragments. Marsh, in turn, disliked Ferdinand Hayden because the Hayden survey supported many of Cope's excavations.

To Cope and Marsh, people were either pro-Cope or pro-Marsh. If not, such people should simply stay away from the field of vertebrate paleontology. At one point, Marsh reportedly hijacked a trainload of fossil bones from Cope and sent it back to Yale. Once the fossils were stored with Marsh's other material, it was difficult to determine whether Cope's claims had merit.

Although the Smithsonian Institution and the U.S. Geological Survey did some collecting and archiving of fossils, the federal government was hardly in the same financial or even academic league with Cope and Marsh. So, eventually, O. C. Marsh was asked to collect directly for the U.S. government. At first, Marsh declined, stating that, since his expeditions were privately financed, he was under no obligation to the federal government or anyone else. His specimens were and would continue to be his personal property.

Eventually, however, Marsh relented and agreed to become paleontologist with the U.S. Geological Survey. Later, he also added the title of honorary curator of the Department of Paleontology at the U.S. National Museum. He even agreed to donate duplicate specimens to government museums, and several times before his death in 1899 (just two years after the death of his rival), Marsh sent freight train loads of specimens to Washington. After his death, he had arranged for another five freight car loads—some 80 tons—to be deposited in Washington.

Clearly, both Marsh and Cope were authorities in the field of vertebrate paleontology, and their discoveries captured the imagination of the general public, especially after full skeletons of primitive animals began to be exhibited widely in museums. But neither man was considered prolific in publishing the fruits of his knowledge.

What work Marsh did publish was significant. His *Odontornithes, or The Extinct Toothed Birds of North America*, published in 1880, and a part of the results from the King survey, was a classic. And his discoveries of fossil horses in Nebraska essentially made his reputation. Although Joseph Leidy first explored the evolution of fossil horses in North America, Marsh's work was a substantial improvement, based on considerably more fossil evidence of the existence of horses back to the Miocene era. But so much of O. C. Marsh's collections remained undescribed at the time of his death that it took federal scientists decades to bring their knowledge up to the level of Marsh's.

Edward Cope also was slow to publish his material. He disliked criticism, especially editorial comments, and fought with Lieutenant George Wheeler constantly during the publication of the Wheeler survey reports. Cope wanted to make changes in the galley proofs—when the text is set in type—something few scientists would consider doing at such a late stage, except for printer's errors. Yet, like Marsh, the contributions of Edward Cope to paleontology were noteworthy. While Joseph Leidy published his monograph on *The Ancient Fauna of Nebraska*, Cope did an early paper on such prehistoric animals of Kansas.

Cope claimed the discovery of the flying saurian, *Ornithochirus harpyia*—a discovery also claimed and named by Marsh. Cope did discover the *Eobasileus*, a rhinoceros-like animal that Cope modestly called, "The most extraordinary fossil mammal found in North America."

Publications aside, two of Cope's enduring legacies were the discovery of Eocene fossil beds in northern New Mexico, while working with the Wheeler survey in 1874, and his excavations along Bitter Creek and Bridger Basin in Wyoming in 1872. In the summer of 1872, Cope returned home with 50 new species of fossil birds, lizards, fishes, turtles, snakes, crocodiles, and quadrupeds from those Wyoming sites—only to be struck down by a debilitating bout of mountain fever for most of that winter.

Fortunately for the progress of paleontology in North America, both O. C. Marsh and Edward Cope were gone from the scene by 1899. Later scientists could pursue their excavations at a slower pace. Public interest in dinosaurs would remain high, but the pace of wanton excavation slowed significantly.

Chapter 14

THE NEW ENTHUSIASTIC
AMATEURS

To many people, the living legacy of John Muir is Yosemite National Park. One can scarcely think of Muir without associating him with the Sierra Nevada and its most famous national park.

But Muir's contribution to natural history extends much further. Before Muir, in the era of the great surveys, plants, animals, and fossils were regarded as objects to collect, illustrate, and describe. It was important to classify all new forms of life encountered in the American west into appropriate scientific categories. As theories of evolution and selection were becoming widely accepted, naturalists attempted to place things in some sort of universal order.

After Muir, and because of his writings, there was little need to collect what was now largely familiar. It was now more important to think not which plants and animals were in the west, but why they were there and how they fit into their environment and with humans.

This change in approach did not occur overnight, nor has the collection phase completely disappeared. New species are discovered every year, but modern scientists rely on more molecular methods of description—genetics rather than solely meristics. Or the new naturalists seek more specialized areas of natural history, where previous collectors have not been as thorough.

One such specialist was Elam Bartholomew, a Kansas farmer and occasional politician. His avocation was horticulture and, in particular, fungal biology.

This interest grew from his farming. Many of the plant diseases that he encountered seemed to be related to fungi of one form or another. But Elam's interest in botany extended back even further. When he was 30 years old, in 1882, he noted in his journal about going "up the creek about two miles in the a.m. collecting botanical specimens."

Bartholomew spent his early years in Illinois and most of his adult life in Kansas. But it was the western prairies where he pursued his interests in plants. He tried to identify everything that he encountered. For almost half a century, he was at least a part-time plant naturalist. Since many of the species had been discovered and described years before, Bartholomew's passion was discovering new species for his personal list. Eventually, though, despite botanizing in an area of the west that had been scoured by naturalists for decades, Bartholomew began to encounter rare and undescribed species, and in 1886, Bartholomew noted in his journal his discovery of several plants new to his county.

In 1884, Bartholomew spent time collecting with Professor E. Plank, a botanist of regional notoriety who was compiling a monograph on the flora of Kansas. During the following years, Bartholomew increased his practical knowledge of botany by undertaking repeated field excursions with Plank and two other professors from the Agricultural College at Manhattan (now Kansas State University), William Kellerman and George Failyer.

Some of these trips were on foot, while others were on horseback, and on many occasions, students from the college (now university) sought out Bartholomew's expertise. One day, Elam awoke to find his horse dead beside him. It was apparently due to natural causes and hardly a life-threatening event (except for the horse) as it might have been in the days of Thomas Nuttall, but it nevertheless was traumatic and caused delays in the botanical collecting.

One piece of advice from the college professors would prove fruitful to Bartholomew. Kansas flora was becoming widely recognized, and Elam was advised to specialize—to find a niche where knowledge was sparse. He started to pursue this in his journal entry of February 19, 1887: "Spent the forenoon in botanizing among the mosses, lichens, and stump fungi."

By 1889, Bartholomew was credited with discovering several new species of fungi, and one of them, *Diplodina bartholomi,* was named after him by William Kellerman.

This specialization led to connections between specific fungi and plant and animal diseases, including "corn-stalk disease of cattle." It was Bartholomew who advocated the idea that fungi can act as germs—something that was just then being published by physicians in medical journals.

Bartholomew was not a trained medical scientist, so the specific connection between fungi and disease was left to others. Elam contributed to the identification and classification of the fungi, and he also conducted field tests of the efficacy of various fungicides on crops. Bartholomew's expertise with fungi started to spread, and soon he was being paid to collect specimens for scientists in other parts of the country. Prof. F. S. Earle, of Auburn University, contracted with Elam to obtain 500 specimens of fungi. It took Elam three full days to obtain the samples, then ship them to Alabama—all for his $25.00 fee.

The significance of Bartholomew's work is that, despite his lack of formal education, Kansas State University awarded him an honorary master of science degree in 1898 and an honorary doctor of science degree in 1922. Publication of his treatise, *Fungus Flora of Kansas,* increased the known species in the state from 465 to 1,829. His personal herbarium/fungus collection totaled 40,000 specimens and was incorporated into the Farlow Herbarium Collection at Harvard University. Bartholomew's fungus collection probably accounted for half of the world's known species at that time.

Like Elam Bartholomew, enthusiastic amateurs had the potential to still make important natural history discoveries well into the late nineteenth century. Bartholomew did it by specializing in his curiosity. Others made their contributions by examining animal behavior—not just the quantitative descriptions of dead specimens, but the natural behavior of live animals.

One such pioneer in this field was Florence Merriam.

Florence was born to be a naturalist. Yet, for years, most people would have believed that avocation was more closely suited to her older brother, C. Hart Merriam. Hart and Florence's father encouraged a love of the outdoors for his children growing up in New York.

When the elder Merriam served as a congressman in Washington, D.C., he arranged a meeting with his son, Hart, and Spencer Baird, then the assistant secretary of the Smithsonian Institution. Baird hired Hart as an ornithologist for the Hayden survey that was then exploring the geological features of the Rocky Mountains. Hart had considerable knowledge of wild animals, especially birds, but his father's political position obviously helped. Hart was only 16 years old.

Baird's decision to hire the young man proved correct. When the expedition ended, Hart Merriam returned with 313 bird skins and 67 nests and bird eggs for the Smithsonian collection. That taste of natural history would never leave Hart Merriam, and although he went on to receive his medical degree in 1879 and practiced medicine back in New York for several years, he remained in touch with many avid naturalists.

Florence, meanwhile, maintained an avid curiosity of local bird life, and after being educated at Mrs. Piatt's School in Utica, New York, she went off to Smith College in 1882. Florence was 19 and in somewhat frail health. Yet, she enjoyed herself at the relatively new college.

She was not accepted as a regular student, however. Because she lacked the educational background for regular admission, she was enrolled as a "special student," a stigma that affected her during most of her college career and later in life. In her own mind, she felt inadequate: her father and brother were prominent locally and nationally, yet the daughter carried the label of "special student."

Smith was too new to have formal science programs for an

enrollment exclusively of women. A professor from Amherst was even hired to come over to Northampton, Massachusetts, to teach geology. But, despite that shortcoming, Florence and the others at the college received training in English, writing, ethics, philosophy, religion, art, and music.

During her first years at Smith, Florence maintained a low-key interest in local birds—something she pursued with the encouragement of her brother. Hart, meanwhile, was balancing his medical practice with his continuing interest in natural history. He was one of the founders of the American Ornithologists Union and traveled to Labrador and Greenland as physician/naturalist with an expedition. He followed that experience by traveling to museums and collections in Germany. He became more of a prominent member of the eastern community of naturalists and started associating with naturalist and artist Ernest Thompson Seton (then known as Ernest Seton Thompson). At age 26, Hart gave up his medical practice and turned to natural history full-time with the U.S. Department of Agriculture. Later, his particular group—the Division of Economic Ornithology and Mammalogy— became the U.S. Biological Survey, and in the late 1880s, he became its director. Although he had broad interests in natural history, Hart's lasting legacy was with mammals, especially small mammals of the west. He tended to be a "splitter," rather than a "lumper," when it came to taxonomy and designation of species. Such individuals tend to name many animals that exhibit slight variations in form or color as being separate species, rather than lumping similar forms into a single species. It was a trait that put him at odds with his friend Theodore Roosevelt, who once criticized such practices in an article in the journal *Science*. Despite these differences of opinion, Merriam's colleagues honored the naturalist by naming numerous mammals, reptiles, fishes, and insects after him.

Florence Merriam's career in natural history can probably be traced to a college writing assignment for the Smith College Science Association. Feeling somewhat inadequate about her qualifications for writing about most science subjects, she decided to write an article on local Massachusetts birds—a subject that she knew quite well.

"I thought that, by reading up, I might write an article that would serve to interest or at least call their (the students at Smith) attention to the common birds we have here," she wrote to her brother. "And if at the same time give them a few points on general habits, etc. that they have failed to notice."

Her writing skills were obviously excellent, and two local newspapers reprinted the college assignment. It would be the first of numerous articles and books that Florence would write in her lifetime. Hart nominated his sister for membership in the American Ornithologists Union, and she became its first female associate member in 1885. She immediately plunged into causes related to birds.

At the time, an estimated 5 million birds were being killed annually for their feathers, which largely were used to adorn ladies' hats. The Ornithologists Union was proposing opposition to the bird trade, and Dr. George Grinnell, editor of *Forest and Stream*, formed the Audubon Society for the Protection of Birds—later known simply as the Audubon Society. Grinnell named the group after the man who epitomized the study of birds in North America and one who had tutored Grinnell when he was a child.

Florence Merriam took the lead and organized an Audubon chapter at Smith College and it soon had one-third of the students as members. Years later, she would organize the District of Columbia Chapter of the Audubon Society as well and teach their first bird classes for the public.

Florence became a bird expert, not by shooting and collecting bird skins, but by observing the animals in their natural surroundings. She took the protection issue to heart and was appalled when her friend, Fannie Hardy, an experienced birder and daughter of naturalist Manley Hardy, wore feather-adorned hats in public. After a chastising from Florence, and reading several articles on the bird trade (given to her by Florence), Fannie quit wearing feathers.

Florence wrote to nature writer John Burroughs and invited him to visit the Audubon group at Smith. Burroughs consented, and thoroughly enjoyed talking to a group of young women, all of whom were sitting on the grass beneath a grove of trees on the Smith campus. Burroughs and Merriam maintained a correspondence and he remained a friend and mentor to Florence, encouraging her nature writing.

This she did in newspaper articles and in the Audubon Society's magazine, *Audubon,* which was founded to better inform the society's growing membership. Florence wrote regular articles even after she "graduated" from Smith in 1886. To keep herself occupied, she engaged in various types of social work and continued her local bird watching. Technically, Florence Merriam was not able to graduate with her classmates in June 1886. As a special student, she only was awarded a certificate for completing the years of college courses. She continued to correspond with others in the class of 1886, and even contributed to the periodic class newsletters. But, to Smith College, a special student, originally enrolled with less than adequate qualifications, could never achieve full status as a college graduate.

That attitude eventually changed as college admissions and retention standards changed. Smith College saw the error in its earlier policy, especially for someone who obviously had proven her talents and intelligence, and had brought honor to the college. At the graduation ceremony in 1921, Florence Merriam belatedly received her bachelor of arts degree, 35 years after her formal schooling ended.

When the original *Audubon* ceased publication (it was later resurrected), Florence took her many articles, added some new ones, and turned the essays into a book, *Birds through the Opera Glass,* published in 1889. The same year, she made her first visit to the American west.

Although there were many reasons for visiting the wide-open spaces of the west, Florence went largely due to her frail health. She tired easily and lacked the physical strength that her mind wished that she had. Eventually, she was diagnosed as having tuberculosis. Most people—Florence included—believed that the arid climate of Utah and California would help treat her disease. Apparently it did, because, after repeated trips to sunny climates, her tuberculosis was cured by 1895.

In the meantime, she kept writing, publishing her second book, *My Summer in a Mormon Village*, in 1894; *A-Birding on a Bronco*, in 1896; and *Birds of Village and Field*, in 1899. She studied hummingbirds in California and was appointed a "field assistant" for one of Hart's biological expeditions to the Mount Shasta region of northern California.

Most family and friends of the Merriams—and probably Florence as well— believed that she would forever remain a spinster. Yet, on December 16, 1899, at age 36, she married Vernon Bailey, chief naturalist of the U.S. Biological Survey and a longtime friend of Hart Merriam. For the next three decades, the Baileys made regular trips to the west in spring and summer, returning to Washington, D.C., for the fall and winter. Most trips were devoted to scientific studies—Vernon specialized in mammalogy and herpetology but also was interested in botany. Florence remained an ornithologist. Together, the Baileys collaborated to one degree or another on several books, including *Wild Animals of Glacier National Park* in 1918. Florence continued to write articles for *St. Nicholas*—a children's magazine—as well as *The Auk, Condor,* and *Bird-Lore*. One of her most noted books, *Handbook of Birds of the Western United States*, was published in 1902—the result of many seasons spent in the west—and remained a standard guidebook for decades, much as those of Thomas Nuttall and John James Audubon had been in their day, although this guide was targeted to western birds.

Florence Merriam Bailey eventually visited New Mexico, one of the last areas of the United States with marginally known bird communities, and she and her husband made regular trips to the state. Florence remained productive well into the 1930s, publishing *Birds of New Mexico* in 1928, and *Among the Birds in Grand Canyon Country* in 1939.

Her writing style always conveyed a connection between scientific accuracy and interesting prose, in which she created a visual image of colors, sounds, and movements through words. As an example, she described a group of marsh wrens (in *Birds of Village and Field*) as follows:

The first outburst of the marsh wrens is almost paralyzing. You feel as if you had entered a factory with machines clattering on all sides. Perching atilt of the reeds, with tails on their backs, the excited little music boxes run on chattering and scolding almost in your face, diving out of sight in the cat-tails only to reappear near your hand as you search for their nests.

Florence Bailey became the first woman Fellow of the American Ornithologists Union in 1929 and was awarded the Union's Brewster Medal for her lifelong achievements. The University of New Mexico bestowed an honorary degree on the ornithologist in 1933.

Vernon Bailey, whose contributions to western natural history were far from insignificant, died in May 1942—just two months after the death of C. Hart Merriam. These deaths were devastating for Florence and ended her long string of western trips. But it didn't stop her writing. She was still engaged in nature writing and personal correspondence almost up to the day of her death six years later.

Florence Merriam Bailey epitomized the new amateur naturalists—experts in their field, to be certain, but naturalists who became focused on nature writing, in the footsteps of John Muir and John Burroughs. Yet Bailey always recalled the allure of the west, sleeping under the stars in Arizona, and becoming a part of nature:

Our sleeping bags under the sky afforded us rare moonlight and sunrise pictures and also enabled us to hear choice nocturnal calls and the first morning bird songs.

This was a sentiment expressed by a naturalist of the new order.

But, it many ways, it was similar to the joy expressed by naturalists of an earlier era, such as John Townsend, in 1834:

> *None but a naturalist can appreciate a naturalist's feelings—his delight amounting to ecstacy—when a specimen such as he has never before seen meets his eye.*

Further Reading

GENERAL ACCOUNTS

Allen, William A. *Adventures with Indians and Game,* or *Twenty Years in the Rocky Mountains.* Chicago: A. W. Bowen, 1903; reprint, Time-Life Books, 1983.

Bonta, Marcia Myers, ed. *American Women Afield: Writings by Pioneering Women Naturalists.* College Station: Texas A&M University, 1995.

Botkin, Daniel B. *Our Natural History: The Lessons of Lewis and Clark.* New York: Grosset/Putnam, 1995.

Bowles, Samuel. *Our New West.* Chicago: Hartford, 1869.

Cutter, Donald C. "Spanish Scientific Exploration along the Pacific Coast." Pp. 151–60 in Robert G. Ferris, ed., *The American West: An Appraisal.* Santa Fe: Museum of New Mexico Press, 1963.

Elman, Robert. *America's Pioneering Naturalists.* Tulsa, Okla.: Winchester Press, 1982.

Evans, Howard Ensign. *Pioneer Naturalists.* New York: Henry Holt, 1993.

Every, Dale Van. *The Final Challenge: The American Frontier, 1804–1845.* New York: William Morrow, 1964.

Farber, Paul Lawrence. *Finding Order in Nature: The Naturalist Tradition from Linnaeus to E. O. Wilson.* Baltimore: Johns Hopkins University Press, 2000.

Fleharty, Eugene D. *Wild Animals and Settlers on the Great Plains.* Norman: University of Oklahoma Press, 1995.

Flores, Dan. *The Natural West: Environmental History of the Great Plains and Rocky Mountains.* Norman: University of Oklahoma Press, 2001.

Gilbert, Bil. *The Trailblazers.* New York: Time-Life Books, 1973.

Goetzmann, William H. *New Lands, New Men: America and the Second Great Age of Discovery.* New York: Viking, 1986.

————. *Exploration and Empire: The Explorer and the Scientist in the Winning of the American West*. Austin: Texas State Historical Association, 1993.

Kastner, Joseph. *A Species of Eternity*. New York: Alfred A. Knopf, 1977.

Kohlstedt, Sally Gregory, ed. *The Origins of Natural Science in America: The Essays of George Brown Goode*. Washington, D.C.: Smithsonian Institution Press, 1991.

McKelvey, Susan Delano. *Botanical Exploration of the Trans-Mississippi West, 1790–1850*. Jamaica Plain, Mass.: Arnold Arboretum, Harvard University, 1955.

Peattie, Donald Culross. *Green Laurels: The Lives and Achievements of the Great Naturalists*. New York: Simon & Schuster, The Literary Guild, 1936.

Wild, Peter. *Pioneer Conservationists of Western America*. Missoula, Mont.: Mountain Press, 1979.

INDIVIDUAL NATURALISTS

Barrus, Clara. *Our Friend John Burroughs*. Boston: Houghton Mifflin, 1914.

Benson, Maxine. *Martha Maxwell: Rocky Mountain Naturalist*. Lincoln: University of Nebraska Press, 1986.

Burroughs, Raymond Darwin, ed. *The Natural History of the Lewis and Clark Expedition*. East Lansing: Michigan State University Press, 1995.

Cutright, Paul Russell. *Lewis and Clark: Pioneering Naturalists*. Urbana: University of Illinois Press, 1969.

Cutright, Paul Russell, and Michael J. Brodhead. *Elliott Coues: Naturalist and Frontier Historian*. Urbana: University of Illinois Press, 1981.

Dupree, A. Hunter. *Asa Gray, 1810–1888*. Cambridge, Mass.: Harvard University Press, 1959.

Evans, Howard Ensign. *The Natural History of the Long Expedition to the Rocky Mountains, 1819–1820*. Oxford: Oxford University Press, 1997.

Ford, Alice. *John James Audubon: A Biography*. New York: Abbeville Press, 1988.

Ford, Corey. *Where the Sea Breaks Its Back*. Boston: Little, Brown, 1966.

Goodman, George J., and Cheryl A. Lawson. *Retracing Major Stephen H. Long's 1820 Expedition: The Itinerary and Botany*. Norman: University of Oklahoma Press, 1995.

Harvey, A. G. *Douglas of the Fir*. Cambridge, Mass.: Harvard University Press, 1947.

Kofalk, Harriet. *No Woman Tenderfoot: Florence Merriam Bailey, Pioneer Naturalist.* College Station: Texas A&M University Press, 1989.

McVaugh, Rogers. *Edward Palmer: Plant Explorer of the American West.* Norman: University of Oklahoma Press, 1956.

Merrill, J. C. "In Memoriam: Charles Emil Bendire." *Auk* 15, no. 1: 1–6.

Mitchell, Ann Lindsay, and Syd House. *David Douglas: Explorer and Botanist.* London: Aurum Press, 1999.

Moring, John R. "Fish Discoveries by the Lewis and Clark and Red River Expeditions." *Fisheries* 21, no. 7: 6–12.

Nichols, Roger L., and Patrick L. Halley. *Stephen Long and American Frontier Exploration.* Norman: University of Oklahoma Press, 1995.

Renehan, Edward J., Jr. *John Burroughs: An American Naturalist.* Hensonville, N.Y.: Black Dome, 1992.

Streshinsky, Shirley. *Audubon: Life and Art in the American Wilderness.* New York: Villard Books, 1993.

Stroud, Patricia Tyson. *Thomas Say: New World Naturalist.* Philadelphia: University of Pennsylvania Press, 1992.

Warren, Leonard. *Joseph Leidy: The Last Man Who Knew Everything.* New Haven, Conn.: Yale University Press, 1998.

JOURNALS AND DIARIES

Bartholomew, David M. *Pioneer Naturalist on the Plains: The Diary of Elam Bartholomew, 1871 to 1934.* Manhattan, Kans.: Sunflower University Press, 1998.

Coues, Elliott, ed. *The History of the Lewis and Clark Expedition.* 3 vols. (originally 4 vols.). Reprint of 1893 edition. New York: Dover.

Davies, John. *Douglas of the Forests: The North American Journals of David Douglas.* Seattle: University of Washington Press, 1980.

Douglas, David. *Journal Kept by David Douglas during His Travels in North America.* London: William Wesley and Son, 1914.

Engberg, Robert. *John Muir: Summering in the Sierra.* Madison: University of Wisconsin Press, 1984.

Engberg, Robert, and Donald Wesling, eds. *John Muir: To Yosemite and Beyond.* Madison: University of Wisconsin Press, 1980.

Flores, Dan L., ed. *Jefferson and Southwestern Exploration.* Norman: University of Oklahoma Press, 1984.

Gordon, Mary McDougall, ed. *Through Indian Country to California: John P. Sherburne's Diary of the Whipple Expedition, 1853–1854*. Stanford, Calif.: Stanford University Press, 1988.

Houston, Stuart, ed. *Arctic Ordeal: The Journal of John Richardson, Surgeon-Naturalist with Franklin, 1820–1822*. Montreal: McGill-Queen's University Press, 1984.

James, Edwin, comp. *Account of an Expedition from Pittsburgh to the Rocky Mountains* (Under the Command of Major Stephen H. Long, From the Notes of Major Long, Mr. T. Say, and Other Gentlemen of the Exploring Party). Several reprint versions. Barre, Mass.: Imprint Society, 1972.

Kohl, Michael F., and John S. McIntosh, eds. *Discovering Dinosaurs in the Old West: The Field Journals of Arthur Lakes*. Washington, D.C.: Smithsonian Institution Press, 1997.

Lincecum, Jerry Bryan, and Edward Hake Phillips, eds. *Adventures of a Frontier Naturalist: The Life and Times of Dr. Gideon Lincecum*. College Station: Texas A&M University Press, 1994.

Lincecum, Jerry Bryan, Edward Hake Phillips, and Peggy A. Redshaw, eds. *Science on the Texas Frontier: Observations of Dr. Gideon Lincecum*. College Station: Texas A&M University, 1997.

Muir, John. *The Story of My Boyhood and Youth*. San Francisco: Sierra Club Books, 1988.

Nuttall, Thomas. *A Journal of Travels into the Arkansas Territory during the Year 1819*. Several editions, one edited by Savoie Lottinville. Fayetteville: University of Arkansas Press, 1999.

O'Sullivan, Timothy, and William Bell. *Wheeler's Photographic Survey of the American West, 1871–1873*. New York: Dover, 1983.

Stetson, Lee, ed. *The Wild Muir*. Yosemite National Park, Calif.: Yosemite Associates, 1994.

Teale, Edwin Way, ed. *The Wilderness World of John Muir*. Boston: Houghton Mifflin, 1954.

Townsend, John Kirk. *Narrative of a Journey across the Rocky Mountains to the Columbia River*. Philadelphia: Henry Perkins, 1839.

———. *Across the Rockies to the Columbia*. Lincoln: University of Nebraska Press, 1978.

Van Doren, Mark, ed. *Travels of William Bartram*. New York: Dover, 1955.

Zwinger, Ann. *John Xantus: The Fort Tejon Letters, 1857–1859*. Tucson: University of Arizona Press, 1986.

Index

Other Cooper Square Press Titles of Interest

Edge of the World: Ross Island, Antarctica
A Personal and Historical Narrative of Exploration, Adventure, Tragedy, and Survival
CHARLES NEIDER
With a new introduction
536 pp., 45 b/w photos, 15 maps
0-8154-1154-5
$19.95

The Fabulous Insects
Essays by the Foremost Nature Writers
EDITED BY CHARLES NEIDER
288 pp.
0-8154-1100-6
$17.95

Great Shipwrecks and Castaways
Firsthand Accounts of Disasters at Sea
EDITED BY CHARLES NEIDER
256 pp.
0-8154-1094-8
$16.95

The Great White South
Traveling with Robert F. Scott's Doomed South Pole Expedition
HERBERT G. PONTING
New introduction by Roland Huntford
440 pp., 175 b/w illustrations, 3 b/w maps & diagrams
0-8154-1161-8
$18.95

In Search of Robinson Crusoe
DAISUKE TAKAHASHI
256 pp., 23 b/w photos
0-8154-1200-2
$25.95 cloth

The Karluk's Last Voyage
An Epic of Death and Survival in the Arctic, 1913–1916
CAPTAIN ROBERT A. BARTLETT
New introduction by Edward E. Leslie
378 pp., 23 b/w photos, 3 maps
0-8154-1124-3
$18.95

Killer 'Cane
The Deadly Hurricane of 1928
ROBERT MYKLE
264 pp., 15 b/w photos
0-8154-1207-X
$26.95 cloth

La Salle
A Perilous Odyssey from Canada to the Gulf of Mexico
DONALD JOHNSON
296 pp., 25 b/w illustrations
0-8154-1240-1
$26.95 cloth

The Life and African Expeditions of Livingstone
DR. DAVID LIVINGSTONE
656 pp., 52 b/w line drawings and maps
0-8154-1208-8
$22.95

Man Against Nature
Firsthand Accounts of Adventure and Exploration
EDITED BY CHARLES NEIDER
512 pp.
0-8154-1040-9
$18.95

My Arctic Journal
A Year among Ice-Fields and Eskimos
JOSEPHINE PEARY
Foreword by Robert E. Peary
New introduction by Robert M. Bryce
280 pp., 67 b/w illustrations, maps, &
diagrams
0-8154-1198-7
$18.95

My Attainment of the Pole
FREDERICK A. COOK
New introduction by Robert M. Bryce
680 pp., 45 b/w illustrations
0-8154-1137-5
$22.95

A Negro Explorer at the North Pole
MATTHEW A. HENSON
Preface by Booker T. Washington
Foreword by Robert E. Peary, Rear
Admiral, U.S.N.
New introduction by Robert A. Bryce
232 pp., 6 b/w photos
0-8154-1125-1
$15.95

The North Pole
ROBERT PEARY
Foreword by Theodore Roosevelt
New introduction by Robert M. Bryce
480 pp., 109 b/w illustrations, 1 map
0-8154-1138-3
$22.95

The South Pole
An Account of the Norwegian Antarctic
Expedition in the Fram, 1910–1912
CAPTAIN ROALD AMUNDSEN
Foreword by Fridtjof Nansen
New introduction by Roland Huntford
960 pp., 155 b/w illustrations
0-8154-1127-8
$29.95

Stanley
The Making of an African Explorer
FRANK MCLYNN
424 pp., 19 b/w illustrations
0-8154-1167-7
$18.95

Through the Brazilian Wilderness
THEODORE ROOSEVELT
New introduction by H. W. Brands
448 pp., 9 b/w photos, 3 maps
0-8154-1095-6
$19.95

Tutankhamun
The Untold Story
THOMAS HOVING
408 pp., 43 b/w photos
0-8154-1186-3
$18.95

The Voyage of the Discovery
Scott's First Antarctic Expedition,
1901–1904
CAPTAIN ROBERT F. SCOTT
Preface by Fridtjof Nansen
New introduction by Ross MacPhee
Volumes I & II

Volume I
712 pp., 147 b/w illustrations
0-8154-1079-4
$35.00 cloth

Volume II
656 pp., 123 b/w illustrations
0-8154-1151-0
$35.00 cloth

Available at bookstores; or call
1-800-462-6420.

COOPER SQUARE PRESS
200 Park Avenue South
Suite 1109
New York, NY 10003-1503